J. A. K. THOMSON

THE ETHICS OF
ARISTOTLE

THE NICOMACHEAN ETHICS
TRANSLATED

PENGUIN BOOKS

Penguin Books Ltd, Harmondsworth, Middlesex, England
Penguin Books Inc., 3300 Clipper Mill Road, Baltimore 11, Md, U.S.A.
Penguin Books Pty Ltd, Ringwood, Victoria, Australia

—

First published 1953
Published in Penguin Books 1955
Reprinted 1956, 1958, 1959, 1961, 1962, 1963, 1965

—

This translation Copyright © the Estate of
J. A. K. Thomson, 1953

—

Made and printed in Great Britain
by The Whitefriars Press Ltd
London and Tonbridge
Set in Monotype Baskerville

THE PENGUIN CLASSICS

FOUNDER EDITOR (1944–64): E. V. RIEU

PRESENT EDITORS:

Betty Radice and Robert Baldick

L55

ALSO BY J. A. K. THOMSON

—

Shakespeare and the Classics (*1952*)

Classical Influences on English Poetry (*1951*)

The Classical Background of
English Literature (*1948*)

The Art of the Logos (*1935*)

The Greek Tradition:
Essays in the Reconstruction of
Ancient Thought (*1927*)

—

The above are published by
George Allen and Unwin Ltd, London,
who also issue a cloth-bound edition
of the present translation of
Aristotle's *Ethics*

NOTE ON THE TEXT

For the most part I have followed the text of
Mr H. Rackham as it appears in the second
edition of his *Nicomachean Ethics* in the Loeb
series. Everything has been translated except
a few sentences of recapitulation and the like
which are now entirely superfluous.
These omissions are marked
by dots.

CONTENTS

INTRODUCTION

I

THE LIFE OF ARISTOTLE

THE life of Aristotle was spent in learning and teaching and writing. It was therefore what people call uneventful. Yet of intellectual and spiritual experiences, in which a man may be considered most truly to live, he had his full share. It is largely because these have been disregarded that he assumed the appearance of an impersonal 'authority' – a mechanical brain always giving the same answers to the same questions. But the real man was not like that.

He was born in 385, or perhaps 384, B.C. at Stageira (or Stageiros), a town of some importance in what was known as Chalcidice, the trident-shaped peninsula trending south-east of Salonica into the Aegean Sea. Stageira lay on the northern base of it not far from the sea and overlooked by a range of mountains. It had been a colony of Chalcis in Euboea, though the connexion in Aristotle's time was mainly sentimental. Stageira had gone its own way and developed a local culture of its own, of which in 385 B.C. Aristotle's father, Nicomachus, was perhaps the leading representative. In particular he was considered a master of the medical science of his time. This brought him an invitation to stay at the Macedonian court in Pella as physician to the king, Amyntas. The reader is invited to note three things: Aristotle was not an Athenian; his father was a doctor, which in those days implied being something of a biologist too; he had some acquaintance with the Macedonian court. These things were to exercise a powerful influence on his life.

When he was about seventeen he became a member of Plato's Academy. What led him to take this step we cannot now discover, but it shows how strong was the attraction then exercised by the Academy. That institution was not, as is too often said or implied, a kind of university, for it provided no organized teaching; it was a fellowship of intellectually disposed persons drawn to the centre of Greek culture by the prospect of exchanging ideas and of listening to Plato. Young Aristotle must have felt a little like a Rhodes Scholar going up to Oxford. It is certain that he surrendered at

once to the enchantment of the Master. In course of time no doubt
– after nearly twenty years of devoted discipleship – he came more
and more emphatically to dissent from much of Plato's teaching.
But of Plato himself he never ceased to think with affection and admiration. After he is supposed (by some) to have broken with him
he composed an inscription for an altar in which he described
Plato as 'a man whom it is not lawful for the bad even to praise.'
Admiration could hardly go higher than that.

Nevertheless when the older man died in 348/7 B.C. Aristotle
felt that he must discover how he stood in regard to Platonism,
about which he had begun to feel certain doubts. The Academy
was now under a new head, Speusippus, to whom Aristotle could
not be expected to feel a personal loyalty. Accordingly for the next
three years we find him living at Assos, in Asia Minor, in the society
of two friends, members of the Academy like himself. Assos was not
far from the site of Homer's Troy and the friends lived under the
protection of Hermeias, who then ruled the Troad. Aristotle came
to know him well, and Hermeias was a man worth knowing. He
had sprung from the very lowest rank of society and was endowed
by nature with strong and perhaps unscrupulous passions. Having
come for some reason to Athens he had chanced to hear Plato, and
the words of Plato had changed his life. His ability raised him to
princely power, in the exercise of which he evidently did his best
to realize the Platonic ideal of the good ruler. But he had made
enemies and through the treachery of one of these fell into the
hands of the Persians, whose empire was run on very different
principles. They put him to death after he had refused, under torture, to betray his friends. The effect upon Aristotle was extraordinary. His passionate grief found expression in a beautiful and
long-remembered poem (of which the beginning has been preserved) in which he said that his friend had proved, as well
as any hero of old, that goodness is worth dying for, being so beautiful. And that is not the whole story. Hermeias had a niece and
adopted daughter called Pythias. Aristotle and she fell in love and
they were married. She died young. Long afterwards, when Aristotle himself came to die, he left instructions in his will that her
bones – reduced to ashes no doubt and enclosed as the custom was
in an urn – should be buried with him 'according to her own
express desire.'

From Assos Aristotle went to Mytilene in the island of Lesbos,
attracted there no doubt by Theophrastus, his friend of Academy
times and all times, who was a native of Lesbos. There he spent

about three years thinking out his position and probably collecting material for his remarkable studies in biology. Then something happened in the quiet existence of Aristotle with which all the world is familiar. He was invited to become what people call the 'tutor' of the boy who became Alexander the Great. The invitation came from Alexander's father, the famous 'Philip of Macedon', and the reasons for it are not perfectly clear. If he knew Aristotle personally at all it must have been on very slight acquaintance. True, Aristotle was the son of Nicomachus, and that would be a recommendation. No doubt too Philip, who was dipped if not imbued in culture, would hear of Aristotle as a man of high character and extraordinary powers of mind. It may have been such considerations that influenced Philip to give the invitation. But what made Aristotle accept it? He must have known that he would hate living at the Macedonian court with its murderous intrigues and orgies of drunkenness; he never mentions such places without strong expressions of disapproval and distaste. The question, however, admits of an almost certain answer. Aristotle accepted the proposal because in this respect at least he was a good Platonist. Plato had said that there would be no very good government until philosophers were kings or kings philosophers. If then the opportunity came to a philosopher of guiding the policy of a state, either directly or by instructing a young prince, he could not in conscience reject it. In this belief Plato himself had gone, at some risk to his life and liberty, to see what he could do with the rulers of Sicily. Several members of the Academy had undertaken similar enterprises. Aristotle then would feel it his duty to go to Pella, the more so perhaps because Macedonia was then the strongest power in Europe and so presented the finest opportunity. Accordingly in 342 B.C. we find him at the Macedonian court. A legend was born and Aristotle came to be thought of as he

who bred
Great Alexander to subdue the world

Alexander, however, was formed by nature, not study, to subdue the world, nor can we suppose that the best general in Europe called in a philosopher to teach his son the art of war. But the art of government – Aristotle might have tried to communicate that, although we are bound to consider that his pupil, however intelligent, was only fourteen. We have also to consider that when Alexander came to govern his own conquests he went on a principle to which Aristotle was altogether opposed. In 336 B.C. Philip was assassinated and Alexander at twenty years of age ascended the throne of Macedonia. From that moment he never had a day to spare for more tuition under Aristotle. There is no reason to doubt his respect and admiration for his teacher, who may have instilled in him his love of Homer and his interest in the collection of scientific evidence. But they had to go different ways, and the ways diverged more and more widely as time went on. Their friendship was strained by at least one painful incident. Alexander had been accompanied in his invasion of the Persian empire by Callisthenes, a nephew of Aristotle. Callisthenes was a promising young man but, as Aristotle himself seems to have admitted, he was tactless. In court circles to be tactless is fatal. It was represented to Alexander by the ill-wishers of Callisthenes that he was involved in a plot against the king, who thereupon had him executed. Aristotle did not know the facts and therefore could not judge whether his nephew was guilty or not. But the incident could not fail to increase his dislike of courts.

The result was that in 335/4 B.C., after an absence of thirteen years, he decided to go back to Athens. He cannot have been altogether sure of his reception. Although he kept out of active politics, his connexion with Alexander made it certain that he would be accused of Macedonian sympathies, and Athens, where Demosthenes was still alive, was under the surface still fiercely anti-Macedonian. But Aristotle would also know that the Athenians had a still deeper feeling – pride in their reputation as the great defenders of liberty of speech and of thought. On his side he was soon able to claim that he brought fresh fame to the city. His school attracted many distinguished pupils and collaborators. It was built, the material part of it, on a piece of once consecrated ground called the Lyceum, to which was added a garden called the *Peripatos*, or 'Walk'. Aristotle is supposed to have used this garden a good deal and his habit of walking there led to his teaching being referred to in later times by the name or nickname of the 'Peripatetic Philosophy'. The Lyceum flourished some twelve or thirteen years under Aristotle, who was by no means a figure-head but a very active teacher and director of studies and research – probably, all things considered, the greatest teacher who ever lived.

Then Alexander died in far-off Babylon. There was a new wave of anti-Macedonian feeling in Athens, and Aristotle was threatened with prosecution, ostensibly on the ground that his praise of Hermeias went beyond what could be given to any mortal without impiety. He therefore considered it prudent to leave the city 'in case,' as he expressed it, 'the Athenians should sin a second time against philosophy.' (The first time had been against Socrates.) He retired to Chalcis, where his mother had some property, and in Chalcis he not long afterwards died. This was in 322 B.C. He was in his sixty-third year.

II

THE WORKS OF ARISTOTLE

THE works of Aristotle have gone through the strangest vicissitudes. To follow these a little explanation is necessary. The writings which we now possess belong substantially to the later period of his life, the period when he was teaching in the Lyceum. But he had been at an earlier date a somewhat prolific author in a very different manner. The works of this period have been lost, all but some fragments, yet it was this and not our Aristotle that was read in classical antiquity. This must always be remembered when we read what the ancients say about him as late as the beginning of the present era. Thus Cicero speaks of the 'golden stream' (*aureum flumen*) of Aristotle's style. At this description we stare in astonishment until we realize that Cicero is speaking of the lost books, which he knows very well, for he imitates at least the form of them in his own philosophical writings. From this and from other indications it is evident that these early works of Aristotle were written in a manner suited to the needs of 'the general reader'. What is more important, the doctrine taught in them was, as an examination of the fragments clearly reveals, more or less pure Platonism. It was of course well known to every educated man in the three centuries before Cicero that Aristotle had founded a school which in many ways had diverged from the teaching of the Academy. But in what ways? No one exactly knew, for the lectures in which Aristotle had made his position clear – the lectures which *we* now read – had been lost or had survived only in the notebooks of pupils who had 'taken them down'. The story of what happened is so interesting, and indeed so important, that it may be summarized here. There is no good reason for doubting its truth, for it explains the facts and it rests on the unexceptionable authority of Strabo, a learned and careful scholar who lived in the generation after Cicero.

Before he died Aristotle bequeathed his library – the first systematically arranged and catalogued library in Europe – to his successor, Theophrastus. Among these manuscripts were his un-published lectures. Theophrastus, when he himself came to die, bequeathed *his* books, including of course Aristotle's, to his pupil Neleus, who was allowed to carry them off from the Lyceum to his native town, Scepsis, in the Troad. When in his turn Neleus died his property, including his books, fell to his heirs, who were in-capable of understanding them and stored them somewhere in the house. But now the price of old books began to rise. There was rivalry between the Ptolemies of Egypt and the rulers of Pergamum as to which should acquire the best and largest library. Agents with purchasing power were sent to all the likely places, especially of course to Athens. There can be no doubt that they tried the Lyceum, which in fact bred the kind of scholars who created the new libraries, but the Lyceum did not know what had happened to the manuscripts of Aristotle. The family at Scepsis evidently got wind of these inquiries; at any rate they hastily unpacked the books and hid them in an underground cellar. It seems a curious pro-ceeding but it can be explained. Scepsis was in the Troad, and the Troad was part of the dominions ruled over by the princes of Pergamum. The Scepsis family may very well have taken a dim view of what they were likely to get for the books from their own government, especially if they could not produce the title deeds of their possessions. So they decided not to be in the market yet and hid the volumes. These had already suffered from neglect, and now they were exposed to the damp of that cellar and the moths infest-ing it. And they lay there a long time – a century and a half or longer. At last something was done about it. A wealthy book col-lector named Apellicon got news of the hidden treasure and offered a price for it which the owners could not resist. With Apellicon the books now travelled to Athens. Not long afterwards, in 86 B.C. to be exact, Athens was captured by the Roman general Sulla. The library of Apellicon was part of the loot. Sulla was an educated person, fully capable of seeing the value of his prize. So he had the books shipped to Rome, where they were suitably housed and put under the care of a librarian. But what an escape for Aristotle!

And if he had not escaped, the history of Europe – there is not the smallest exaggeration in saying this – would have been ex-tremely different. To make this clear we must go back to the mo-ment when Apellicon became master of the Aristotelian manu-scripts. When he examined them – they would be papyrus rolls – he found that they had suffered greatly from the damp and the moths and from general neglect. He tried to fill the gaps by writing in suitable words of his own. But he was not much of a philosopher and the task he had undertaken was quite beyond his powers. Then his treasure had come to Rome, where presumably it was now the property of the state. There was great excitement among professional philosophers, especially of course among those who regarded themselves as Aristotelians. Apparently, however, there was still some difficulty in obtaining copies of the originals owing perhaps to the scruples of the librarian. If he had them it was not without justification. For when he was at last induced, by a scholar called Tyrannio, to lend the manuscripts for expert examination, Tyrannio hastened with them to a firm of publishers, who rushed out an edition. It was scandalously incorrect, because the originals were in bad condition, while the professional scribes who copied them, not being properly supervised and not understanding what they so hastily copied, introduced new blunders of their own. Yet this act of piracy – for it seems to have been that or little better – had one good result. It led to a revival of interest in Aristotle. A series of genuine scholars and philosophers, of whom Aristonicus was the most important, set to work on producing a better text, and gradually succeeded. It is due in the main to them that we possess these later works in a not unsatisfactory form. On the other hand the works of Aristotle's Platonizing period have disappeared. We can guess what happened. The rediscovered lectures were much more interesting to philosophers, especially of course to Peripatetics, because they were an authoritative statement of the Master's distinctive opinions. So they were carefully preserved and studied, while the popular writings were left to the general public, who did not care enough for them to see that they were protected, with the result that in the decline of ancient culture they perished altogether. So when Albertus of Cologne helped to revive the study of Aristotle in the thirteenth century he had little to go upon except such of the later discourses as had been translated, or partly translated, into Latin. He was the teacher of Thomas Aquinas, the greatest of the medieval schoolmen, who based all his work, wide-ranging as it was, on the Aristotelian method, as he understood it. His authority combined with other influences, not all sympathetic to Thomas, quickly raised Aristotle to the supreme position he held in the higher education of the later Middle Ages.

It would serve no useful purpose to set down here a detailed list of the surviving works of Aristotle. They cover an unparalleled range of subjects and it would take too long to describe them even in outline. They deal with physics and metaphysics, with zoology and biology, with logic, with political and moral science, with psychology, with literary style and literary criticism, and much else. All these matters he put on a systematic basis so well founded that, broadly speaking, the history of science has hitherto been a story of following, or breaking away from, Aristotle. Like a Colossus he bestrides the centuries.

But these famous treatises are composed in a strictly technical style with only the rarest attempt at grace in the writing. One may in this age of emotional self-expression feel a good deal of sympathy with the old, perhaps fabulous, don who said, 'I do like Aristotle, he is so nice and dry.' But had he to be so dry as all that? The explanation is simple. Aristotle was not writing here for the general public but what was in effect a programme of studies in the Lyceum, which (and not the Academy) was the first true university. In a university the teaching of the different subjects must be organized and co-ordinated, and it must have a Head who sees to that. The Head of the Lyceum was Aristotle, and what he did in his capacity of Head was to work out in an unusually systematic and detailed way the general lines to be followed by the students. But the result has been that we are left with only what might be called the articulated skeleton of his thought.

III

THE MEDIEVAL VIEW OF ARISTOTLE

In the later Middle Ages – in the earlier he was inadequately known – the authority of Aristotle was absolute. Thomas refers to him simply as 'the Philosopher', as if other philosophers hardly counted; for Dante he is 'the Master of those that know.' This led to many strange results, for Aristotle was thought to be right about everything, which is far from being true. It was particularly unfortunate that astronomy, the only one of the natural sciences, unless we regard alchemy as a science, which deeply engaged the interest of the Middle Ages, was precisely the subject in which Aristotle went farthest astray. Astronomy depends on mathematics, and he had not so good a head for mathematics as he had for other disciplines. He believed that the earth was a solid stationary ball at the centre of the universe and that the sun and moon and stars revolved about the earth. This theory was later elaborated into the 'Ptolemaic System'. Up to a point it worked well enough, and to the Middle Ages it appeared entirely satisfactory; its truth is assumed by Dante and by Chaucer, both of whom display a considerable knowledge of the subject. It was, we all remember, superseded by the 'Copernican System', itself the elaboration of a Greek hypothesis, stated by Aristarchus of Samos (about 310–230 B.C.), who argued that the earth moved round the sun. Yet when Galileo supported the view of Aristarchus and Copernicus he got into trouble with the authorities, who felt that to doubt the truth of anything said by Aristotle was a kind of impiety. In this field then, and in the whole field of physics, which holds so great a place in modern science, Aristotle was less of a help than a hindrance.

But what completely enthralled these centuries was Aristotelian logic, especially that division of it which is called deductive logic. Aristotle himself undoubtedly spent a great deal of time and thought on perfecting his logic, and we can see that he was proud of the result. But he regarded it as a means not an end. This appears from the name given to it, *organon*, which is Greek for a 'tool'. It was not a science in itself but an instrument for the use of the scientist. Yet we cannot be surprised at the importance which Aristotle attached to it. Before his time even philosophers were capable of adducing quite fallacious arguments without seeing that they were fallacious. It is very much to Aristotle's credit that he perceived that this would never do; science is possible only when valid inferences are drawn. Hence all those rules of his for correct argumentation. Modern philosophers have given them the name of 'Formal Logic' and are inclined to think that they prove nothing. That may be true, but they have still some value in preventing people, even modern philosophers, from drawing wrong conclusions from their premises. Yet it need not be denied that detecting fallacies, or even drawing valid conclusions from given premises, is not the most direct way of reaching the truth. And in general it must be said that the medieval philosophers were hardly aware of this. Their best work – and their best is marvellously fine and subtle – takes the form of rigorously correct deduction from one or more first principles which are taken as self-evidently true. It is not, however, the habit of Aristotle himself to accept first principles without examination. Actually he is not a logical martinet and often surprises us by the looseness – which is not a synonym of inaccuracy – of his own reasoning. But he was followed by such martinets, and even in antiquity logic, in the hands of certain Stoics, became an intimidating instrument. We shall understand better what happened afterwards if we remember that it was not so much Aristotle in his own Greek that was read by the School-men as Aristotle translated into Latin, refined upon by subsequent logicians and expounded by Latin and Arabic commentators. The result was that the Schoolmen turned him into a Schoolman. The event was not entirely regrettable. The discipline of logic was infinitely valuable to the medieval mind, which might otherwise have lost itself in the wrong kind of mysticism. If that is disputed, there is something else which does not admit of dispute. Thinking logically compels one to write grammatically, since to be ungram-matical is to be illogical. Scientific grammar is in fact an invention of the logicians; Aristotle was the first to 'analyse sentences'.

Finally it may be said that in these later medieval centuries Aristotle more than any other single influence formed the Euro-pean mind. Whether we like it or not, he has been our great edu-cator. Everyone remembers Chaucer's Clerk of Oxenford, who 'unto logyk hadde longe y-go' – had gone deep into logic – and would rather have 'twenty bokes clad in blak or reed of Aristotle and his philosophie' than anything else in the world. That is what Aristotle meant to the Middle Ages.

Then came the Renaissance and the attack on him, led in England by Bacon. The attack drove Aristotle from some of his positions but not from all, and he is still in the field. Aristotle has come back.

IV

THE MODERN VIEW OF ARISTOTLE

THE presentation of Aristotle's philosophy as a cast-iron system has broken down. When we look at it closely and as a whole we see that it is nothing of the kind. We should see this even more clearly if we had the lost earlier works, for then we could trace step by step the process by which he ceased to be a Platonist and be-came a Peripatetic. But in fact we can, thanks in the main to Werner Jaeger, trace it to some extent even in the lectures or dis-courses which we have. They are in many, perhaps in most, cases not homogeneous compositions. Parts of them belong to an earlier, parts to a later, stage in the intellectual history of the author. There are inconsistencies, sometimes even self-contradictions. It is pretty clear what happened. In the dozen or so years in which Aristotle was lecturing at the Lyceum he would find reason to change his mind or modify his views of certain questions. But in-

stead of recasting or rewriting his lectures he simply added what
he now had to say to the original draft. No doubt if he had published his lectures he would have taken care to remove anomalies.
Yet in some ways the discourses are more instructive as they stand.
In them we read the speaker's intellectual autobiography. We can,
though of course only partially, follow the movement of his thought
from Platonism to something more distinctively his own. The tendency of Platonism, perhaps inherited from Socrates, was to be dis-
satisfied with a final explanation which did not show that the
thing explained was in the best condition of which it was capable,
for the good is the true and the true the good. The tendency of
Aristotelianism was to accept whatever explanation seemed to account for the facts. That of course is a gross over-simplification, but
it suggests the difference between them. Science hitherto has followed Aristotle rather than Plato. All that can be said within our
limits here is that Aristotle came more and more to think of the
universe as a vast complex of organisms each striving to attain the
end assigned by Nature to it. The Greek word for 'end' is *telos*, and
this is why the Aristotelian system is often described as 'teleo-
logical'.

A world of organisms tending to fulfil their natures is the conception of a biologist rather than a mathematician. For a long time
before it was the mathematicians who had upon the whole determined the quality of Greek philosophical speculation, including
that of Plato. But what chiefly interests Aristotle is development.
Where he is unique is in combining this interest with an analytical
genius of the first order. It was this combination which enabled
him to become the true founder of science; that is of the natural or
physical sciences, for the Greeks had already made astonishing ad-
vances in mathematics. These sciences call for two operations: the
collection of material or evidence, and its analysis and classification. It is common knowledge that Aristotle introduced the method
of classification by genus and species; it is perhaps generally known
that he was the first to explain the nature of an organism. What
has scarcely been understood and is only now being recognized is
that he is the father of 'research'. This all-important fact was overlooked, partly because the collections of data and specimens
formed by himself and his pupils have disappeared, partly because
the Middle Ages, having no turn for the physical sciences, concentrated on his logic and metaphysics. The result was that the notion
became implanted in the minds of those who revived science at the
Renaissance that Aristotle was their grand enemy, the embodi-

ment of reactionary dogmatism. The truth is that Aristotle, at least the later and independent Aristotle, continually insists on testing every hypothesis by all the evidence at his disposal. And this insistence is the chief characteristic of the modern man of science.

It is a true, though hardly a fair, criticism of such Greek science as existed before the work of Aristotle that it indulged in speculation upon an insufficient basis of observed and tested evidence. It is hardly fair, because these early thinkers were working alone, without textbooks, without microscopes or telescopes, without even instruments for exact weighing and measuring. What could they do except ask questions and suggest answers? Yet in the nature of the questions they asked and the quality of the answers they gave they revealed the scientific genius of the Hellenic race. Aristotle suffered from most of their disabilities, but he perceived that they might be largely overcome by planned co-operation. To achieve this was probably his main object in founding the Lyceum. The lack of instruments of precision still hampered him in subjects like physics and astronomy. But it was different in subjects like political and moral science. To qualify himself for writing about politics he had more than a hundred and fifty distinct political constitutions described in detail, he himself undertaking the most important, the constitution of Athens. In order to introduce, what was sorely needed, some kind of generally acceptable system into the chronology of Greek historians he had a list made of all the victors at the Pythian Games from their foundation to his own day – a task of great labour and research. In the same spirit he caused his pupils to excerpt from the Athenian archives the records kept there of all the dramas that had been performed at Athens – and there were hundreds of them – the dates of their performance, their titles and their authors. In this way he founded the science which we now call the history of literature. He saw the importance, or rather the necessity, of a sufficient library to enable his pupils to carry on their work, and with that end in view collected and arranged an unprecedented number of books. He made a collection of maps . . . He applied the same methods, so far as his means and opportunities allowed, to the biological sciences. He formed a museum which he equipped with 'specimens' to illustrate his lectures. It is said that Alexander took great interest in this and maintained a constant supply to it of the creatures found in his immense empire. We have reason to think that, like Darwin, he put himself in touch with hunters and fishers and other amateur naturalists. Many of his specimens he caused to be carefully drawn, dissected, described, and classified. Too often he was forced to rely on the reports of credulous travellers, but where he could control his material he is said by zoologists to be extremely accurate, being particularly good, as one might expect in a Greek, on Aegean fishes, of which he knew a surprising number. Botany he left to Theophrastus, who followed as well as he could the methods of the Master, collecting, examining, and describing a great many plants. In view of all this and much more it should be no longer possible for any self-respecting historian of science to repeat the nonsense that Aristotle did not understand the value of research, though it may be true to say that he did not understand the value of experiment as an instrument of research.

V

THE NICOMACHEAN ETHICS

THERE are as many as three ethical treatises preserved among the works attributed to Aristotle, of which that called after Nicomachus is the most authoritative; the other two are called respectively the *Eudemian Ethics* and the *Magna Moralia*. How they got these titles is no longer known.

It might be possible to extract from the Dialogues of Plato something like a system of morals; in fact this has been attempted or done. Before Plato, Socrates in conversation and Democritus in writing had dealt with ethical problems. But Aristotle appears to have been the first to reduce the principles of human conduct to a science. It is therefore natural that he should give the impression of feeling his way. A less dogmatic treatise on the subject by an original thinker it would not be easy to find. He declares more than once that he will be content if what he says is only roughly true. He sometimes goes back upon himself, as when he restates his position on the subject of pleasure. That shows how erroneous is the idea that Aristotle seeks to impose on us a system which he maintains to be incapable of improvement or alteration. You might say this perhaps of Hegel or Karl Marx or Herbert Spencer; but not of Aristotle. He thinks his system can, and hopes it may, be worked out in more convincing detail; at present he offers it as a sketch. He does not close his mind to other suggestions. The consciousness of an intellectual superiority makes him perhaps overweening, but hardly any major philosopher has been more careful to record and

consider the views of other thinkers. He may not always understand them or represent them fairly–almost all ancient criticism is
open to that objection–but at any rate he takes them into account.
Unlike many sages he makes more of their agreement with him
than their disagreement. And if *hoi polloi*, the mass of ordinary men
and women, think certain actions are right or wrong, Aristotle
listens with respectful attention on the ground that in a question of
morals the mass of ordinary men and women are very likely to be
right.

How good a book is the *Nicomachean Ethics*? That it has had so
much fame and influence is not an answer to this question. It may
fairly be said that there is something good on almost every page,
while on some matters of the greatest importance – money for instance or equity – what Aristotle said (more than two thousand
years ago) can hardly be improved upon. But a good deal of what
we read in the *Ethics* does not now appear convincing or even quite
true. Much seems disputable, more perhaps obvious or commonplace. But this is the fate of pioneers; the path they opened up becomes a public highway. 'Man is a social animal' is now a truism,
perhaps a platitude, but it was a new and striking observation
when Aristotle first uttered it. We must read him with some
measure of historical imagination. Judged by modern standards
the weakest part of the book is probably its descriptive psychology.
But here again the historical explanation helps us to understand.
Aristotle did not command the terminology which would have
enabled him to describe the states of soul which he attempted – so
ill, it often seems to us – to define. He is well aware of this himself
and he more than once complains of it. He had to do the best he
could with the loose popular terminology current in his time, and
it was totally inadequate for his purpose. This puts him at a hopeless disadvantage compared with the modern psychologist with his
array of carefully distinguished terms. For all that the reader comes
to perceive that Aristotle has a genuine understanding of human
nature; at least he never produces in us that odd feeling which we
sometimes get in reading a modern, that the writer believes he has
laid bare the secrets of man's heart because he has an endless number of tickets with which to label it. Aristotle knows how, if not
exactly why, people behave as they do; and that is perhaps the
better part of such knowledge.

In what then do the interest and importance of the *Ethics* consist
for us now? It may be suggested that they consist in this, that
Aristotle had the boldness and originality to base ethics of psy-

chology. He might have made his position clearer, but he could not rid himself all at once of his ·Platonic prepossessions, and this clouds his language with some ambiguity. Plato believed in the existence of an absolute standard to which human conduct must be referred and by which its ethical quality must be measured. Aristotle did not deny this, but he came to believe that Plato had approached the question from the wrong end. It was no good, he thought, evolving an ideal from your inner consciousness and then bidding ordinary men and women pursue that. You must learn how people do behave before you are qualified to tell them how they ought to behave. As he puts it, in ethics we must proceed from what is 'known to us' before we can reach what is 'known absolutely'. Of course we must form hypotheses, but these must always be tested by the facts. That is the procedure followed in the natural sciences. In fact, whether he fully realizes it or not, Aristotle is for turning ethics into the study of human behaviour. He does indeed insist that this study must be guided by a disposition to believe that virtuous are intrinsically superior to vicious activities. But this disposition is a natural product of the direction given to his studies by the 'Law-giver' or, as we might put it, by Church and State. Though Aristotle would not be Aristotle if he did not theorize, he is really concerned in the *Ethics* with the practice rather than the theory of morals. To become a good man you must behave like a good man. *Then* you will know what goodness is. Ethics is the science or, if you like, the art of making that discovery. It can be made, but it can be made only in that way. Perhaps this does not amount to much more than a rooted distrust of ethical systems which frame themselves on a number of deductions from first principles which are incapable of proof. Aristotle agreed that such principles existed in some of the sciences – metaphysics, for example – but he thought they should be kept as far as possible out of the science which deals with good and bad, with right and wrong, in human conduct.

As for his method, it is surely not difficult to see in the *Ethics* that Aristotle had collected material, just as a modern psychologist collects it, on which to base his observations. Consider the number, variety and aptness of his illustrations of type psychology; they are obviously drawn from a case-book. In Plato's *Republic* we find studies of human types, the 'Oligarchic Man', the 'Democratic Man', and so on. The New Comedy, which flourished contemporaneously with Aristotle, was crowded with typical characters. Such studies then were not new. But we can get closer to him than that.

His friend, colleague and successor Theophrastus has left a famous little book entitled *Characters*, which contains a number of what we should call thumb-nail sketches of types – the 'Superstitious Man', the 'Officious Man', and so forth. Here we have a collection of traits of character – for that is what 'characters' means in Greek – made actually in the Lyceum. As it stands it can hardly have been published by Theophrastus himself and it has much the appearance of what the eighteenth century would have called 'elegant extracts' drawn from his note-books and published after his death. We can hardly doubt that Aristotle had a mass of such material to draw upon. In fact on his own principles of research he was bound to assemble it. He meant the *Ethics* to be studied in intimate connexion with the *Politics*, and he would not adopt one method for the former and another for the latter. The man who collected 158 constitutions for his *Politics* must have collected many descriptions of human types for his *Ethics*.

The book must be left to speak for itself. 'Speak' is here the proper word, for what we have in the *Nicomachean Ethics* is the substance of lectures delivered to students at the Lyceum. The reader will understand it best if he remembers that Aristotle did not himself publish the book, and perhaps would not have published it in any circumstances. Let him not think that he is reading a book but that he is listening to a man speaking. He will find that it makes a great difference, especially when he remembers who this speaker is.

J. A. K. THOMSON

BOOK ONE

*Aristotle begins, in a way characteristic of his method, with a genera-
lization which, if accepted, will lead to a more exact account of his
subject. It is a generalization which is fundamental to his philosophy
and in his own mind there is no doubt about the truth of it. Yet he
is not at this point asserting its truth. He is content to state a position
which he has found reason to hold. It may be defined in some such
words as these :* The good is that at which all things aim. *If we
are to understand this, we must form to ourselves a clear notion of
what is meant by an aim or, in more technical language, an 'end'.
The first chapter of the* Ethics *is concerned with making the notion
clear.*

CHAPTER ONE

IT is thought that every activity, artistic or scientific, in
fact every deliberate action or pursuit, has for its object
the attainment of some good. We may therefore assent to
the view which has been expressed that 'the good' is 'that
at which all things aim'.* Since modes of action involving
the practised hand and the instructed brain are numerous,
the number of their ends is proportionately large. For instance, the end of medical science is health; of military
science, victory; of economic science, wealth. All skills of
that kind which come under a single 'faculty' – a skill in
making bridles or any other part of a horse's gear comes
under the faculty or art of horsemanship, while horsemanship itself and every branch of military practice comes under
the art of war, and in like manner other arts and techniques
are subordinate to yet others – in all these the ends of the

---

* It is of course obvious that to a certain extent they do not all aim at
the same thing, for in some cases the end will be an activity, in others the
product which goes beyond the actual activity. In the arts which aim
at results of this kind the results or products are intrinsically superior to
the activities.

master arts are to be preferred to those of the subordinate skills, for it is the former that provide the motive for pursuing the latter.*

CHAPTER TWO

Now if there is an end which as moral agents we seek for its own sake, and which is the cause of our seeking all the other ends – if we are not to go on choosing one act for the sake of another, thus landing ourselves in an infinite progression with the result that desire will be frustrated and ineffectual – it is clear that this must be the good, that is the absolutely good. May we not then argue from this that a knowledge of the good is a great advantage to us in the conduct of our lives? Are we not more likely to hit the mark if we have a target? If this be true, we must do our best to get at least a rough idea of what the good really is, and which of the sciences, pure or applied, is concerned with the business of achieving it.

Ethics is a branch of politics. That is to say, it is the duty of the statesman to create for the citizen the best possible opportunity of living the good life. It will be seen that the effect of this injunction is not to degrade morality but to moralize politics. The modern view that 'you cannot make men better by act of parliament' would have been repudiated by Aristotle as certainly as by Plato and indeed by ancient philosophers in general.

Now most people would regard the good as the end pursued by that study which has most authority and control over the rest. Need I say that this is the science of politics? It is political science that prescribes what subjects are to be taught in states, which of these the different sections of the population are to learn, and up to what point. We see also

* It makes no difference if the ends of the activities are the activities themselves or something over and above these, as in the case of the sciences I have mentioned.

that the faculties which obtain most regard come under this science: for example, the art of war, the management of property, the ability to state a case. Since, therefore, politics makes use of the other practical sciences, and lays it down besides what we must do and what we must not do, its end must include theirs. And that end, in politics as well as in ethics, can only be the good for man. For even if the good of the community coincides with that of the individual, the good of the community is clearly a greater and more perfect good both to get and to keep. This is not to deny that the good of the individual is worth while. But what is good for a nation or a city has a higher, a diviner, quality.

Such being the matters we seek to investigate, the investigation may fairly be represented as the study of politics.

The study of politics is not an exact science.

CHAPTER THREE

IN studying this subject we must be content if we attain as high a degree of certainty as the matter of it admits. The same accuracy or finish is not to be looked for in all discussions any more than in all the productions of the studio and the workshop. The question of the morally fine and the just – for this is what political science attempts to answer – admits of so much divergence and variation of opinion that it is widely believed that morality is a convention and not part of the nature of things. We find a similar fluctuation of opinion about the character of the good. The reason for this is that quite often good things have hurtful consequences. There are instances of men who have been ruined by their money or killed by their courage. Such being the nature of our subject and such our way of arguing in our discussions of it, we must be satisfied with a rough outline of the truth, and for the same reason we must be content with broad conclusions. Indeed we must preserve this attitude when it comes to a more detailed statement of the views that are held. It is a mark of the educated man and a proof of his culture that in every subject he looks for only so much precision as its nature permits. For example, it is absurd to demand logical demonstrations from a professional speaker; we might as well accept mere probabilities from a mathematician.

Political science is not studied with profit by the young.

Every man is a good judge of what he understands: in special subjects the specialist, over the whole field of knowledge the man of general culture. This is the reason why political science is not a proper study for the young. The young man is not versed in the practical business of life from which politics draws its premises and its data. He is, besides, swayed by his feelings, with the result that he will make no headway and derive no benefit from a study the end of which is not *knowing* but *doing*. It makes no difference whether the immaturity is in age or in character. The defect is not due to lack of years but to living the kind of life which is a succession of unrelated emotional experiences. To one who is like that, knowledge is as unprofitable as it is to the morally unstable. On the other hand for those whose desires and actions have a rational basis a knowledge of these principles of morals must be of great advantage. ...

This, however, is something of a digression. Let us resume our consideration of what is the end of political science. For want of a better word we call it 'Happiness'. People are agreed on the word but not on its meaning.

CHAPTER FOUR

To resume. Since every activity involving some acquired skill or some moral decision aims at some good, what do we take to be the end of politics – what is the supreme good attainable in our actions? Well, so far as the name goes there is pretty general agreement. 'It is happiness,' say both intellectuals and the unsophisticated, meaning by 'happiness' living well or faring well. But when it comes to saying in what happiness consists, opinions differ, and the account given by the generality of mankind is not at all like that given by the philosophers. The masses take it to be something plain and tangible, like pleasure or money or social standing. Some maintain that it is one of these, some that it is another, and the same man will change his opinion about it more than once. When he has caught an illness he will say that it is health, and when he is hard up he will say that it is money. Conscious that they are out of their depths in such discussions, most people are impressed by anyone who pontificates and says something that is over their heads. Now it would no doubt be a waste of time to examine all these opinions; enough if we consider those which are most in evidence or have something to be said for them. Among these we shall have to discuss the view held by some that, over and above particular goods like those I have just mentioned, there is another which is good in itself and the cause of whatever goodness there is in all these others.

A digression on method.

We must be careful not to overlook the difference that it makes whether we argue *from* or *to* first principles. Plato used very properly to advert to this distinction. Employing a metaphor from the race-course, where the competitors run from the starting-point and back to it again, he would ask whether the appropriate procedure in a particular enquiry was *from* or *to* first principles. Of course we must start from what is known. But that is an ambiguous expression, for things are known in two ways. Some are known 'to us' and some are known absolutely. For members of the Lyceum there can be little doubt that we must start from what is known to us. So the future student of ethics and politics, if he is to study them to advantage, must have been well brought up. For we begin with the *fact*, and if there is sufficient reason for accepting it as such, there will be no need to ascertain also the *why* of the fact. Now a lad with such an upbringing will have no difficulty in grasping the first principles of morals, if he is not in possession of them already. If he has neither of these qualifications, he had better take to heart what Hesiod says:

> That man is best who sees the truth himself;
> Good too is he who hearkens to wise counsel.
> But who is neither wise himself nor willing
> To ponder wisdom, is not worth a straw.

A man's way of life may afford a clue to his genuine views upon the nature of happiness. It is therefore worth our while to glance at the different types of life.

CHAPTER FIVE

LET us return from this digression. There is a general assumption that the manner of a man's life is a clue to what he on reflection regards as the good – in other words, happiness. Persons of low tastes (always in the majority) hold that it is pleasure. Accordingly they ask for nothing better than the sort of life which consists in having a good time. (I have in mind the three well-known types of life – that just mentioned, that of the man of affairs, that of the philosophic student.) The utter vulgarity of the herd of men comes out in their preference for the sort of existence a cow leads. Their view would hardly get a respectful hearing, were it not that those who occupy great positions sympathize with a monster of sensuality like Sardanapalus. The gentleman, however, and the man of affairs identify the good with honour, which may fairly be described as the end which men pursue in political or public life. Yet honour is surely too superficial a thing to be the good we are seeking. Honour depends more on those who confer than on him who receives it, and we cannot but feel that the good is something personal and almost inseparable from its possessor. Again, why do men seek honour? Surely in order to confirm the favourable opinion they have formed of themselves. It is at all events by intelligent men who know them personally that they seek to be honoured. And for what? For their moral qualities. The inference is clear; public men prefer virtue to honour. It might therefore seem reasonable to suppose that virtue rather than honour is the end pursued in the life of the public servant. But clearly even virtue cannot be quite the end. It is possible, most people think, to possess virtue while you are asleep, to possess it without acting under its influence during any portion of one's life. Besides, the virtuous man may meet with the most atrocious luck or ill-treatment; and nobody, who was not arguing for argument's sake, would maintain that a man with an existence of that sort was 'happy'.* The third type of life is the 'contemplative', and this we shall discuss later.

As for the life of the business man, it does not give him much freedom of action. Besides, wealth obviously is not the good we seek, for the sole purpose it serves is to provide the means of getting something else. So far as that goes, the ends we have already mentioned would have a better title to be considered the good, for they are desired on their own account. But in fact even their claim must be disallowed. We may say that they have furnished the ground for many arguments, and leave the matter at that.

* I am absolved from a more detailed discussion of this point by the full treatment it has received in current literature.

Aristotle now passes to a criticism of the Platonic theory of a 'universal good', often called the 'idea' or 'form' of the Good. The criticism is too famous, and in parts too acute, to be omitted, but it does not show Aristotle at his best. Plato thought of his forms as 'eternal' in the sense in which God is eternal, that is, as existing out of space and time. This Aristotle either could not or would not understand. It is true of course that Plato represents the forms as coming into some kind of relation with objects of sense, and Aristotle is fully entitled to criticize his account of this relation. But the existence of the forms – if they exist – is not thereby disproved.

CHAPTER SIX

But we can hardly avoid examining the problem raised by the concept of a universal good. One approaches it with reluctance because the theory of 'forms' was brought into philosophy by friends of mine. Yet surely it is the better, or rather the unavoidable, course, above all for philosophers, to defend the truth even at the cost of our most intimate feelings, since, though both are dear, it would be wrong to put friendship before the truth.

Those who introduced the theory of forms did not suppose that there existed forms of *groups* of things in which one of the things is thought of as prior in nature to another. This accounts for their not attempting to construct a form of 'number' as distinct from particular numbers. Now a thing may be called good in three ways: in itself, in some quality it has, in some relation it bears to something else. But the 'essence' of a thing – what it is in itself – is by its very nature prior to any relation it may have, such a relation being an offshoot or 'accident' of it. Therefore there cannot be one form embracing *both* the absolutely *and* the relatively good.

Again, the word 'good' is used in as many senses as the word 'is'. We may describe a person or a thing – God, for instance, or the reasoning faculty – as good in the sense of absolutely good. Or we may speak of things as good when we are thinking of their qualities or special excellences. Or we may use the word in connexion with the quantity of something, when we mean that there is a right amount of it; or in connexion with its relation to something else, as when we say that it is 'useful', meaning good as means to an end; or in connexion with its occurrence in time, describing it as 'the right moment', or in connexion with its position in space, as 'a good place to live in.' And so on. Using technical language we may predicate 'good' in the categories of (a) substance, (b) quality, (c) quantity, (d) relation, (e) time, (f) space. Clearly then 'good' is not something that can be said in one and the same sense of everything called 'good'. For then it could not be said in all these *different* senses, but only in one.

Again, things of which there is a single form must be things of which there is a single science. Consequently there should be (if the view we are discussing is right) a single science dealing with *all* good things. But what do we find? An indefinite number of sciences dealing with the goods coming under even one of the heads we have mentioned. Take 'the right moment'. The right moment in war is studied under military science, the right moment in sickness under the science of medicine. Similarly the right quantity in diet is considered by medicine, in bodily exercise by physical training.

Next, what do they mean by 'the thing as it really is'? The question deserves some answer. For in their own terminology 'man as he really is' is just another way of saying 'man'. In this respect, then, there will be no difference between them – they are both 'man'. But, if we are allowed to argue on these lines, we shall find no difference either between the really good and the good, in so far as both are good. Nor will the really good be any more good by being 'eternal'. You might as well say that a white thing which lasts a long time is whiter than one which lasts only a day.*

To the arguments we have been using the objection may

* On this point it may be thought that the Pythagoreans (followed, it would seem, by Speusippus) have a more probable doctrine; they place unity in their column of 'goods'. But we must leave the discussion of this point to another occasion.

present itself that the champions of the forms did not mean their words to apply to *every* good. What they meant (it may be argued) was this. Those things, and those things only, which are pursued and desired on their own account are good. They are good as belonging to one species, while things tending in any way to produce or conserve them, or to check their opposites, are good in a different way, namely as means of achieving them. Clearly then there would be two kinds of 'goods' – things good in themselves and things good as means to these. Let us take them separately. Consider first the things that are good in themselves. Are they called 'good' because they come under a single form? Then what sort of things are the good in themselves? Are they all those things – intelligence, for example, or sight or certain pleasures and honours – that are sought entirely on their own merits? For these are things which, even if we pursue them with some remoter object in view, might be classified as things good in themselves. Or is there nothing good in itself except the form of the good? That would leave the class empty of content. If on the other hand things of the kind I have mentioned do form a class of things good in themselves, it will follow that the same notion of good will be as clearly recognizable in them as the same notion of whiteness presents itself to us in snow and in white lead. But when it comes to honour and sagacity and pleasure, the notions we have of them in respect of their goodness are different and distinguishable. Therefore 'good' is not a general term corresponding to a single form. How then does it happen that these different things are all called 'good'? It can hardly be a mere coincidence. Various answers suggest themselves. All goods may derive from a single good, or all may contribute to form a single good. Or perhaps the answer may be expressed in an equation: 'As sight is good in the body, so is rationality in the mind.' We could frame a series of such equations. But perhaps it is better to drop the discussion of that point here, since a full examination of it is more suited to another branch of philosophy. And we must follow the same course in dealing with the form of the good. For, even if the good which is predicated of a number of different things exists only in one element common to them all, or has a separate existence of its own, clearly it cannot be realized in action or acquired by man. Yet it is just a good of that kind that is the subject of our present inquiry. The thought may indeed suggest itself that a knowledge of the absolute good may be desirable as a means of attaining to those goods which a man may acquire and realize in practice. Might we not use it as a pattern to guide us in acquiring a better knowledge of the things that are good 'for us' and, so knowing, obtaining them? The argument has a certain plausibility, but it manifestly does not accord with the procedure followed by the sciences. For all these aim at some *particular* good and seek to fill up the gaps in their knowledge of how to attain *it*. They do not think it any business of theirs to learn the nature of the *absolute* good. Now it will take some persuading to make us believe that all the masters of technique do not possess, or even make an effort to possess, this knowledge, if it be so powerful an aid to them as is pretended. And there is another puzzle. What advantage in his art will a weaver or a joiner get from a knowledge of the absolute good? Or how shall a doctor or a general who has had a vision of Very Form become thereby a better doctor or general? As a matter of fact it does not appear that the doctor makes a study even of health in the abstract. What he studies is the health of the human subject or rather of a particular patient. For it is on such a patient that he exercises his skill. . . .

What then is the good? If it is what all men in the last resort aim at, it must be happiness. And that for two reasons: (1) happiness is everything it needs to be, (2) it has everything it needs to have.

CHAPTER SEVEN

FROM this digression we may return to the good which is the object of our search. What is it? The question must be asked because good seems to vary with the art or pursuit in which

B 2

it appears. It is one thing in medicine and another in strategy, and so in the other branches of human skill. We must inquire, then, what is the good which is the end common to all of them. Shall we say it is that for the sake of which everything else is done? In medicine this is health, in military science victory, in architecture a building, and so on – different ends in different arts; every consciously directed activity has an end for the sake of which everything that it does is done. This end may be described as its good. Consequently, if there be some one thing which is the end of all things consciously done, this will be the doable good; or, if there be more than one end, then it will be all of these. Thus the ground on which our argument proceeds is shifted, but the conclusion arrived at is the same.

I must try, however, to make my meaning clearer.

In our actions we aim at more ends than one – that seems to be certain – but, since we choose some (wealth, for example, or flutes and tools or instruments generally) as means to something else, it is clear that not all of them are ends in the full sense of the word, whereas the good, that is the supreme good, is surely such an end. Assuming then that there is some one thing which alone is an end beyond which there are no further ends, we may call *that* the good of which we are in search. If there be more than one such final end, the good will be that end which has the highest degree of finality. An object pursued for its own sake possesses a higher degree of finality than one pursued with an eye to something else. A corollary to that is that a thing which is never chosen as a means to some remoter object has a higher degree of finality than things which are chosen both as ends in themselves and as means to such ends. We may conclude, then, that something which is always chosen for its own sake and never for the sake of something else is without qualification a final end.

Now happiness more than anything else appears to be just such an end, for we always choose it for its own sake and never for the sake of some other thing. It is different with honour, pleasure, intelligence and good qualities generally. We choose them indeed for their own sake in the sense that we should be glad to have them irrespective of any advantage which might accrue from them. But we also choose them for the sake of our happiness in the belief that they will be instrumental in promoting that. On the other hand nobody chooses happiness as a means of achieving them or anything else whatsoever than just happiness.

The same conclusion would seem to follow from another consideration. It is a generally accepted view that the final good is self-sufficient. By 'self-sufficient' is meant not what is sufficient for oneself living the life of a solitary but includes parents, wife and children, friends and fellow-citizens in general. For man is a social animal.* A self-sufficient thing, then, we take to be one which on its own footing tends to make life desirable and lacking in nothing. And we regard happiness as such a thing. Add to this that we regard it as the most desirable of all things without having it counted in with some other desirable thing. For, if such an addition were possible, clearly we should regard it as more desirable when even the smallest advantage was added to it. For the result would be an increase in the number of advantages, and the larger sum of advantages is preferable to the smaller.

Happiness then, the end to which all our conscious acts are directed, is found to be something final and self-sufficient.

But we desire a clearer definition of happiness. The way to this may be prepared by a discussion of what is meant by the 'function' of a man.

But no doubt people will say, 'To call happiness the highest good is a truism. We want a more distinct account of what it is.' We might arrive at this if we could grasp what is meant by the 'function' of a human being. If we take a flautist or a sculptor or any craftsman – in fact any class of men at all who have some special job or profession – we find that his special talent and excellence comes out in that job, and this

* Of course we must draw the line somewhere. For, if we stretch it to include ancestors and descendants and friends' friends, there will be no end to it. But there will be another opportunity of considering this point.

is his function. The same thing will be true of man simply as man – that is of course if 'man' does have a function. But is it likely that joiners and shoemakers have certain functions or specialized activities, while man as such has none but has been left by Nature a functionless being? Seeing that eye and hand and foot and every one of our members has some obvious function, must we not believe that in like manner a human being has a function over and above these particular functions? Then what exactly is it? The mere act of living is not peculiar to man – we find it even in the vegetable kingdom – and what we are looking for is something peculiar to him. We must therefore exclude from our definition the life that manifests itself in mere nurture and growth. A step higher should come the life that is confined to experiencing sensations. But that we see is shared by horses, cows, and the brute creation as a whole. We are left, then, with a life concerning which we can make two statements. First, it belongs to the rational part of man. Secondly, it finds expression in actions. The rational part may be either active or passive: passive in so far as it follows the dictates of reason, active in so far as it possesses and exercises the power of reasoning. A similar distinction can be drawn within the rational life; that is to say, the reasonable element in it may be active or passive. Let us take it that what we are concerned with here is the reasoning power in action, for it will be generally allowed that when we speak of 'reasoning' we really mean *exercising* our reasoning faculties. (This seems the more correct use of the word.) Now let us assume for the moment the truth of the following propositions. (*a*) The function of a man is the exercise of his non-corporeal faculties or 'soul' in accordance with, or at least not divorced from, a rational principle. (*b*) The function of an individual and of a *good* individual in the same class – a harp player, for example, and a good harp player, and so through the classes – is generically the same, except that we must add superiority in accomplishment to the function, the function of the harp player being merely to play on the harp; while the function of the good harp player is to play on it well. (*c*) The function of man is a certain form of life, namely an activity of the soul exercised in combination with a rational principle or reasonable ground of action. (*d*) The function of a good man is to exert such activity well. (*e*) A function is performed well when performed in accordance with the excellence proper to it. – If these assumptions are granted, we conclude that the good for man is 'an activity of soul in accordance with goodness' or (on the supposition that there may be more than one form of goodness) 'in accordance with the best and most complete form of goodness.'

Happiness is more than momentary bliss.

There is another condition of happiness; it cannot be achieved in less than a complete lifetime. One swallow does not make a summer; neither does one fine day. And one day, or indeed any brief period of felicity, does not make a man entirely and perfectly happy.

So far, however, we have merely drawn the outline of happiness; the details must be filled in gradually. In the exact sciences precise conclusions are reached, and reached once for all. In ethics we can only approximate to such conclusions.

It is not pretended that we have given more than an outline of the good. But we must be content with that at this stage, for doubtless the proper way of going to work is to draw an outline and fill in the details afterwards – when the sketch is well done, anybody can finish the picture. In this work Time is believed to put his shoulder to the wheel and even point the way to new discoveries. In fact progress in the arts has usually been made in that fashion, for anybody can fill in the gaps in a formula. But we must not forget what we said before about not looking for the same exactness in all we study or labour at, but only as much as the subject-matter in each case allows, or is appropriate to the particular method followed by the student or workman. For example the carpenter and the geometrician alike try to find the right angle, but they do it in different ways, the carpenter being content with such precision as satisfies the requirements of his job, the geometrician as a student of scientific truth seeking to discover the nature and attributes of the right angle. We ought to follow this procedure in other studies as well, always asking ourselves what degree of accuracy is to be expected in them, in order that we may not unnecessarily complicate the facts by introducing side issues.

Nor must we demand in every subject an account of the cause or reason why it is what it is, for there are cases in which it is quite enough if the fact itself is proved. We shall find that this applies to 'beginnings', which is our name for first principles; in them the fact *is* the beginning. Some are grasped by a process of induction, some by a kind of perception, some at the end of a period of training or habituation, others in other ways. On every occasion we must seek to arrive at first principles in the way natural to them in the instance that presents itself. We must also make a point of finding good definitions of them, because such definitions are an immense advantage to us as we pursue the subject. The proverb says that 'the half is greater than the whole,' but we may go further and say that the beginning is greater than the whole, for the beginning clears up many obscurities together in the matter we may be investigating.

It follows that our first principle – our definition of happiness – should be tested not only by the rules of logic but also by the application to it of current opinions on the subject.

CHAPTER EIGHT

So we must examine our first principle not only logically, that is as a conclusion from premises, but also in the light of what is currently said about it. For if a thing be true, the evidence will be found in harmony with it; and, if it be false, the evidence is quickly shown to be discordant with it.

But first a note about 'goods'. They have been classified as (*a*) external, (*b*) of the soul, (*c*) of the body. Of these we may express our belief that goods of the soul are the best and are most properly designated as 'good'. Now according to our definition happiness is an expression of the soul in considered actions, and that definition seems to be confirmed by this belief, which is not only an old popular notion but is accepted by philosophers. We are justified, too, in saying that the end consists in certain acts or activities, for this enables us to count it among goods of the soul and not among external goods. We may also claim that our description of the happy man as the man who lives or fares well chimes in with our definition. For happiness has pretty much been stated to be a form of such living or faring well. Again, our definition seems to include the elements detected in the various analyses of happiness – virtue, practical wisdom, speculative wisdom, or a combination of these, or one of them in more or less intimate association with pleasure. All these definitions have their supporters, while still others are for adding material prosperity to the conditions of a happy life. Some of these views are popular convictions of long standing; others are set forth by a distinguished minority. It is reasonable to think that neither the mass of men nor the sages are mistaken altogether, but that on this point or that, or indeed on most points, there is justice in what they say.

Now our definition of happiness as an activity in accordance with virtue is so far in agreement with that of those who say that it *is* virtue, that such an activity *involves* virtue. But of course it makes a great difference whether we think of the highest good as consisting in the *possession* or in the *exercise* of virtue. It is possible for a disposition to goodness to exist in a man without anything coming of it; he might be asleep or in some other way have ceased to exercise his function of a man. But that is not possible with the activity in our definition. For in 'doing well' the happy man will of necessity *do*. Just as at the Olympic Games it is not the best-looking or the strongest men present who are crowned with victory but competitors – the successful competitors – so in the arena of human life the honours and rewards fall to those who show their good qualities in action.

Observe, moreover, that the life of the actively good is inherently pleasant. Pleasure is a psychological experience, and every man finds that pleasant for which he has a liking – 'fond of' so-and-so is the expression people use. For example, a horse is a source of pleasure to a man who is fond of horses, a show to a man who is fond of sight-seeing. In the same way just actions are a source of pleasure to a man who likes to see justice done, and good actions in general to one who likes goodness. Now the mass of men do not follow any consistent plan in the pursuit of their pleasures, because their pleasures are not inherently pleasurable. But men of more elevated tastes and sentiments find pleasure in things which are in their own nature pleasant, for instance virtuous actions, which are pleasant in themselves and not merely to such men. So their life does not need to have pleasure fastened about it like a necklace, but possesses it as a part of itself. We may go further and assert that he is no good man who does not find pleasure in noble deeds. Nobody would admit that a man is just, unless he takes pleasure in just actions; or liberal, unless he takes pleasure in acts of liberality; and so with the other virtues. Grant this, and you must grant that virtuous actions are a source of pleasure in themselves. And surely they are also both good and noble, and that always in the highest degree, if we are to accept, as accept we must, the judgement of the good man about them, he judging in the way I have described. Thus, happiness is the best, the noblest, the most delightful thing in the world, and in it meet all those qualities which are separately enumerated in the inscription upon the temple at Delos:

> Justice is loveliest, and health is best,
> And sweetest to obtain is heart's desire.

All these good qualities inhere in the activities of the virtuous soul, and it is these, or the best of them, which we say constitute happiness.

For all that those are clearly right who, as I remarked,

maintain the necessity to a happy life of an addition in the form of material goods. It is difficult, if not impossible, to engage in noble enterprises without money to spend on them; many can only be performed through friends, or wealth, or political influence. There are also certain advantages, such as the possession of honoured ancestors or children, or personal beauty, the absence of which takes the bloom from our felicity. For you cannot quite regard a man as happy if he be very ugly to look at, or of humble origin, or alone in the world and childless, or – what is probably worse – with children or friends who have not a single good quality or whose virtues died with them. Well, as I said, happiness seems to require a modicum of external prosperity – thus leading some to identify it with the condition of those who are 'favourites of fortune. ....'

However, we must guard against misunderstanding. Fortune can supply the happy man with the means, and create for him the conditions of his happiness; it cannot create his happiness.

CHAPTER NINE

FROM this springs another problem. Is happiness (a) capable of being acquired by some intellectual process or the formation of a habit or some other method of training, or (b) does it come to us simply by some divine dispensation, or even by the caprice of events? Well, in the first place, if anything is a gift of the gods to men, it is reasonable to suppose that happiness is such a gift, particularly as of all human possessions it is the best.* Yet, even if happiness is not sent by a special providence but is acquired by virtue, or study, or practice, we look on it as one of our greatest blessings. For the crown and end of goodness is surely of all things the best, and the best we may also call divine and blissful. In the second place we look on happiness as something that may

* This, however, is a topic which appears more germane to another branch of study, such as theology.

be widely spread. For through some process – of study or application of our mental powers – it may fall to any man who does not suffer from some disability or incapacity to achieve excellence. Thirdly, assuming that it is a better thing to reach happiness by these efforts of our own than by a stroke of luck, we may reasonably think that happiness is in fact reached in that way. The productions of nature have an innate tendency in the direction of the best condition of which they are capable, and so have the creations of the craftsman and artist and whatever has an efficient cause of any kind, especially if that cause ranks highest in the scale of excellence. But that the greatest and finest thing of all should be at the mercy of chance is a thought that strikes a very jarring note.

The problem may receive some illumination from our description of happiness as an activity of the soul, all the other good things of life being either necessary adjuncts of happiness or useful in helping it to perform its function in the way that tools are helpful to the workman. The conclusion that happiness depends upon ourselves is in harmony with what I said in the first of these lectures, when I laid it down that the highest good is the end which is sought by political science. What the statesman is most anxious to produce is a certain moral character in his fellow-citizens, namely a disposition to virtue and the performance of virtuous actions. That is why we do not naturally speak of a cow or a horse or other beast as 'happy', for none of the brute creation can take part in moral activities. For the same reason no child is 'happy' either, for its age precludes it from taking part as yet in such actions; if we choose to call one happy, it is because he gives promise of being so. For, as I have already observed, we cannot have happiness unless we have complete goodness in a complete lifetime. Life is full of chances and changes, and the most prosperous of men may in the evening of his days meet with great misfortunes, like Priam in the stories we read in the epic poets. A man who has encountered such blows of fate and suffered a tragic death is called happy by no one.

Aristotle goes on to discuss an ancient saying, attributed to Solon, Call no man happy before his death. *It is only after his death, the saying implies, that we can finally strike a balance between the good and ill that have befallen him. The modern reader may be excused if he feels that this paradox is hardly worth discussion. We may say in justification of Aristotle that he held the conviction that there was pretty sure to be some truth in any long-established popular belief, and that this was worth extracting. The truth he extracts here is that, while external things cannot destroy a man's happiness, he cannot help feeling their effects.*

CHAPTER TEN

MUST we go further and call no man happy so long as he is alive? Must we, in Solon's phrase, 'look to the end'? And, if we feel bound to accept this dictum, are we committed to the further admission that a man may be happy when he is dead? Surely that is a paradox if ever there was one, especially for us whose very definition of happiness makes it out to be a form of activity. On the other hand if we deny the possibility of happiness for the dead – if Solon's words mean something else, namely that only when he is dead is it safe to call a man happy as one beyond the arrows of outrageous fortune – even this does not meet all the difficulties involved in the question. For a dead man is popularly believed to be capable of experiencing both good and ill – honour and dishonour, prosperity and the loss of it among his children and descendants generally – in exactly the same way as if he were alive but unaware or unobservant of what was happening. But this raises another question. Suppose a man had lived an exceptionally happy life and was no less happy in his death. Many vicissitudes of fortune may overtake his descendants, some of whom may be good and enjoy such a life as the good deserve, while others may be bad and fare badly.* Is the dead man, then, to change with all their

* These descendants may of course stand to their progenitors in every degree of kinship.

changes and become happy at one time and unhappy at another? It seems unlikely, to say the least. Yet it would also be an odd position to maintain that ancestors are not affected at all, even for a moment, by the ups and downs of the family fortunes. Suppose we go back to the question whether a man can be happy while he is still alive, for perhaps a solution of that will help us in our study of this problem about ancestors and descendants. If we are to 'look to the end' and call a (dead) man happy not because he is but because he was so, how absurd it will be not to tell the truth about him when he actually *is* happy, for no better reason than this, that we are not prepared to call the living happy because of the chopping and changing of fortune and because we have got it into our heads that happiness is something permanent and hard to change, although in fact the wheel of fortune is often turned full circle for the same people! Don't you see that, if we go by this, we shall often have to call the same person now happy and now miserable? That is to make the happy man 'a chameleon' and a 'lodger in a tumble-down house.' I suggest that in following these changes of fortune we are getting off the straight path. Our happiness or unhappiness is not bound up with them; they are only, as I said, the inevitable concomitants of human life. It is the direction of the soul's energies on sound moral principles that makes us happy, their direction towards evil that makes us unhappy.

Now the point we have raised in this discussion is further evidence in support of our definition, since our virtuous activities have a permanence denied to the rest. For it will be agreed that they last longer than the mental exertion demanded by the special sciences. And among these activities themselves the degree of permanence is in proportion to their intrinsic value. This appears from the circumstance that it is in them that those who enjoy true felicity are most deeply and continuously engaged. And this no doubt accounts for the fact that these higher activities do not let us forget them. We conclude, then, that the happy man will have that desideratum of permanence in his happiness – in fact will be happy throughout his whole existence. For to do and to 'contemplate' what is in conformity with goodness is the chief or the only business of his life. And he will take what fortune sends him in the finest spirit and in exactly the right way as being, in the words of Simonides, 'good in very truth' and 'foursquare without a flaw.'

Yet the accidents of fortune are many, though they vary in importance. Little bits of good or bad luck clearly do not much affect the balance of our happiness in life. On the other hand repeated strokes of good fortune cannot, if considerable, fail to increase that happiness, since they must inevitably add to the brilliance of life, and they can be used to fine and lofty ends. But great misfortunes coming in battalions crush and maim our felicity in two ways, by inflicting pain and by putting a check on many of our activities. For all that, even in our calamities, the beauty of the soul shines out when a man bears with composure one heavy mischance after another, not because he does not feel them, but because he is a man of high and heroic temper. Besides, if it be true, as I affirmed, that the quality of a life is determined by its activities, it is impossible for the entirely happy man to become miserable. For he will never be guilty of base or detestable actions. The truly good and wise man, we are convinced, bears with dignity all that fortune sends him and invariably takes the most honourable line of conduct that is open to him in the circumstances, just as a good general employs the forces at his disposal in the most scientific way, and the shoemaker makes the neatest shoe out of the leather given him by the customer, and so with all other craftsmen whatsoever. This being so, never can the happy man become unhappy, though doubtless he can hardly be supposed to enjoy supreme felicity if his woes should rival those of Priam. And surely he will not be full of change and mutability. It will be no easy matter to dislodge him from his happiness, nor will everyday mishaps effect this. It will need a succession of hard blows from which it will take him a long time to recover and be happy again. Indeed, if he recovers at all, it will only be at the end of a protracted period in the course of which he has had every opportunity of winning great and shining prizes for his renewed endeavours.

We are now in a position to describe the happy man as 'one who realizes in action a goodness that is complete and that is adequately furnished with external goods, and that not for some limited period but throughout a fully rounded life spent in that way.' And perhaps we must add to our definition 'one who shall live in this way and whose death shall be consistent with his life.' For the future is dark to us, and happiness we maintain to be an 'end' and in every way final and complete. If this be so, then those who have or shall have the blessings we have enumerated shall be pronounced by us entirely happy in terms of human happiness. . . .

In the short chapter which follows the question whether the dead are touched by the fortunes of the living is revived. It is unnecessary to suppose that Aristotle himself is responsible for the insertion of this unimportant excursus, but he must have said something of the kind, and what we now read may be a note from his hand found and introduced into the treatise by an editor.

CHAPTER ELEVEN

THE notion that the dead are not touched at all by the fortunes of their descendants or any of their friends has a chilling effect on us and is generally repudiated. But the subject is a perplexed one in consequence of the number and variety of the things that happen to us, some of which come home to us more than others. To distinguish between them individually is a business of endless length, so we shall have to be content with a broad statement of a general character. This embraces two affirmations. (1) The misfortunes of our friends of whatever degree, just like those which happen to ourselves, have sometimes a weighty influence upon our lives, and sometimes appear to be comparatively trifling. (2) It makes a great difference whether a particular misfor-

tune befalls men while they are living or after they are dead
– a far greater difference than it makes in a tragedy whether
the grim and lawless deeds precede the action or are performed in the course of it. It is a difference we must take into
our reckoning; still more, perhaps, the problem of whether
the dead participate in any form of good or evil. For the
obvious inference from what we have been saying is that, if
any sense of good or evil penetrates to their consciousness at
all, it must be a weak and slight one either in itself or as they
feel it – slight or at any rate not of such force and quality as
to make the unhappy happy or to rob the happy of their
happiness. . . .

*Aristotle now produces a new argument designed to show that happi-
ness is the end of life – happiness as he has defined it. He draws a
distinction between things that are praised and things that are regarded as above or beyond praise. The end of life must be something
beyond praise; and such is happiness.*

CHAPTER TWELVE

Now after settling these questions let us see if we can discover whether happiness is something to be *praised* or something to be *valued*. (One thing is clear, it is not a mere potentiality of good.) By a thing to be praised we evidently
mean always something that is commended for a certain
quality it has or a certain relation which it bears to something else. Thus we praise the just and the brave and the
good and goodness generally on the strength of what they do
or produce. In like manner we praise the strong and the
swift and so on, on the ground of their possessing certain
native gifts and standing in a certain relation to something
good and excellent. Another way of apprehending the truth
of this is to think of praise addressed to the gods. Praise is
relative, and if the gods are praised, it can only be in comparison with us mortals. This shows that to praise them is a
manifest absurdity. Since praise is of things capable of being

49

related to other things, it is clear that the supremely good things call not for praise but for something greater and better, as plainly appears in the case of the gods, whom we are content to call 'happy' or 'blessed', an epithet we apply also to such men as most closely resemble the gods. We see that it is so also with *things* that are good. No one praises happiness as he praises justice – no, we think it something more divine and higher in the scale of values. Hence Eudoxus is held to have made a good point in his plea for awarding the first prize to pleasure when he adduced the following argument. The fact that pleasure (which is one of the things recognized as good) is not praised is evidence that it is superior to the goods that are praised. And this character, he thought, belongs also to God and to the supreme good, which is the standard to which all other goods are referred.

While praise is given to goodness – for goodness is the inspiration to noble actions – panegyrics or encomiums are bestowed on the high deed done, whether bodily feat or intellectual achievement. We must, however, leave the detailed examination of this subject to those who have made a special study of the encomium, for no doubt it is more in their line than in ours. But so far as we are concerned the arguments that have been adduced must have convinced us that happiness is one of those things that are perfect and beyond praise. We might infer as much from the consideration that it is a first principle, as is proved by the fact that everything we do is done with a view to it, and we regard it as fundamental that the first principle and cause of the things called good should be something above price and divine.

Our definition of happiness compels us to consider the nature of virtue.
But before we can do this we must have some conception of how the
human soul is constituted. It will serve our purpose to take over (for
what it is worth) the current psychology which divides the soul into
'parts'. (Section 18 of the chapter which follows is omitted as unintel-
ligible except to a specialist in Greek mathematics and unimportant
event to him.)

CHAPTER THIRTEEN

HAPPINESS, then, being an activity of the soul in conformity with perfect goodness, it follows that we must examine
the nature of goodness. When we have done this we should
be in a better position to investigate the nature of happiness.
There is this, too. The genuine statesman is thought of as a
man who has taken peculiar pains to master this problem,
desiring as he does to make his fellow-citizens good men
obedient to the laws.* Now, if the study of moral goodness is
a part of political science, our inquiry into its nature will
clearly follow the lines laid down in our preliminary observations.

Well, the goodness we have to consider is human goodness. This – I mean human goodness or (if you prefer to put
it that way) human happiness – was what we set out to find.
By human goodness is meant not fineness of physique but a
right condition of the soul, and by happiness a condition of
the soul. That being so, it is evident that the statesman ought
to have some inkling of psychology, just as the doctor who is
to specialize in diseases of the eye must have a general
knowledge of physiology. Indeed, such a general background
is even more necessary for the statesman in view of the fact
that his science is of a higher order than the doctor's. Now
the best kind of doctor takes a good deal of trouble to acquire
a knowledge of the human body as a whole. Therefore the
statesman should also be a psychologist and study the soul
with an eye to his profession. Yet he will do so only as far as

* We may point to the lawgivers of Crete and Sparta, and similar historical characters.

his own problems make it necessary; to go into greater detail on the subject would hardly be worth the labour spent on it.

Psychology has been studied elsewhere and some of the doctrines stated there may be accepted as adequate for our present purpose and used by us here. The soul is represented as consisting of two parts, a rational and an irrational.* As regards the irrational part there is one subdivision of it which appears to be common to all living things, and this we may designate as having a 'vegetative' nature, by which I mean that it is the cause of nutrition and growth, since one must assume the existence of some such vital force in all things that assimilate food.† Now the excellence peculiar to this power is evidently common to the whole of animated nature and not confined to man. This view is supported by the admitted fact that the vegetative part of us is particularly active in sleep, when the good and the bad are hardest to distinguish.‡ Such a phenomenon would be only natural, for sleep is a cessation of that function on the operation of which depends the goodness or badness of the soul.§ But enough of this, let us say no more about the nutritive part of the soul, since it forms no portion of goodness in the specifically *human* character.

But there would seem to be another constituent of the soul which, while irrational, contains an element of rationality. It may be observed in the types of men we call 'continent' and 'incontinent'. They have a principle – a rational element in their souls – which we commend, because it en-

* Whether the parts are separate like the parts of the body or anything that is physically divisible, or, like the concave and convex aspects of the arc of a circle, are distinguishable only by definition and in thought, is here an irrelevant question.

† I include embryos, which share this power with fully developed organisms. That is more reasonable than to assume that the latter can assimilate food in a different way.

‡ Hence the saying, 'For half their lives no man is happier than another.'

§ This statement requires some modification, because there are some bodily processes which can reach the centres of consciousness during sleep, thus providing us with the reason why virtuous persons have better dreams than the average man.

courages them to perform the best actions in the right way. But such natures appear at the same time to contain an irrational element in active opposition to the rational. In paralytic cases it often happens that when the patient wills to move his limbs to the right they swing instead to the left. Exactly the same thing may happen to the soul; the impulses of the incontinent man carry him in the opposite direction from that towards which he was aiming. The only difference is that, where the body is concerned, we see the uncontrolled limb, while the erratic impulse we do not see. Yet this should not prevent us from believing that besides the rational an irrational principle exists running opposite and counter to the other.* Yet, as I said, it is not altogether irrational; at all events it submits to direction in the continent man, and may be assumed to be still more amenable to reason in the 'temperate' and in the brave man, in whose moral make-up there is nothing which is at variance with reason.

We have, then, this clear result. The irrational part of the soul, like the soul itself, consists of two parts. The first of these is the vegetative, which has nothing rational about it at all. The second is that from which spring the appetites and desire in general; and this does in a way participate in reason, seeing that it is submissive and obedient to it. ... That the irrational element in us need not be heedless of the rational is proved by the fact that we find admonition, indeed every form of censure and exhortation, not ineffective. It may be, however, that we ought to speak of the appetitive part of the soul as rational, too. In that event it will rather be the rational part that is divided in two, one division rational in the proper sense of the word and in its nature, the other in the derivative sense in which we speak of a child as 'listening to reason' in the person of its father.

These distinctions within the soul supply us with a classification of the virtues. Some are called 'intellectual', as wisdom, intelligence, prudence. Others are 'moral', as liberality

* What forms the difference between them is a question which does not here arise.

and temperance. When we are speaking of a man's *character* we do not describe him as wise or intelligent but as gentle or temperate. Yet we praise a wise man, too, on the ground of his 'disposition' or settled habit of acting wisely. The dispositions so praised are what we mean by 'virtues'.

BOOK TWO

This book is the first of a series (II–V) dealing with the moral virtues. But first we have to ask what moral virtue or goodness is. It is a confirmed disposition to act rightly, the disposition being itself formed by a continuous series of right actions.

CHAPTER ONE

VIRTUE, then, is of two kinds, intellectual and moral. Of these the intellectual is in the main indebted to teaching for its production and growth, and this calls for time and experience. Moral goodness, on the other hand, is the child of habit, from which it has got its very name, ethics being derived from *ethos*, 'habit', by a slight alteration in the quantity of the *e*. This is an indication that none of the moral virtues is implanted in us by Nature, since nothing that Nature creates can be taught by habit to change the direction of its development. For instance a stone, the natural tendency of which is to fall down, could never, however often you threw it up in the air, be trained to go in that direction. No more can you train fire to burn downwards. Nothing in fact, if the law of its being is to behave in one way, can be habituated to behave in another. The moral virtues, then, are produced in us neither *by* Nature nor *against* Nature. Nature, indeed, prepares in us the ground for their reception, but their complete formation is the product of habit.

Consider again these powers or faculties with which Nature endows us. We acquire the ability to use them before we do use them. The senses provide us with a good illustration of this truth. We have not acquired the sense of sight from repeated acts of seeing, or the sense of hearing from repeated acts of hearing. It is the other way round. We had these senses before we used them, we did not acquire them as a result of using them. But the moral virtues we do acquire by first exercising them. The same is true of the arts and crafts in general. The craftsman has to learn how to make things, but he learns in the process of making them. So men become builders by building, harp players by playing the harp. By a similar process we become just by performing just actions, temperate by performing temperate actions, brave by performing brave actions. Look at what happens in political societies – it confirms our view. We find legislators seeking to make good men of their fellows by making good behaviour habitual with them. That is the aim of every law-giver, and when he is unable to carry it out effectively, he is a failure; nay, success or failure in this is what makes the difference between a good constitution and a bad.

Again, the creation and the destruction of any virtue are effected by identical causes and identical means; and this may be said, too, of every art. It is as a result of playing the harp that harpers become good or bad in their art. The same is true of builders and all other craftsmen. Men will become good builders as a result of building well, and bad builders as a result of building badly. Otherwise what would be the use of having anyone to teach a trade? Craftsmen would all be born either good or bad. Now this holds also of the virtues. It is in the course of our dealings with our fellow-men that we become just or unjust. It is our behaviour in a crisis and our habitual reactions to danger that make us brave or cowardly, as it may be. So with our desires and passions. Some men are made temperate and gentle, others profligate and passionate, the former by conducting themselves in one way, the latter by conducting themselves in another, in situations in which their feelings are involved. We may sum it all up in the generalization, 'Like activities produce like dispositions'. This makes it our duty to see that our activities have the right character, since the differences of quality in them are repeated in the dispositions that follow in their train. So it is a matter of real importance whether our early education confirms us in one set of habits or another. It would be nearer the truth to say that it makes a very great difference indeed, in fact all the difference in the world.

If, then, everything depends upon the way in which we act, clearly it is incumbent on us to inquire what this way is, never forgetting that we must not look for the precision attainable in the exact sciences.

CHAPTER TWO

SINCE the branch of philosophy on which we are at present engaged differs from the others in not being a subject of merely intellectual interest – I mean we are not concerned to know what goodness essentially is, but how we are to become good men, for this alone gives the study its practical value – we must apply our minds to the solution of the problems of conduct. For, as I remarked, it is our actions that determine our dispositions.

Now that when we act we should do so according to the right principle, is common ground and I propose to take it as a basis of discussion.* But we must begin with the admission that any theory of conduct must be content with an outline without much precision in details. We noted this when I said at the beginning of our discussion of this part of our subject that the measure of exactness of statement in any field of study must be determined by the nature of the matter studied. Now matters of conduct and considerations of what is to our advantage have no fixity about them any more than matters affecting our health. And if this be true of moral philosophy as a whole, it is still more true that the discussion of particular problems in ethics admits of no exactitude. For they do not fall under any science or professional tradition, but those who are following some line of conduct are forced in every collocation of circumstances to think out for themselves what is suited to these circumstances, just as doctors and navigators have to do in their different *métiers*. We can do no more than give our arguments, inexact as they necessarily are, such support as is available.

* There will be an opportunity later of considering what is meant by this formula, in particular what is meant by 'the right principle' and how, in its ethical aspect, it is related to the moral virtues.

After this reminder Aristotle proceeds to lay down a proposition or generalization which is cardinal in his system of ethics. Excess or deficiency in his actions impairs the moral quality of the agent.

Let us begin with the following observation. It is in the nature of moral qualities that they can be destroyed by deficiency on the one hand and excess on the other. We can see this in the instances of bodily health and strength.* Physical strength is destroyed by too much and also by too little exercise. Similarly health is ruined by eating and drinking either too much or too little, while it is produced, increased, and preserved by taking the right quantity of drink and victuals. Well, it is the same with temperance, courage, and the other virtues. The man who shuns and fears everything and can stand up to nothing becomes a coward. The man who is afraid of nothing at all, but marches up to every danger, becomes foolhardy. In the same way the man who indulges in every pleasure without refraining from a single one becomes incontinent. If, on the other hand, a man behaves like the Boor in comedy and turns his back on every pleasure, he will find his sensibilities becoming blunted. So also temperance and courage are destroyed both by excess and deficiency, and they are kept alive by observance of the mean.

Our virtues are employed in the same kinds of action as established them.

Let us go back to our statement that the virtues are produced and fostered as a result, and by the agency, of actions of the same quality as effect their destruction. It is also true that after the virtues have been formed they find expression in actions of that kind. We may see this in a concrete instance – bodily strength. It results from taking plenty of nourishment and going in for hard training, and it is the strong man who is best fitted to cope with such conditions. So with the virtues. It is by refraining from pleasures that we

* If we are to illustrate the material, it must be by concrete images.

become temperate, and it is when we have become temperate that we are most able to abstain from pleasures. Or take
courage. It is by habituating ourselves to make light of
alarming situations and to confront them that we become
brave, and it is when we have become brave that we shall
be most able to face an alarming situation.

There is one way of discovering whether we are in full possession of a
virtue or not. We possess it if we feel pleasure in its exercise; indeed,
it is just with pleasures and pains that virtue is concerned.

CHAPTER THREE

WE may use the pleasure (or pain) that accompanies the
exercise of our dispositions as an index of how far they have
established themselves. A man is temperate who abstaining
from bodily pleasures finds this abstinence pleasant; if he
finds it irksome, he is intemperate. Again, it is the man who
encounters danger gladly, or at least without painful sensations, who is brave; the man who has these sensations is a
coward. In a word, moral virtue has to do with pains and
pleasures. There are a number of reasons for believing this.
(1) Pleasure has a way of making us do what is disgraceful;
pain deters us from doing what is right and fine. Hence the
importance – I quote Plato – of having been brought up to
find pleasure and pain in the right things. True education is
just such a training. (2) The virtues operate with actions and
emotions, each of which is accompanied by pleasure or pain.
This is only another way of saying that virtue has to do with
pleasures and pains. (3) Pain is used as an instrument of
punishment. For in her remedies Nature works by opposites,
and pain can be remedial. (4) When any disposition finds its
complete expression it is, as we noted, in dealing with just
those things by which it is its nature to be made better or
worse, and which constitute the sphere of its operations.
Now when men become bad it is under the influence of
pleasures and pains when they seek the wrong ones among

them, or seek them at the wrong time, or in the wrong manner, or in any of the wrong forms which such offences may take; and in seeking the wrong pleasures and pains they shun the right. This has led some thinkers to identify the moral virtues with conditions of the soul in which passion is eliminated or reduced to a minimum. But this is to make too absolute a statement – it needs to be qualified by adding that such a condition must be attained 'in the right manner and at the right time' together with the other modifying circumstances.

So far, then, we have got this result. Moral goodness is a quality disposing us to act in the best way when we are dealing with pleasures and pains, while vice is one which leads us to act in the worst way when we deal with them.

The point may be brought out more clearly by some other considerations. (5) There are three kinds of things that determine our choice in all our actions – the morally fine, the expedient, the pleasant; and three that we shun – the base, the harmful, the painful. Now in his dealings with all of these it is the good man who is most likely to go right, and the bad man who tends to go wrong, and that most notably in the matter of pleasure. The sensation of pleasure is felt by us in common with all animals, accompanying everything we choose, for even the fine and the expedient have a pleasurable effect upon us. (6) The capacity for experiencing pleasure has grown in us from infancy as part of our general development, and human life, being dyed in grain with it, receives therefrom a colour hard to scrape off. (7) Pleasure and pain are also the standards by which with greater or less strictness we regulate our considered actions. Since to feel pleasure and pain rightly or wrongly is an important factor in human behaviour, it follows that we are primarily concerned with these sensations. (8) Heraclitus says it is hard to fight against anger, but it is harder still to fight against pleasure. Yet to grapple with the harder has always been the business, as of art, so of goodness, success in a task being proportionate to its difficulty. This gives us another reason for believing that morality and statesmanship must concentrate on pleasures and pains, seeing it is the man who deals rightly with them who will be good, and the man who deals with them wrongly who will be bad.

Here, then, are our conclusions. (*a*) Virtue is concerned with pains and pleasures. (*b*) The actions which produce virtue are identical in character with those which increase it. (*c*) These actions differently performed destroy it. (*d*) The actions which produced it are identical with those in which it finds expression.

Aristotle now meets an obvious objection: How can a man perform (say) just actions unless he is already just?

CHAPTER FOUR

A DIFFICULTY, however, may be raised as to what we mean when we say that we must perform just actions if we are to become just, and temperate actions if we are to be temperate. It may be argued that, if I do what is just and temperate, I am just and temperate already, exactly as, if I spell words or play music correctly, I must already be literate or musical. This I take to be a false analogy, even in the arts. It is possible to spell a word right by accident or because somebody tips you the answer. But you will be a scholar only if your spelling is done as a scholar does it, that is thanks to the scholarship in your own mind. Nor will the suggested analogy with the arts bear scrutiny. A work of art is good or bad in itself – let it possess a certain quality, and that is all we ask of it. But virtuous actions are not done in a virtuous – a just or temperate – way merely because *they* have the appropriate quality. The *doer* must be in a certain frame of mind when he does them. Three conditions are involved. (1) The agent must act in full consciousness of what he is doing. (2) He must 'will' his action, and will it for its own sake. (3) The act must proceed from a fixed and unchangeable disposition. Now these requirements, if we except mere knowledge, are not counted among the necessary qualifications of an artist. For the acquisition of virtue, on the other hand, knowledge is of little or no value, but the other requirements are of immense, of sovran, importance, since it is the repeated performance of just and temperate actions that produces virtue. Actions, to be sure, are *called* just and temperate when they are such as a just or temperate man would do. But the doer is just or temperate not because he does such things but when he does them in the way of just and temperate persons. It is therefore quite fair to say that a man becomes just by the performance of just, and temperate by the performance of temperate, actions; nor is there the smallest likelihood of a man's becoming good by any other course of conduct. It is not, however, a popular line to take, most men preferring theory to practice under the impression that arguing about morals proves them to be philosophers, and that in this way they will turn out to be fine characters. Herein they resemble invalids, who listen carefully to all the doctor says but do not carry out a single one of his orders. The bodies of such people will never respond to treatment – nor will the souls of such 'philosophers'.

It is now time to produce a formal definition of virtue. In the Aristotelian system this means stating its genus and differentia – that is to say, the class of things to which it belongs and the point or points which distinguish it from other members of the class.

CHAPTER FIVE

WE now come to the formal definition of virtue. Note first, however, that the human soul is conditioned in three ways. It may have (1) feelings, (2) capacities, (3) dispositions; so virtue must be one of these three. By 'feelings' I mean desire, anger, fear, daring, envy, gratification, friendliness, hatred, longing, jealousy, pity and in general all states of mind that are attended by pleasure or pain. By 'capacities' I mean those faculties in virtue of which we may be described as capable of the feelings in question – anger, for instance, or pain, or pity. By 'dispositions' I mean states of mind in virtue of which we are well or ill disposed in respect

of the feelings concerned. We have, for instance, a bad disposition where angry feelings are concerned if we are disposed
to become excessively or insufficiently angry, and a good
disposition in this respect if we consistently feel the due
amount of anger, which comes between these extremes. So
with the other feelings.

Now, neither the virtues nor the vices are feelings. We
are not spoken of as good or bad in respect of our feelings
but of our virtues and vices. Neither are we praised or
blamed for the way we feel. A man is not praised for being
frightened or angry, nor is he blamed just for being angry;
it is for being angry in a particular way. But we *are* praised
and blamed for our virtues and vices. Again, feeling angry
or frightened is something we can't help, but our virtues are
in a manner expressions of our will; at any rate there is an
element of will in their formation. Finally, we are said to be
'moved' when our feelings are affected, but when it is a
question of moral goodness or badness we are not said to be
'moved' but to be 'disposed' in a particular way. A similar
line of reasoning will prove that the virtues and vices are not
capacities either. We are not spoken of as good or bad, nor
are we praised or blamed, merely because we are *capable* of
feeling. Again, what capacities we have, we have by nature;
but it is not nature that makes us good or bad. ... So, if the
virtues are neither feelings nor capacities, it remains that
they must be dispositions. ...

We have now to state the 'differentia' of virtue. Virtue is a disposi-
tion; but how are we to distinguish it from other dispositions? We
may say that it is such a disposition as enables the good man to per-
form his function well. And he performs it well when he avoids the
extremes and chooses the mean in actions and feelings.

CHAPTER SIX

IT is not, however, enough to give this account of the *genus*
of virtue – that it is a disposition; we must describe its
species. Let us begin, then, with this proposition. Excellence

of whatever kind affects that of which it is the excellence in two ways. (1) It produces a good state in it. (2) It enables it to perform its function well. Take eyesight. The goodness of your eye is not only that which makes your eye good, it is also that which makes it function well. Or take the case of a horse. The goodness of a horse makes him a good horse, but it also makes him good at running, carrying a rider, and facing the enemy. Our proposition, then, seems to be true, and it enables us to say that virtue in a man will be the disposition which (a) makes him a good man, (b) enables him to perform his function well. We have already touched on this point, but more light will be thrown upon it if we consider what is the specific nature of virtue.

To make his meaning clearer Aristotle draws an illustration from mathematics. It is Greek mathematics, and the terminology is no longer quite the same as ours; for example, what he calls 'arithmetical proportion' we should rather call 'arithmetical progression'. It may be doubted whether the illustration makes his meaning – which after all is simple – any clearer. Perhaps it only disguises the danger of passing from mathematical to ethical values. Like other Greek thinkers Aristotle cannot always shake himself free from the associations clustering about Greek words, Greek being the only language he knew. Dividing a material object in half instead of in two unequal parts is not, or is not necessarily, moral action. It cannot be said that Aristotle is unaware of this, for he sees that in conduct the too much and the too little and the mean vary for each agent – a thing abhorrent to the mathematician. So his illustration rather hinders than helps him.

In anything continuous and divisible it is possible to take the half, or more than the half, or less than the half. Now these parts may be larger, smaller, and equal either in relation to the thing divided or in relation to us. The equal part may be described as a mean between too much and too little. By the mean of the thing I understand a point equidistant from the extremes; and this is one and the same for everybody. Let me give an illustration. Ten, let us say, is 'many' and two is 'few' of something. We get the mean of the thing if we take six; * that is, six exceeds and is exceeded by an equal number. This is the rule which gives us the arithmetical mean. But such a method will not give us the mean in relation to ourselves. Let ten pounds of food be a large, and two pounds a small, allowance for an athlete. It does not follow that the trainer will prescribe six pounds. That might be a large or it might be a small allowance for the particular athlete who is to get it. It would be little for Milo but a lot for a man who has just begun his training.† It is the same in all walks of life. The man who knows his business avoids both too much and too little. It is the mean he seeks and adopts – not the mean of the thing but the relative mean.

Every form, then, of applied knowledge, when it performs its function well, looks to the mean and works to the standard set by that. It is because people feel this that they apply the *cliché*, 'You couldn't add anything to it or take anything from it' to an artistic masterpiece, the implication being that too much and too little alike destroy perfection, while the mean preserves it. Now if this be so, and if it be true, as we say, that good craftsmen work to the standard of the mean, then, since goodness like Nature is more exact and of a higher character than any art, it follows that goodness is the quality that hits the mean. By 'goodness' I mean goodness of moral character, since it is moral goodness that deals with feelings and actions, and it is in them that we find excess, deficiency, and a mean. It is possible, for example, to experience fear, boldness, desire, anger, pity, and pleasures and pains generally, too much or too little or to the right amount. If we feel them too much or too little, we are wrong. But to have these feelings at the right times on the right occasions towards the right people for the right motive and in the right way is to have them in the right measure, that is, somewhere between the extremes; and this

* $6 - 2 = 10 - 6$.

† What applies to gymnastics applies also to running and wrestling.

is what characterizes goodness. The same may be said of the mean and extremes in actions. Now it is in the field of actions and feelings that goodness operates; in them we find excess, deficiency, and, between them, the mean, the first two being wrong, the mean right and praised as such.* Goodness, then, is a mean condition in the sense that it aims at and hits the mean.

Consider, too, that it is possible to go wrong in more ways than one. (In Pythagorean terminology evil is a form of the Unlimited, good of the Limited.) But there is only one way of being right. That is why going wrong is easy, and going right difficult; it is easy to miss the bull's-eye and difficult to hit it. Here, then, is another explanation of why the too much and the too little are connected with evil and the mean with good. As the poet says,

Goodness is one, evil is multiform.

We are now in a position to state our definition of virtue with more precision. Observe that the kind of virtue meant here is moral, not intellectual, and that Aristotle must not be taken as saying that the kind of virtue which he regards as the highest and truest is any sort of mean.

We may now define virtue as a disposition of the soul in which, when it has to choose among actions and feelings, it observes the mean relative to us, this being determined by such a rule or principle as would take shape in the mind of a man of sense or practical wisdom. We call it a mean condition as lying between two forms of badness, one being excess and the other deficiency; and also for this reason, that, whereas badness either falls short of or exceeds the right measure in feelings and actions, virtue discovers the mean and deliberately chooses it. Thus, looked at from the point of view of its essence as embodied in its definition, virtue no

* Being right or successful and being praised are both indicative of excellence.

doubt is a mean; judged by the standard of what is right and best, it is an extreme.

Aristotle enters a caution. Though we have said that virtue observes the mean in actions and passions, we do not say this of all acts and all feelings. Some are essentially evil and, when these are involved, our rule of applying the mean cannot be brought into operation.

But choice of a mean is not possible in every action or every feeling. The very names of some have an immediate connotation of evil. Such are malice, shamelessness, envy among feelings, and among actions adultery, theft, murder. All these and more like them have a bad name as being evil in themselves; it is not merely the excess or deficiency of them that we censure. In their case, then, it is impossible to act rightly; whatever we do is wrong. Nor do circumstances make any difference in the rightness or wrongness of them. When a man commits adultery there is no point in asking whether it is with the right woman or at the right time or in the right way, for to do anything like that is simply wrong. It would amount to claiming that there is a mean and excess and defect in unjust or cowardly or intemperate actions If such a thing were possible, we should find ourselves with a mean quantity of excess, a mean of deficiency, an excess of excess and a deficiency of deficiency. But just as in temperance and justice there can be no mean or excess or deficiency, because the mean in a sense *is* an extreme, so there can be no mean or excess or deficiency in those vicious actions – however done, they are wrong. Putting the matter into general language, we may say that there is no mean in the extremes, and no extreme in the mean, to be observed by anybody.

After the definition comes its application to the particular virtues. In these it is always possible to discover a mean — at which the virtue aims — between an excess and a deficiency. Here Aristotle found that a table or diagram of the virtues between their corresponding vices would be useful, and we are to imagine him referring to this in the course of his lectures.

CHAPTER SEVEN

But a generalization of this kind is not enough; we must show that our definition fits particular cases. When we are discussing actions particular statements come nearer the heart of the matter, though general statements cover a wider field. The reason is that human behaviour consists in the performance of particular acts, and our theories must be brought into harmony with them.

You see here a diagram of the virtues. Let us take our particular instances from that.

In the section confined to the feelings inspired by danger you will observe that the mean state is 'courage'. Of those who go to extremes in one direction or the other the man who shows an excess of fearlessness has no name to describe him,* the man who exceeds in confidence or daring is called 'rash' or 'foolhardy', the man who shows an excess of fear and a deficiency of confidence is called a 'coward'. In the pleasures and pains — though not all pleasures and pains, especially pains — the virtue which observes the mean is 'temperance', the excess is the vice of 'intemperance'. Persons defective in the power to enjoy pleasures are a somewhat rare class, and so have not had a name assigned to them: suppose we call them 'unimpressionable'. Coming to the giving and acquiring of money, we find that the mean is 'liberality', the excess 'prodigality', the deficiency 'meanness'. But here we meet a complication. The prodigal man and the mean man exceed and fall short in opposite ways. The prodigal exceeds in giving and falls short in getting money, whereas the mean man exceeds in getting and falls

* We shall often have to make similar admissions.

short in giving it away. Of course this is but a summary account of the matter – a bare outline. But it meets our immediate requirements. Later on these types of character will be more accurately delineated.

But there are other dispositions which declare themselves in the way they deal with money. One is 'lordliness' or 'magnificence', which differs from liberality in that the lordly man deals in large sums, the liberal man in small. Magnificence is the mean state here, the excess is 'bad taste' or 'vulgarity', the defect is 'shabbiness'. These are not the same as the excess and defect on either side of liberality. How they differ is a point which will be discussed later. In the matter of honour the mean is 'proper pride', the excess 'vanity', the defect 'poor-spiritedness'. And just as liberality differs, as I said, from magnificence in being concerned with small sums of money, so there is a state related to proper pride in the same way, being concerned with small honours, while pride is concerned with great. For it is possible to aspire to small honours in the right way, or to a greater or less extent than is right. The man who has this aspiration to excess is called 'ambitious'; if he does not cherish it enough, he is 'unambitious'; but the man who has it to the right extent – that is, strikes the mean – has no special designation. This is true also of the corresponding dispositions with one exception, that of the ambitious man, which is called 'ambitiousness'. This will explain why each of the extreme characters stakes out a claim in the middle region. Indeed we ourselves call the character between the extremes sometimes 'ambitious' and sometimes 'unambitious'. That is proved by our sometimes praising a man for being ambitious and sometimes for being unambitious. The reason will appear later. In the meantime let us continue our discussion of the remaining virtues and vices, following the method already laid down.

Let us next take anger. Here too we find excess, deficiency, and the mean. Hardly one of the states of mind involved has a special name; but, since we call the man who attains the mean in this sphere 'gentle', we may call his disposition 'gentleness'. Of the extremes the man who is angry over-

much may be called 'irascible', and his vice 'irascibility';
while the man who reacts too feebly to anger may be called
'poor-spirited' and his disposition 'poor-spiritedness'.

Some virtues and vices appear in social intercourse.

There are, in addition to those we have named, three other
modes of observing the mean which in some ways resemble
and in other ways differ from one another. They are all concerned with what we do and say in social intercourse, but
they differ in this respect, that one is concerned with truthfulness in such intercourse, the other two with the agreeable,
one of these two with the agreeable in amusement, the other
with the agreeable element in every relation of life. About
these two, then, we must say a word, in order that we may
more fully convince ourselves that in all things the mean is
to be commended, while the extremes are neither commendable nor right but reprehensible. I am afraid most of
these too are nameless; but, as in the other cases, we must
try to coin names for them in the interests of clearness and
to make it easy to follow the argument. Well then, as regards
veracity, the character who aims at the mean may be called
'truthful' and what he aims at 'truthfulness'. Pretending,
when it goes too far, is 'boastfulness' and the man who
shows it is a 'boaster' or 'braggart'. If it takes the form of
understatement, the pretence is called 'irony' and the man
who shows it 'ironical'. In agreeableness in social amusement the man who hits the mean is 'witty' and what characterizes him is 'wittiness'. The excess is 'buffoonery' and the
man who exhibits that is a 'buffoon'. The opposite of the
buffoon is the 'boor' and his characteristic is 'boorishness'.
In the other sphere of the agreeable – the general business of
life – the person who is agreeable in the right way is
'friendly' and his disposition 'friendliness'. The man who
makes himself too agreeable, supposing him to have no ulterior object, is 'obsequious'; if he has such an object, he is a
'flatterer'. The man who is deficient in this quality and takes

every opportunity of making himself disagreeable may be called 'peevish' or 'sulky' or 'surly'.

But it is not only in settled dispositions that a mean may be observed; it may be observed in passing states of emotion.

Even when feelings and emotional states are involved one notes that mean conditions exist. And here also, it would be agreed, we may find one man observing the mean and another going beyond it, for instance, the 'shamefaced' man, who is put out of countenance by anything. Or a man may fall short here of the due mean. Thus any one who is deficient in a sense of shame, or has none at all, is called 'shameless'. The man who avoids both extremes is 'modest', and him we praise. For, while modesty is not a form of goodness, it is praised; it and the modest man. Then there is 'righteous indignation'. This is felt by any one who strikes the mean between 'envy' and 'malice', by which last word I mean a pleased feeling at the misfortunes of other people. These are emotions concerned with the pains and pleasures we feel at the fortunes of our neighbours. The man who feels righteous indignation is pained by undeserved good fortune; but the envious man goes beyond that and is pained at anybody's success. The malicious man, on the other hand, is so far from being pained by the misfortunes of another that he is actually tickled by them.

However, a fitting opportunity of discussing these matters will present itself in another place. And after that we shall treat of justice. In that connexion we shall have to distinguish between the various kinds of justice – for the word is used in more senses than one – and show in what way each of them is a mean. . . .

But after all, proceeds Aristotle, the true determinant of the mean is not the geometer's rod but the guiding principle in the good man's soul. The diagram of the virtues and vices, then, is just an arrangement and, as Aristotle goes on to show, an unimportant one at that.

CHAPTER EIGHT

Thus there are three dispositions, two of them taking a vicious form (one in the direction of excess, the other of defect) and one a good form, namely, the observance of the mean. They are all opposed to one another, though not all in the same way. The extreme states are opposed both to the mean and one another, and the mean is opposed to both extremes. For just as the equal is greater compared with the less, and less compared with the greater, so the mean states (whether in feelings or actions) are in excess if compared with the deficient, and deficient if compared with the excessive, states. Thus a brave man appears rash when set beside a coward, and cowardly when set beside a rash man; a temperate man appears intemperate beside a man of dull sensibilities, and dull if contrasted with an intemperate man. This is the reason why each extreme character tries to push the mean nearer the other. The coward calls the brave man rash, the rash man calls him a coward. And so in the other cases. But, while all the dispositions are opposed to one another in this way, the greatest degree of opposition is that which is found between the two extremes. For they are separated by a greater interval from one another than from the mean, as the great is more widely removed from the small, and the small from the great, than either from the equal. It may be added that sometimes an extreme bears a certain resemblance to a mean. For example, rashness resembles courage, and prodigality resembles liberality. But between the extremes there is always the maximum dissimilarity. Now opposites are by definition things as far removed as possible from one another. Hence the farther apart things are, the more opposite they will be. Sometimes it is the deficiency, in other instances it is the excess, that is more directly opposed to the mean. Thus cowardice, a deficiency, is more opposed to courage than is rashness, an excess. And it is not insensibility, the deficiency, that is more opposed to temperance but intemperance, the excess. This arises from one or other of two causes. One lies in the nature of the thing itself and may be explained as follows. When one extreme is nearer to the mean and resembles it more, it is not that extreme but the other which we tend to oppose to the mean. For instance, since rashness is held to be nearer and liker to courage than is cowardice, it is cowardice which we tend to oppose to courage on the principle that the extremes which are remoter from the mean strike us as more opposite to it. The other cause lies in ourselves. It is the things to which we are naturally inclined that appear to us more opposed to the mean. For example, we have a natural inclination to pleasure, which makes us prone to fall into intemperance. Accordingly we tend to describe as opposite to the mean those things towards which we have an instinctive inclination. For this reason intemperance, the excess, is more opposed to temperance than is insensibility to pleasure, the deficiency.

CHAPTER NINE

I HAVE said enough to show that moral excellence is a mean, and I have shown in what sense it is so. It is, namely, a mean between two forms of badness, one of excess and the other of defect, and is so described because it aims at hitting the mean point in feelings and in actions. This makes virtue hard of achievement, because finding the middle point is never easy. It is not everybody, for instance, who can find the centre of a circle – that calls for a geometrician. Thus, too, it is easy to fly into a passion – anybody can do that – but to be angry with the right person and to the right extent and at the right time and with the right object and in the right way – that is not easy, and it is not everyone who can do it. This is equally true of giving or spending money. Hence we infer that to do these things properly is rare, laudable and fine.

Aristotle now suggests some rules for our guidance.

In view of this we shall find it useful when aiming at the mean to observe these rules. (1) *Keep away from that extreme which is the more opposed to the mean.* It is Calypso's advice:

> Swing round the ship clear of this surf and surge.

For one of the extremes is always a more dangerous error than the other; and – since it is hard to hit the bull's-eye – we must take the next best course and choose the least of the evils. And it will be easiest for us to do this if we follow the rule I have suggested. (2) *Note the errors into which we personally are most liable to fall.* (Each of us has his natural bias in one direction or another.) We shall find out what ours are by noting what gives us pleasure and pain. After that we must drag ourselves in the opposite direction. For our best way of reaching the middle is by giving a wide berth to our darling sin. It is the method used by a carpenter when he is straightening a warped board. (3) *Always be particularly on your guard against pleasure and pleasant things.* When Pleasure is at the bar the jury is not impartial. So it will be best for us if we feel towards her as the Trojan elders felt towards Helen, and regularly apply their words to her. If we are for packing her off, as they were with Helen, we shall be the less likely to go wrong.

To sum up. These are the rules by observation of which we have the best chance of hitting the mean. But of course difficulties spring up, especially when we are confronted with an exceptional case. For example, it is not easy to say precisely what is the right way to be angry and with whom and on what grounds and for how long. In fact we are inconsistent on this point, sometimes praising people who are deficient in the capacity for anger and calling them 'gentle', sometimes praising the choleric and calling them 'stout fellows'. To be sure we are not hard on a man who goes off the straight path in the direction of too much or too little, if he goes off only a little way. We reserve our censure for the man who swerves widely from the course, because then we are bound to notice it. Yet it is not easy to find a formula by which we may determine how far and up to what point a man may go wrong before he incurs blame. But this difficulty of definition is inherent in every object of perception; such questions of degree are bound up with the circumstances of the individual case, where our only criterion *is* the perception.

So much, then, has become clear. In all our conduct it is the mean state that is to be praised. But one should lean sometimes in the direction of the more, sometimes in that of the less, because that is the readiest way of attaining to goodness and the mean.

BOOK THREE

Aristotle now approaches the question of moral responsibility, so important in modern ethics. It never occurred to him to doubt the freedom of the will, but he is as much alive as any modern thinker to the fact — and the importance of the fact — that our acts are not all voluntary. In the following chapter he distinguishes between the degrees of their voluntariness.

CHAPTER ONE

WE have found that moral excellence or virtue has to do with feelings and actions. These may be voluntary or involuntary. It is only to the former that we assign praise or blame, though when the involuntary are concerned we may find ourselves ready to condone and on occasion to pity. It is clearly, then, incumbent on the student of moral philosophy to determine the limits of the voluntary and involuntary. Legislators also find such a definition useful when they are seeking to prescribe appropriate rewards and punishments.

Actions are commonly regarded as involuntary when they are performed (*a*) under compulsion, (*b*) as the result of ignorance. An act, it is thought, is done under compulsion when it originates in some external cause of such a nature that the agent or person subject to the compulsion contributes nothing to it. Such a situation is created, for example, when a sea captain is carried out of his course by a contrary wind or by men who have got him in their power. But the case is not always so clear. One might have to consider an action performed for some fine end or through fear of something worse to follow. For example, a tyrant who had a man's parents or children in his power might order him to to do something dishonourable on condition that, if the man did it, their lives would be spared; otherwise not. In such cases it might be hard to say whether the actions are voluntary or not. A similar difficulty is created by the jettison of cargo in a storm. When the situation has no complications you never get a man voluntarily throwing away his property. But if it is to save the life of himself and his mates, any sensible person will do it. Such actions partake of both qualities, though they look more like voluntary than involuntary acts. For at the time they are performed they are the result of a deliberate choice between alternatives, and when an action is performed the end or object of that action is held to be the end it had at the moment of its performance. It follows that the terms 'voluntary' and 'involuntary' should be used with reference to the time when the acts were being performed. Now in the imaginary cases we have stated the acts are voluntary. For the movement of the limbs instrumental to the action originates in the agent himself, and when this is so it is in a man's own power to act or not to act. Such actions therefore are voluntary. But they are so only in the special circumstances; otherwise of course they would be involuntary. For nobody would choose to do anything of the sort purely for its own sake. Occasionally indeed the performance of such actions is held to do a man credit. This happens when he submits to some disgrace or pain as the only way of achieving some great or splendid result. But if his case is just the opposite he is blamed, for it shows a degraded nature to submit to humiliations with only a paltry object in view, or at any rate not a high one. But there are also cases which are thought to merit, I will not say praise, but condonation. An example is provided when a man does something wrong because he is afraid of torture too severe for flesh and blood to endure. Though surely there are some things which a man cannot be compelled to do – which he will rather die than do, however painful the mode of death. Such a deed is matricide; the reasons which 'compelled' Alcmaeon in Euripides' play to kill his mother carry their absurdity on the face of them. Yet it is not always easy to make up our minds what is our best course in choosing one of two alternatives – such and such an action instead of such and such another – or in facing one penalty instead of another. Still harder is it to stick to our decision when made. For, generally speaking, the consequences we expect in such imbroglios are painful, and what we are forced to do far from honourable. Then we get praised or blamed according as we succumb to the compulsion or resist it.

What class of actions, then, ought we to distinguish as 'compulsory'? It is arguable that the bare description will apply to any case where the cause of the action is found in things external to the agent when he contributes nothing to the result. But it may happen that actions, though, abstractly considered, involuntary, are deliberately chosen at a given time and in given circumstances in preference to a given alternative. In that case, their origin being in the agent, these actions must be pronounced voluntary in the particular circumstances and because they are preferred to their alternatives. In themselves they are involuntary, yet they have more of the voluntary about them, since conduct is a sequence of particular acts, and the particular things done in the circumstances we have supposed are voluntary. But when it comes to saying which of two alternative lines of action should be preferred – then difficulties arise. For the differences in particular cases are many.

If it should be argued that pleasurable and honourable things exercise constraint upon us from without, and therefore actions performed under their influence are compulsory, it may be replied that this would make every action compulsory. For we all have some pleasurable or honourable motive in everything we do. Secondly, people acting under compulsion and against their will find it painful, whereas those whose actions are inspired by the pleasurable and the honourable find that these actions are accompanied by pleasure. In the third place it is absurd to accuse external influences instead of ourselves when we fall an easy prey to such inducements and to lay the blame for all dishonourable deeds on the seductions of pleasure, while claiming for ourselves credit for any fine thing we have done. It appears, then, that an action is compulsory only when it is caused by something external to itself which is not influenced by anything contributed by the person under compulsion.

Then there are acts done through ignorance. Any act of this nature is other than voluntary, but it is involuntary only when it causes the doer subsequent pain and regret. For a man who has been led into some action by ignorance and yet has no regrets, while he cannot be said to have been a voluntary agent – he did not know what he was doing – nevertheless cannot be said to have acted involuntarily, since he feels no compunction. We therefore draw a distinction. (a) When a man who has done something as the result of ignorance is sorry for it, we take it that he has acted involuntarily. (b) When such a man is not sorry, the case is different and we shall have to call him a 'non-voluntary' agent. For it is better that he should have a distinctive name in order to mark the distinction. Note, further, that there is evidently a difference between acting *in consequence* of ignorance and acting *in* ignorance. When a man is drunk or in a passion his actions are not supposed to be the result of ignorance but of one or other of these conditions. But, as he does not realize what he is doing, he is acting *in* ignorance. To be sure every bad man is ignorant of what he ought to do and refrain from doing, and it is just this ignorance that makes people unjust and otherwise wicked. But when we use the word 'involuntary' we do not apply it in a case where the agent does not know what is for his own good. For involuntary acts are not the consequence of ignorance when the ignorance is shown in our choice of ends; what does result from such ignorance is a completely vicious condition. No, what I mean is not general ignorance – which is what gives ground for censure – but particular ignorance, ignorance that is to say of the particular circumstances or the particular persons concerned. In such cases there may be room for pity and pardon, because a man who acts in ignorance of such details is an involuntary agent. It will therefore no doubt be well to define the nature and determine the number of these particular circumstances. They are (1) the agent, (2) the act, (3) that which is the object or within the range of the act. Sometimes we must add (4) the instrument (e.g. a tool), (5) the effect or result (e.g. when a man's life is saved), (6) the manner (e.g. gently or roughly). Now nobody in his right mind could be ignorant of *all* these circumstances. Obviously he cannot be ignorant of (1) the agent – how can he fail to know himself? But a man may fail to know (2) what he is doing, as when people say that a remark 'escaped' them or that they did not know they were betraying secrets. (A good instance is that of Aeschylus' supposed revelation of the Mysteries.) Or like the man who was accused of killing another with a catapult, you might say you only wanted to show him how the thing worked. Then (3) you might mistake, say, your son for an enemy, like Merope in the play, or (4) take a naked spear instead of one with the button on, or a lump of rock in mistake for a pumice stone, or (5) you might be the death of a man with a medicine which you hoped would save his life, or (6) hit your antagonist a blow when you only meant to grip his hand, as in 'open' wrestling. Seeing then that there is the possibility of ignorance in any of these special circumstances, one who has acted in ignorance of any one of them is considered to have acted involuntarily, especially if it was the most important of them that he did not know, which by general agreement are (2) the act and (3) the effect of the act.

An involuntary act being one performed under compulsion or as the result of ignorance, a voluntary act would seem to be one of which the origin or efficient cause lies in the agent, he knowing the particular circumstances in which he is acting. I believe it to be an error to say that acts occasioned by anger or desire are involuntary. For in the first place if we maintain this we shall have to give up the view that any of the lower animals, or even children, are capable of voluntary action. In the second place, when we act from desire or anger are none of our actions voluntary? Or are our fine actions voluntary, our ignoble actions involuntary? It is an absurd distinction, since the agent is one and the same person. It is surely paradoxical to describe as 'involuntary' acts inspired by sentiments which we quite properly desire to have. There are some things at which we *ought* to feel angry, and others which we *ought* to desire – health, for instance, and the acquisition of knowledge. Thirdly, people assume that what is involuntary must be painful and what falls in with our own wishes must be pleasant. Fourthly, what difference is there in point of voluntariness between wrong actions which are calculated and wrong actions which are done on impulse? Both are to be avoided; and the further reflection suggests itself, that the irrational emotions are no less typically human than our considered judgement. Whence it follows that actions inspired by anger or desire are equally typical of the human being who performs them. Therefore to classify these actions as 'involuntary' is surely a very strange proceeding.

Aristotle is now led to consider the nature of proairesis, *a word which he uses to express the choice both of ends and of the means to an end. In the medieval Latin versions it was translated by* electio. *We can hardly revive that use of 'election' now, but so long as we keep in mind that* proairesis *always implies an act of* deliberate *choice, we shall follow his meaning well enough.*

CHAPTER TWO

HAVING distinguished between voluntary and involuntary actions, we must now examine what is meant by *proairesis* or 'deliberate choice'. It is evidently related to goodness in a specially intimate way, and we may take it as affording a better test of character than is supplied by actions.

Now such choice is clearly a voluntary act. But 'choice' and 'the voluntary' are not interchangeable expressions, the voluntary having a wider connotation. Thus children and animals are as capable of voluntary action as adult men; but they have not the same capacity for deliberate choice. Also things done on the inspiration of the moment, though we may call them voluntary, are not said to be done of deliberate choice. Some identify it with desire, some with passion, others with wish, others with belief or opinion of some kind. But none of these theories carries conviction. Let us consider them one by one.

(1) The brutes do not share with man the power of deliberate choice, but like him they feel desire and passion. Moreover, the man who lacks self-control feels desire when he acts but does not exercise choice, while the exact opposite is true of the man who is master of his passions. Again, desire may be in conflict with choice, but not one desire with another. Finally, the object of desire presents itself as painful or pleasant, but the object of choice is neither the one nor the other. (2) Still less is choice to be identified with passion. Acts which are the effects of passion are surely the very last that can be called acts of deliberate choice. (3) Nor is choice anything like a wish, though there is a superficial connexion between them. There can be no choice where impossibilities are involved; a man who should declare that he 'chose' something incapable of realization would be considered a half-wit. On the other hand it is just impossibilities for which we do tend to wish – for instance, to live for ever. Again, we may form a wish for some result which could never be achieved by our own efforts – for instance, the success of a particular actor or athlete. Nobody, however, *chooses* things like that but only what he imagines he could accomplish by his own efforts. Again, our wishes are directed more to ends than to means. For example, our *wish* is to be healthy, but what we *choose* are things which will make us healthy. We 'wish' – it is the regular word in this connexion – to be happy, but it would be an incorrect expression to say we 'choose' to be happy. In fine, choice is evidently concerned with things which we regard as attainable. (4) Neither can it be opinion, for it seems possible to entertain an opinion about anything – about things that are eternal and impossible – just as much as about things which we suppose attainable. Besides, we distinguish opinions as true or false, not as good or bad, which is the distinction drawn when we make a choice. Probably, then, no one goes so far as to identify choice with opinion in general. But neither can it be identi-

fied with any particular opinion. For it is on our choice of good or evil, not on our opinion about it, that it depends whether we are to be good or bad. Again, when we choose, it is to take or avoid something good or bad. But, when we form an opinion, it is of what a thing is, or for whom it is profitable and in what way, whereas taking or avoiding something is hardly a matter of opinion. Again, when a choice is commended, it is because the right thing or the right course has been chosen rather than for any other reason. But when we praise an opinion, it is on the ground that it has been arrived at in the right way. And when we choose it is those things which we know for certain to be good, but when we form an opinion it is about things which we do not certainly know to be true. Again, it is generally believed that the same people are not equally good at choosing the best actions and forming the best opinions; there are people whose opinions tend to be true but who choose the wrong actions out of sheer devilry. That an act of choice must be preceded or accompanied by an opinion respecting it is true but immaterial. It is not that we are investigating, but whether choice is just a kind of opinion.

Now if none of the definitions we have enumerated is right, what *is* the nature and character of *proairesis* – its genus and differentia? Obviously it belongs to the genus of things voluntary. But not everything that is voluntary is chosen. May we then define it as a voluntary act preceded by deliberation? The qualification is suggested by the fact that you cannot have a choice without reasoning and reflecting. Such previous deliberation seems to be indicated by the very word *proaireton*, which means chosen *before* something else.

Our next step, then, must be to ascertain what we mean by 'deliberation'.

CHAPTER THREE

WE must now ask ourselves about 'deliberation'. May anything be matter for deliberation, or are there some things that cannot be deliberated about at all? (I assume that we ought not to apply the expression 'object of deliberation' to something about which a fool or a lunatic might deliberate; it should be applied only to something about which a reasonable person might deliberate.) Surely nobody 'deliberates' about eternal things, such as the stellar system or the incommensurability of the diagonal with the side of a square. Nor is deliberation concerned with things in motion when the motions are regular, whether the cause of this is the necessity of their being, or the law of their growth, or something else – things, I mean, like the solstices or the dawn. Neither do we deliberate about things that do not happen in regular sequences – droughts, for example, or abnormal rainfalls. Nor about things that are the result of luck or accident, like finding a crock of gold. In all these cases the reason why we do not deliberate about them is that nothing we can do affects the issue. No, it is about things which we can influence by our action that we deliberate.* Even here we have to admit exceptions in deliberating about human affairs. Thus you will not find a Spartan deliberating about the best form of constitution for the Scythians. What we find is that particular groups or societies deliberate about matters which can be brought to an issue by their own exertions. Again, deliberation is out of place when the subject of it is some branch of art or science that has been worked out in detail and is complete within its own limits. An instance of this is spelling. We have never any doubt how a word should be spelt. It is things where our own agency is effective (though not always to the same extent) which engage our deliberations. Such are the practice of medicine and business methods, to which we may add navigation, though here there is a greater call for deliberation than in the case of gymnastic training, because navigation has not been reduced to such exact rules. These observations may be applied to other forms of skill. Finally, deliberation is more in place

* These in fact are all we need consider, for nature, necessity, chance *plus* intelligence and human agency may be taken as forming a complete list of the generally admitted causes.

when it is applied to the arts than to the sciences, because the arts present us with more grounds for a difference of opinion. Deliberation, then, is concerned with things which, while in general following certain definite lines, have no predictable issues, or the result of which cannot be clearly stated, or in which, when important decisions have to be made, we take others into our counsels, distrusting our own ability to settle the point.

Observe also that we do not deliberate about ends but always about means. A doctor does not deliberate whether or not he will cure his patients, nor an orator whether or not he is to win over his audience, nor a statesman whether or not he is to produce law and order, nor does anyone else deliberate about the end at which he is aiming. No, they set some end before themselves and then proceed to consider how and by what means it can be attained. If it appears that there is a variety of means of doing this, they consider which of these will be the easiest and most effective. If it appears that there is only one way of achieving the result, they go on to consider how it will be achieved thereby, and by what means that in turn is to be realized, until they come at last to the cause which, although it is the last in the order of discovery, is the first in the chain of causes.* If they then discover that they have run into an impossibility – if for example they find that a business they would like to start needs capital and they have not got the means of supplying it – they drop the scheme. But, if the thing seems feasible, they try to push it through. By 'feasible' is to be understood what can be achieved by the efforts of ourselves and our friends, since what we do through them is pretty much what we do ourselves, for the cause of their so acting has its origin in us.

---

* Anyone deliberating in the manner I have described seems to be engaged in a process of investigation or analysis, like a mathematician studying a geometrical figure – of course not every investigation (mathematical investigation, for instance) is deliberation, but every deliberation is investigation – and what comes last in the analysis comes first in the process as a result of which the subject investigated is brought into being.

For the craftsman the question sometimes is what tools he is to use, sometimes what use he is to make of them; and in the same way in other activities it is sometimes what means we are to use, sometimes how we are to use whatever means we find to hand.

To repeat our conclusions. A man is the originating cause of his actions; deliberation has for the sphere of its operation acts which are within his own power of doing them; all that we do is done with an eye to something else. It follows that when we deliberate it is about means and not ends. And in our deliberations we are not concerned with particular facts. When we see a loaf we do not deliberate whether it is a loaf, or whether it has been long enough in the oven; we have only to look at it or taste it to find out that. There must be a limit somewhere to deliberation; otherwise there will be no end to it.

Now the thing we deliberate about and the thing we choose are one and the same. The only difference is that, when a thing is chosen, it is already set apart, inasmuch as it has been already selected as a result of the deliberation. We all stop asking how we are going to act when we have traced the origin of action back to ourselves, that is to the ruling or rational part of ourselves, for that it is which makes deliberate choice. The procedure is exemplified in the prehistoric constitutions which we find depicted in the Homeric poems – the kings merely announced their decisions to the people.

Since, therefore, when we choose, we choose something within our reach which we desire as the result of deliberation, we may describe *proairesis* as 'the deliberate desire of something within our power.' The deliberation comes first, then the selection, lastly the desire of following the result of the deliberation. ...

We choose the means and wish the end. What then is it that we do when we wish? It is all very well to say that we wish for the good. The question is, Do we wish for what is really good or only what seems good to us?

CHAPTER FOUR

I HAVE said that wishing, as distinguished from choosing, is directed to ends. Now there are two views about it. (1) It is directed to the good. (2) It is directed to what *appears* to be good. But there are objections to both. (1) Those who maintain that the object of wish is the good are bound to argue that what a man wishes is not wished at all when the end he chooses is chosen under a misapprehension. For according to them if a thing is wished, it must be good. But what is to prevent a man from wishing something bad? (2) Those who say that what we wish is the apparent good are bound to maintain that there is no such thing as a 'natural' object of wish, but that every man wishes what appears to him personally to be good. Yet different persons have different, and sometimes contradictory, views of what is good. Clearly this will not do. In the circumstances we may content ourselves with the proposition that in the true and absolute sense we wish for the good, so long as the personal factor does not come in. When it does, each man wishes what seems to him individually to be good. This allows us to believe that what the good man wishes is truly wished, while what the bad man wishes is just anything that happens to attract him.* For in every moral problem the good man's view of the truth corresponds to the truth, and so he forms a correct judgement. Moral beauty and the sources of pleasure manifest themselves in special forms corresponding to each disposition that is capable of feeling them, and the good man

---

* Thus when a regimen s ollowed you find, if you are in good health, that what is truly wholesome is wholesome to you; but, if you are not well, you will find that other things suit you. You will get the same result if you try the experiment with things that are bitter or sweet or hot or heavy and so on.

shows his superiority above all in his power of seeing the truth in every department of conduct. He is, so to speak, the standard and yardstick of what is fine and pleasant. Most men, it seems only too clear, are led astray by the siren Pleasure. To them she falsely seems a blessing; her they choose as a good, and shun pain as an evil.

The question is now raised whether it is at all times in our power to be good and to do the right. The answer is yes. And it is also in our power at all times to be vicious.

CHAPTER FIVE

SINCE then it is the end that is the object of our wishing, and the means to the end that is the object of our deliberating and choosing, the actions which deal with means must be done by choice and must be voluntary. Now when the virtues are exercised it is upon means. So virtue also is attainable by our own exertions. And so is vice. For what it lies in our power to do, it lies in our power not to do; when we can say 'no', we can say 'yes'. If, then, it is in our power to perform an action when it is right, it will be equally in our power to refrain from performing it when it is wrong; and if it lies with us to refrain from doing a thing when that is right, it will also lie with us to do it when that is wrong. But if it is in our power to do the right or the wrong thing, and equally in our power to refrain from doing so; and if doing right or wrong is, as we saw, the same as being good or bad ourselves, we must conclude that it depends upon ourselves whether we are to be virtuous or vicious. The words

> To sin and suffer – that offends us still:
> But who is ever blest against his will?

must be regarded as a half-truth. It is true that no one is blest against his will, but untrue that wickedness is involuntary. Otherwise we shall have to deny the truth of what we have just been saying and maintain that a man is not the originator of his own actions, of which he might be described as the begetter. But if he demonstrably is so, and we cannot trace our actions to any other springs than those which are found within ourselves, then actions which have such an origin are themselves within our control and are voluntary. In support of this conclusion it seems possible to call in evidence the practice of both private individuals and of legislators. For they inflict pains and penalties for misbehaviour, except in cases where the offender is not held responsible, because he has acted from ignorance or under duress. On the other hand they bestow honours on those who have done some fine action. Their motive in the first case is to stop evil practices, in the second to encourage the well-doer. Now nobody encourages us to do things which it is not in our power to do and which are not voluntary. It does not help at all to be made to believe that there is no such thing as getting hot, or feeling pain or anger, and so on. We shall feel them all the same. We even find that the circumstance that an offence was committed out of ignorance is made a reason for punishment when the offender is held responsible for his ignorance, as is shown, for instance, by the sentence in a case where the accused had been drunk. It may then be doubled on the ground that the offence originated with the offender, since it was open to him to refrain from getting drunk and his drunkenness was responsible for his not knowing what he was doing when he committed the offence. We punish people, too, for breaking the law through ignorance of some point in it which it was their business to know and which they could have known without much trouble. And punishment follows also when the ignorance is thought to have been due to carelessness, it being held that the guilty party need not have shown this ignorance. He should have noticed what he was doing – it was his duty to notice. You may say that very likely he could not help it, he is just that sort of man. But there is an answer to that. Such people have only themselves to blame for having acquired a character like that by their loose living, just as they have only themselves to blame for being unjust, if they make a practice of unjust behaviour, or intemperate, if they spend their time in drinking or other forms of dissipation. It is their persistent activities in certain directions that make them what they are. This is well illustrated by the behaviour of men who are training for some competition or performance: they devote their whole time to the appropriate exercises. The man, then, must be a perfect fool who is unaware that people's characters take their bias from the steady direction of their activities. If a man, well aware of what he is doing, behaves in such a way that he is bound to become unjust, we can only say that he is voluntarily unjust.

Again, while we cannot fairly argue that when a man behaves unjustly he does not wish to be unjust, or that when he plunges into dissipation he has no wish to be dissipated, it is by no means true that he can stop being unjust or dissolute merely by wishing it. You might as well expect a sick man to get better by wishing it. Yet the illness may be voluntary in the sense that it has been caused by loose living and neglecting the doctor's orders. There was a time when he need not have been ill; but once he let himself go, the opportunity was lost. When once you have thrown a stone, it is gone for good and all. Still it lay with yourself to let it lie instead of picking it up and throwing it; the origin of the act was in you. Similarly it was open to the dishonest and dissolute fellow to avoid becoming such a character; so that his original action was voluntary. But once he is hardened in vice the possibility of reforming disappears. Nor is it only vices of character that are voluntary. It is not rare to find bodily defects which are so too. Doubtless nobody blames a man for being born ugly, but we do blame those who lose their looks from want of exercise and neglect of hygiene. We may have the same feeling when a man's physique is weakened or impaired. Thus blindness is not an object of censure but of compassion when it is the result of a congenital defect or an illness or a blow. But if it is the result of alcoholic poisoning or general debauchery, then no one has any sympathy with the blind man. It comes to this. Physical defects which could have been avoided are blamed, but not those which a man cannot help and for which he is therefore not responsible. But, this granted, we must be held responsible for moral failings which are generally reprobated.

But someone may say, 'We all aim at what appears to us to be good, but over this appearance we have no control. How the end appears is determined by the character of the individual. Now one of two things. Either the individual is in a manner responsible for his moral character or he is not. If he is, he will also be in a manner responsible for the way in which the end – that is the good – appears to him. If he is not, then none of us will be responsible for his own misdeeds. The wrongdoer will be acting wrongly because he is ignorant of the true end and thinks that by such wrongdoing he will attain the highest good. That he should aim at the end in this fashion is not a matter of his own choosing. We must be born with an eye for a moral issue which will enable us to form a correct judgement and choose what is truly good. A man who has this natural gift is one of Nature's favourites, and such an endowment is one of the greatest and noblest in the world. It is something that cannot be acquired or learned; and if a man possesses it just as it was when it was bestowed upon him at birth, he will have all the native gifts and graces in their genuine and fullest form.' But if this be a sound argument, how will it be possible to maintain that virtue is more voluntary than vice? To the good and the bad man alike the end presents and establishes itself in the same way, whatever that may be, whether an instinctive process or not; and whatever they do, they do it somehow with reference to the end as they see it. One is driven then to hold one of two positions. Either (a) the view one takes of the end – whatever that view may be – is not imposed on us by Nature but is partly due to oneself. Or (b) the end is given by Nature but virtue is voluntary, because the virtuous man does voluntarily whatever he has left himself to do in order to attain his end. In either case vice will be just as voluntary as virtue. For the free agency of the bad man is just as important for his conduct as the free agency of the good man for his, even if we agree that it does not appear in the bad man's choice of an end. So if we say that the virtues are voluntary,* then our vices are voluntary too. The cases are identical. ...

Our dispositions, however, have a different kind of voluntariness from that of our actions. We are masters of an action of ours from start to finish, and it is present to our minds at every stage, so that we know what we are doing. But with dispositions it is otherwise. Their beginning is something we can control, but as they develop step by step the stages of their development elude our observation – it is like the progress of a disease. They are, however, voluntary in the sense that it was originally in our power to exercise them for good or for evil.

Let us now resume our discussion of the virtues, taking them one by one, saying what each is, in what sort of things it finds its expression and in what way. From this method it will transpire how many virtues there are.

Aristotle now embarks upon a long analysis of the virtues and vices. These do not include the characteristically Christian virtues of piety, chastity and humility, which are not regarded by him as independent virtues at all. Yet, however he may classify and name the moral feelings and habits which form the material for his analysis, that material is substantially the same for him as for us. The picture of the good man which emerges is perfectly recognizable and even familiar to us.

CHAPTER SIX

LET us begin with courage.

We have seen that it is a disposition which aims at the mean in situations inspiring fear and confidence. What we fear are of course things of a nature to inspire fear. Now these are, speaking generally, evil things, so that we get the

---

* As a matter of fact we ourselves in a way contribute something to the causes which produce our moral character, and it is because we have such and such a character that we set before ourselves such and such an end.

definition of fear as 'an anticipation of evil.' Well, we do fear all evil things – ill-repute, poverty, sickness, friendlessness, death and so on – but in the opinion of most people courage is to be distinguished from the simple fear of all these. There are some evils which it is proper and honourable to fear and discreditable not to fear – disgrace, for example. The man who fears disgrace has a sense of what is due to himself as a man of character and to other people; the man who does not fear it has a forehead of brass. Such a man indeed is occasionally styled a brave fellow, but only by a transference of epithet made possible by the fact that there is one point of similarity between him and the truly brave man, namely, their freedom from timidity. Then one ought not, of course, to fear poverty or illness or, indeed, anything at all that is not a consequence of vice or of one's own misconduct; still we do not call a man who is fearless in facing these things 'brave' except once more by analogy. For we find individuals who are cowardly on the field of battle and yet spend money lavishly and meet the loss of it with equanimity. And surely a man is not to be dubbed a coward because he dreads brutality to his wife and children, or the effects of envy towards himself, or anything of that nature. Nor is a man described as brave if he does not turn a hair at the prospect of a whipping.

What, then, are the objects of fear confronting which the brave man comes out in his true colours? Surely one would say the greatest, for it is just in facing fearful issues that the brave man excels. Now the most fearful thing is death; for death is an end, and to the dead man nothing seems good or evil any more for ever. Yet even death may be attended by circumstances which make it seem inappropriate to describe the man confronted by it as 'brave'. For instance, he might be drowned at sea or pass away in his bed. In what dangers, then, is courage most clearly displayed? Shall we not say, in the noblest? Well, the noblest death is the soldier's, for he meets it in the midst of the greatest and most glorious dangers. This is recognized in the honours conferred on the fallen by republics and monarchs alike. So in the strict meaning of the word the brave man will be one who fear-lessly meets an honourable death or some instant threat to life; and it is war which presents most opportunities of that sort. Not but what the brave man will be fearless in plague, or in peril by sea, although it will be a different kind of fear-lessness from that of the old salt. For in a shipwreck the brave man does not expect to be rescued, and he hates the thought of the inglorious end which threatens him, whereas the seaman who has weathered many a storm never gives up hope. Courage, too, may be shown on occasions when a man can put up a fight or meet a glorious death. But there is no opportunity for either when you are going down in a ship.

CHAPTER SEVEN

ALL men have not the same views about what is to be feared, although there are some terrors which are admitted to be more than human nature can face. Terrors of that order are experienced of course by every sane person. But there are great diversities in the extent and degree of the dangers that are humanly tolerable; and there is the same variety in the objects which instil courage. What characterizes the brave man is his unshaken courage wherever courage is humanly possible. No doubt even then he will not always be exempt from fear; but when he fears it will be in the right way, and he will meet the danger according to the rule or principle he has taken to guide his conduct, his object being to achieve moral dignity or beauty in what he does, for that is the end of virtue. Yet it is possible to feel such dangers too much, and possible to fear them too little, and possible also to fear things that are not fearful as much as if they were. One may fear what one ought not to fear, and that is one kind of error; one may fear it in the wrong way, and that is another. A third error is committed when one fears at the wrong time. And so on. We have the same possibilities of error when we deal with things that give us confidence. The brave man is the man who faces or fears the right thing for the right purpose in the right manner at the right moment, or who shows courage in the corresponding ways.*

The consideration of courage naturally leads to the consideration of rashness and cowardice.

We must now speak of the characters which show too much or too little courage. The man who goes to an extreme in fearlessness has no distinctive name.† But we should call a man mad or impervious to impressions, if he was afraid of nothing whatever –

> Nor trembling earth nor swelling seas,

which people say the Celts do not fear. The man who is overbold is called 'rash'. He gives the impression of over-acting the part, and his courage is a little suspect. At all events he would like people to believe that he is animated by the same feelings as the brave man when danger threatens. So he imitates him whenever he can. For this reason most rash men are of the forcible feeble type. They swagger a good deal when things look bright, but make themselves scarce in the presence of actual danger.

The man who goes to the extreme in fear is a coward – one who fears the wrong things in the wrong way and all the rest of it. He also exhibits a deficiency in boldness. But what one particularly notices is the extremity of his fear in the face of pain. We may therefore describe the coward as a poor-spirited person scared of everything. This is the very opposite of the brave man, for a bold heart indicates a confident temper.

* He acts and feels in a way that rises to the occasion and conforms to the principle that governs his conduct. The end of every activity fits the disposition which finds expression in that activity. We see this in the case of the brave man. His courage has the stamp of nobility; therefore nobility is its end, for the essential nature and quality of anything is defined by its end. This leads to the conclusion that the brave man faces danger and acts bravely because his purpose is noble.

† A common case, as we have already noted.

We may say, then, that the coward, the rash man, and the brave man work as it were with the same materials, but their attitudes to them are different. The coward has too much fear and too little courage, the rash man too much courage and too little fear. It is the brave man who has the right attitude, for he has the right disposition, enabling him to observe the mean. We may add that the rash man is foolhardy, ready for anything before the danger arrives; but, when it does, sheering off. On the other hand the brave man is gallant in action but undemonstrative beforehand.

Summing up, let us say that courage is the disposition which aims at the mean in conditions which inspire confidence or fear in the circumstances I have described; it feels confidence and faces danger because it is the fine thing to do so and because it is base to shrink from doing it. Yet to kill oneself as a means of escape from poverty or disappointed love or bodily or mental anguish is the deed of a coward rather than a brave man. To run away from trouble is a form of cowardice and, while it is true that the suicide braves death, he does it not for some noble object but to escape some ill.

So far Aristotle has been speaking of courage in the strict sense of the word. But the name has been extended to include dispositions which resemble true courage. There are some five of them, which he now describes.

CHAPTER EIGHT

Such, then, is the nature of courage. But besides true courage there are five types of behaviour to which the name is commonly applied.

(1) First, as most nearly resembling true courage, let us consider civilian courage, I mean the courage of the citizen soldier. The common view about citizen armies is that they are inspired to confront the perils of war by their fear of the penalties in their laws and of the disgrace attaching to cowardice on the one hand, and by the desire to gain dis-

tinction in the field on the other. Hence those nations are thought bravest among whom cowardice is a reproach and valour is honoured. This is the kind of courage which Homer celebrates in heroes like Hector and Diomede. You will remember what Hector says:

> Should I retreat behind the gates,
> Polydamas will be the first to cast reproach on me.

And Diomede says:

> Hector one day will boast among the assembled men of Troy,
> 'Before my spear was Tydeus' son sent scurrying to his ships.'

This courage has the closest resemblance of all the imperfect types to courage as we have defined it, because it is inspired by a moral excellence – the feeling which makes us ashamed to do wrong – and by the desire of a noble thing, honour, and the wish to escape reproach, which is a thing that carries dishonour with it. And under the same heading we must place the courage shown by men compelled to fight by their commanders. But this we must put lower in the scale of merit, because their motive is lower, since it is not shame but fear, and what they shun is pain and not dishonour. They are forced into courage by those in authority over them. Listen to Hector:

> That man of you that I shall mark skulking behind the lines –
> He shall not save his carcase from the dogs that gnaw the slain.

There are officers who form their men in line before them and beat them if they give ground, and others who make them stand drawn up in front of trenches and similar obstacles. They are all doing the same thing – using compulsion. But bravery ought not to be the effect of compulsion, it should be inspired by its own nobility.

(2) There is an opinion that experience in this or that particular risk may be regarded as courage. Some such idea underlies the belief of Socrates that courage is knowledge. This form of courage is not confined to one set of people in one set of circumstances, but it is specially characteristic of

the professional soldier on active service. Many things which happen in a campaign are alarming in appearance only, as the experienced campaigner knows from his own observation. The others do not know this, and accordingly seem less brave in comparison. Secondly, practice has taught the professional fighting man how to inflict the maximum loss on the enemy at the minimum loss to himself. For he gets the most out of his weapons, which are specially adapted both for offence and defence. So it is like armed men fighting unarmed or professionals versus amateurs.* On the other hand in mortal danger it is the regulars who show the white feather when they are outmatched in numbers and equipment. They are the first to run, while the conscripts die where they stand. We saw this in the battle at the temple of Hermes. The explanation, of course, is that the citizen-soldier thinks it a disgrace to run away and would rather perish than save his skin by doing that. But when professional troops have engaged it is because they were under the impression that they held an initial advantage. When they realize that it is not so they take to their heels, for it is death they fear rather than dishonour. Now the truly brave man is not like that.

(3) People see a connexion between courage and what we may call 'the fighting spirit'. Men who are animated by this spirit, much as wild beasts when they charge the hunters who have wounded them, are generally reckoned courageous, because the courageous man has the fighting spirit which is always ready to advance in face of danger. Hence such expressions in Homer as 'Into their spirit he put strength,' and 'Wrath he aroused and spirit,' and 'Bitter the rage his nostrils filled,' and 'Boiled his blood. ...' All this and the like evidently imply a rousing up of the spirit and a powerful impulse. The motive of the brave, however, is the nobility of what they do; their high spirit merely contributes its aid to their efforts. But when wild animals are 'brave' it is the result of some pain they are feeling. When they turn on

* I say this because in professional sport it is not courage that carries the fight farthest but strength *plus* training.

their hunters it is because they have been wounded or frightened.* It is not then courage that they display, because they need the spur of pain and fury to make them rush into danger blind to the risks they run. If nothing more than that were needed, donkeys would be brave when they are hungry, for when they feel hungry they will go on eating, though blows are showered upon them.† Of the moods which resemble courage this which has a high spirit for its driving force seems the most natural; indeed, when it includes deliberate choice and purpose it is hard to distinguish from courage. We must not forget that it is human to be painfully affected by anger and to find revenge sweet. But the most one can say of those who fight from no higher motive than anger is that they are good fighters; one cannot call them brave. For they are not moved by honour or guided by principle; simply they are swayed by their feelings. Still some resemblance does exist between them and the brave.

(4) Again, we cannot allow that the sanguine are brave. The confidence they derive from a series of successful encounters inspires them with boldness in danger, and so far they resemble the brave, who are also bold. But they are bold in different ways, the brave for the reasons I have stated, the sanguine because they feel sure that they can beat the opposition without much likelihood of being knocked about themselves.‡ But when things go wrong the merely sanguine make themselves scarce, whereas the brave man, as we saw, comes out in his true colours when he has with his eyes open to face dangers as great as human nature can endure, so acting because it is the fine thing to do, while not to do it will hurt his reputation. That is why to remain calm and undismayed in sudden alarms is thought a better proof of courage than to behave with like equanimity when the danger has been foreseen; it is a better test of a man's normal reaction to danger when he has it sprung upon him

* In forest or marshy ground they keep to themselves.

† One could add another illustration – adulterers take great risks to gratify their lust.

‡ A drunk man at the sanguine stage is as bold as you please.

without warning. One might decide to face a peril after weighing the risks run and considering the principle involved. But it calls for a natural disposition to courage to be able to confront the unforeseen.

(5) Another variety of seeming-courage is displayed by those who face a danger without realizing that it is a danger. Their condition is not unlike that of the sanguine, but their courage is of a lower order because they are not so sure of themselves. Their self-confidence enables the sanguine to stand firm for a time; but those who have never been undeceived about their danger run away the moment they suspect that the situation is not what they imagined it to be. This is what happened when the Argives engaged the Spartans under the impression that they were Sicyonians. ...

The relation of courage to pleasure and pain.

CHAPTER NINE

COURAGE is shown in relation to whatever is alarming or encouraging, but it is in relation to the alarming that it is most itself. The man who is composed in the heart of dangers and meets them in the right spirit is more essentially courageous than the man whose nerves are firm in encouraging circumstances. Yet the latter is thought courageous, too. In fact, as I had occasion to observe, men may be credited with courage merely for their patience in bearing pain. This suggests that courage is accompanied by some degree of pain. Hence we are justified in commending courage on the ground that it is harder to bear pain than to abstain from pleasure. No doubt the end at which courage aims is a source of pleasure, but we are blinded to this by the pains incident to its exercise. Think of what happens in our athletic contests, the boxing matches, for instance. No doubt the end which the boxers have before them – the crown of victory – is very sweet. But flesh and blood must feel the pain of taking the punches, not to mention their sufferings

in the course of training. They have so much of this to endure that their final objective seems but a small item in the
account and to lose any pleasure it holds. If, then, the same
is true of the brave man, death and wounds will be painful
to him, and he will not willingly endure them. But endure
them he will, because that is the fine thing to do, while
shunning them is dishonourable. We may even say that the
more completely a man possesses virtue, and the more truly
happy he is, the more painful will death seem to him. For
life has most to offer such a man, and he knows the greatness
of the blessings which he is to lose; and this cannot fail to be
a subject of painful reflection. But that does not make him
any the less brave – he may actually be braver – for he
would rather be a good soldier than have an unbroken con-
tinuance of these blessings. It is not true then that pleasure
accompanies the exercise of every virtue, save in so far as
pleasure is felt when the end is attained. We may easily
credit it that the best professional soldiers are not made out
of men like these but out of such as, though in fact less brave,
meet danger readily, having nothing to lose and being prepared to barter their lives for petty gains.

That is all that need be said in this connexion about
courage, but it should suffice to give us a rough idea of its
nature.

The virtue of which Aristotle now gives an account is Sophrosyne, *a
word which cannot be rendered by any modern English equivalent. It
is, however, what our moralists until quite recently called 'temperance', and this, with its opposite 'intemperance', will be used here.
What Aristotle means by* Sophrosyne *will gradually appear.*

CHAPTER TEN

LET us next say something about temperance, which like
courage is considered to be one of the virtues developed in
the irrational parts of the soul.

We have already described it as aiming at the mean in

pleasurable experiences.* Intemperance is shown in the same field. So we must now say something definite about the quality of the pleasures which are the material on which temperance and its opposite work. Let us begin by drawing a distinction between (*a*) pleasures of the soul and (*b*) pleasures of the body.

(*a*) As an instance of pleasures of the soul consider the love of distinction in public life or in some branch of learning. The devotee in either case takes pleasure in what he loves without any physical sensations. What he feels is a spiritual or intellectual pleasure, and we do not speak of men who seek that kind of pleasure as 'temperate' or 'intemperate'. Nor do we apply these terms to any class of persons whose pleasures are not those of the flesh. For example, the kind of person who likes to swap stories and anecdotes, and wastes his time discussing trivialities, we call a 'gossip' or a 'chatterbox', but not 'intemperate'. Neither should we so describe a man who makes a tragedy out of some loss he has met with of money or of friends.

(*b*) It is then the pleasures of sense that are the concern of temperance, though not all of these. The people who find pleasure in looking at things like colours and forms and pictures are not called temperate or intemperate. At the same time we must suppose that pleasure in these things can be felt too much or too little or in due measure. It is so with the pleasures of listening. A man may take inordinate delight in music or acting. But nobody is prepared to call him intemperate on that account; nor, if he takes neither too much nor too little, do we think of describing him as temperate. It is the same with the pleasures of smell, except when some association comes in. A man is not called intemperate if he happens to like the smell of apples or roses or incense. Yet he may be, if he inhales essences or the emanations of the cuisine, for these are odours which appeal to the voluptuary, because they remind him of the things that arouse his desires. And not only the voluptuary; everybody likes the smell

* It is of course concerned also with pain, but in a different way and to a less extent.

of things to eat when he is hungry. Still the delight in such things is specially characteristic of the voluptuary or intemperate man, because it is on these that his heart is set. And if we extend our observation to the lower animals, we note that they, too, find nothing intrinsically pleasant in these sensations. A hunting-dog gets no pleasure from the scent of a hare. The pleasure is in eating it; all the scent did was to tell him the hare was there. It is not the lowing of an ox that gratifies a lion but the eating it, though the lowing tells him the ox is somewhere about, and that evidently gives him pleasure. Nor does he, as Homer thinks, rejoice when he has caught sight of 'stag or goat of the wild,' but because he is promising himself a meal.

Such are the pleasures with which temperance and intemperance deal, and they are pleasures in which the lower animals also share. On that account they have the name of being illiberal and brutish, confined as they are to touch and taste. And even taste seems to count for little or nothing in the practice of temperance. It is the function of taste to discriminate between flavours, as connoisseurs do when they sample wines, and chefs when they prepare entrées; although it is not exactly the flavours that please (except, perhaps, with the intemperate), it is the enjoyment of the flavorous article, and that is wholly a tactile experience, whether in eating, drinking, or what are called the pleasures of sex. This explains the anecdote of the epicure who prayed that his throat might be made longer than a crane's – the longer the contact, he thought, the more protracted the pleasure. So the sense in respect of which we give an intemperate man that name is the sense that comes nearest to being universal. This may seem to justify its ill-repute, for it belongs to us not as men but as animals. Therefore to delight in such sensations, and to prefer them to any other pleasure, is brutish.*

* There are, of course, tactile pleasures of a different and less vulgar kind – such, for example, as we feel in the gymnasium from the massage and hot bath. But the intemperate man is interested only in the touching of certain parts of the body, not the whole.

CHAPTER ELEVEN

WITH regard to desires, they would seem to fall into two classes, (a) general and (b) particular or adventitious. An example of (a) is the desire for food, which may be described as a natural desire, since every man feels the need of nourishment in liquid or solid form, sometimes in both; also of sexual intercourse when, in Homer's phrase, he is young and lusty. On the other hand there are (b) particular sorts of nourishment which may be one man's meat and another's poison. Similarly one may not always want to eat the same viands. So here personal preference comes in. There is, however, a natural element even in this, for in the first place it is natural that tastes should differ, and in the second there are some delicacies which everybody finds more palatable than his staple diet. In the case of the natural desires, then, men rarely go wrong or, if they do, it is only in the way of desiring too much, since to eat and drink immoderate quantities of ordinary food and liquor is to overburden nature, for all one naturally desires is to satisfy a need. (Hence, gluttons are called 'belly-gods', because they stuff their bellies to excess. The vice is one to which the grosser part of mankind is prone.) But when it comes to particular or private pleasures many a man goes wrong, and he may go wrong in a number of ways. If he is what people call an 'addict' to something, it is either because he finds pleasure in something wrong or feels the pleasure more intensely than other people or in a wrong fashion. The intemperate man, indeed, goes to excess in all these directions at once. For he delights in some wrong, even abominable, things; and in cases where liking is unexceptionable, he carries it too far and feels it more intensely than the average man. Clearly, then, it is excess in pleasures that constitutes intemperance, which is a blameworthy disposition. In the sphere of pains, however, we must remark that temperance and courage are not on the same footing. It is not in virtue of his enduring pain that a man is called temperate, nor in virtue of his not enduring it that he is called intemperate. He is called intemperate because he feels an undue amount of pain at missing pleasures – here you have a pleasure actually causing pain – and temperate because he is not pained by the absence of pleasure. This implies that the intemperate man desires all pleasures, or the most pleasurable, and is led by his desire to prefer them to everything else. The consequence is that he feels pain both when he fails to get these pleasures and when he desires them, since some degree of pain is inseparable from desire, although to say pleasure *causes* pain sounds paradoxical.

As for those who react too weakly to pleasures and feel less than the due degree of gratification in tasting them, they can hardly be said to exist, such insusceptibility being sub-human. Why, even the brute beasts have their preferences in diet, taking pleasure in some kinds of food and disliking others. If there does exist a being to whom nothing gives pleasure, or to whom one thing feels just like another, he cannot be anything like fully human. In fact he is such a *rara avis* that he has not got a name of his own.

The temperate man holds a position between these extremes. So far from taking pleasure in the things which the intemperate man loves best, he has a positive distaste for them. To describe him in general terms – He does not find pleasure in the wrong things, nor, indeed, extreme pleasure in anything of a pleasure-giving sort; he does not feel pain or desire in the absence of pleasures, or, if he does, it is in a moderate degree and not more than he ought, and not at the wrong time or under any of the wrong conditions. But such pleasures as conduce to health and bodily fitness he will desire to have in due measure – that is in the right way – as well as all other pleasures that do not injure his health and physique, and are not sordid, or more expensive than he can afford. The man who scorns these limitations sets too high a value on such pleasures, therein differing from the temperate man, who rates them at their true value.

CHAPTER TWELVE

INTEMPERANCE seems to have a more voluntary character than cowardice. For the motive of intemperance is pleasure, of cowardice pain; and whereas pleasure is deliberately chosen by us, pain is something we avoid. Secondly, pain may drive a man distracted, inducing a pathological condition, but the operation of pleasure is never so violent as that. We may infer that intemperance is more voluntary than cowardice and should therefore incur severer reprehension. It is another count against intemperance that it is easier to train ourselves to resist pleasure, because the opportunities which life presents us of indulging in it are so numerous, and no risk is run in any effort we make to harden ourselves against its seductions, whereas the very contrary is true when we arm ourselves against our fears. We must, however, note a distinction. A cowardly disposition has more of a voluntary character than particular acts of cowardice because cowardliness is not in itself painful, whereas every time a man has an access of cowardice he endures agonies of fear, to the point of discarding his arms and in other ways disgracing himself, which makes it reasonable to suppose that he is acting under some kind of compulsion. But in the intemperate man we see the contrary exemplified. Each action of his, separately considered, is voluntary, for each is the act of one feeling desire and appetite. On a wider view, however, his condition is seen to be less voluntary, for no one *desires* to lose control of his passions.

Note that *akolasia*, our word for 'intemperance', is also applied to the naughtiness of children, which has a certain resemblance to the wantonness of their elders. To which of the two ages it was originally applied is a question which does not concern us here. But it seems obvious that the later must borrow the word from the earlier, since its literal meaning is 'the condition which results from not being chastised.' The metaphor is apt, for chastisement – a form of repression – is just what is needed by that in us which has base desires together with the power of rapid growth, a tendency particularly observable in desire and in the child. For the life of children, as much as that of intemperate men, is wholly governed by their desires, and it is in them that the craving for pleasant things is strongest. So if this appetite is not rendered obedient and submissive to authority, it will swell prodigiously. For in an irrational being like a child the desire for what gives it pleasure is insatiable and draws its gratification from every quarter. The satisfaction of the desire stimulates the innate tendency and, when powerful and intense enough, it knocks the sense of proportion out of one. For that reason such gratifications should be moderate and rare. They should never clash with the rational element – that 'obedient and chastened principle,' as I called it. It is this element or principle which should govern the appetitive part of us as the instructions of his tutor govern the life of a boy. So in the soul of the temperate man the appetitive part should be harmonized with this principle. For the aim both of it and of temperance is the same – the attainment of what is fine and noble. Moreover, the temperate man desires the right things in the right way and at the right time, and this is in accordance with the instructions of the principle. . . .

BOOK FOUR

Proceeding with his discussion of the moral virtues, Aristotle considers a quality which is fairly, though not perfectly, translated by 'liberality'.

CHAPTER ONE

WE are now to speak of liberality, a virtue which may be defined as a disposition to observe the mean in dealing with material goods. For it is not in military matters, nor in those relations in which the temperate man shows his quality, nor again in his management of law-suits that a man is praised as 'liberal'; it is in the acquisition, and more particularly in the distribution, of wealth, meaning by 'wealth' anything that money can buy. Prodigality or extravagance on the one hand, illiberality or meanness on the other, are the corresponding excess and deficiency in this field. 'Mean' is the description we normally apply to people who take any expenditure too much to heart, but the word 'prodigality' has sometimes in our use of it wider implications, since debauchees and men who squander their money on vicious self-indulgence are also called prodigal. For this reason prodigality is looked upon with extreme disfavour as including more than one vice. But this is an improper use of the term, for prodigality does not imply the possession of more than one vice, that of squandering one's means. The man who is the cause of his own ruin is 'past saving',* the general opinion being that to exhaust one's means is much the same as ruining oneself, because our 'means' are our means of living. – This, then, we take to be the meaning of 'prodigality'.

Wealth is a commodity, and commodities may be used in a good or a bad way: every commodity is best used by the man who has the appropriate virtue; therefore wealth will

* *Asotos.*

be used best by the man who has the virtue which comes out in dealing with wealth. This is the liberal man. Now when we speak of using wealth we are thinking of spending it or giving it away; the getting and keeping of money is associated in our minds with the process of making it. So the liberal man is chiefly characterized by his habit of giving to the proper recipients and taking from the proper, and not from the wrong, quarters. The good man thinks it more blessed to give than to receive, and virtue is more clearly shown in the performance of fine actions than in the non-performance of base ones. But it is obvious that doing good and behaving generously go along with giving, while having good done to one and refraining from ignoble practices go with getting. Besides, praise and (though possibly in a less degree) gratitude are bestowed on him who gives, not on him who merely declines to accept. Moreover, it is easier to decline a gift than to bestow it, since it costs us more of an effort to sacrifice what belongs to us than to refrain from taking what belongs to other people. Again, the epithet of 'liberal' is reserved for donors; those who decline a gift are commended not for liberality but for their sense of what is right in the circumstances. And of course no one dreams of praising the *recipient* of a favour. It is probably no exaggeration to say that among good men it is the liberal who are liked best. For they are practically helpful, their help taking the form of a gift.

Since good deeds are morally fine and are inspired by a fine motive, it follows that the liberal man will have a fine object in his giving. And he will give in the right way, which means giving to the right persons to the right amount at the right time, and fulfilling all the other requirements of right giving. And he will have pleasure, or at least no pain, in giving thus. For a really good action should give us pleasure and not pain – pain least of all. As for the man who gives to the wrong persons or from some ignoble motive, he must receive some other description than 'liberal', and so must the man who only gives with a wrench. Such a man puts pocket before principle, and a liberal man would never do that.

One may infer from what has been said that another trait of the liberal man will be this. He will not accept money from a tainted source – receipts of that sort are impossible to one who sets little store by riches. Nor is he the kind of man who looks for favours; the man who confers a favour would rather not be repaid in the same coin. What revenues he receives will come from the proper source, namely, his private means, and in receiving them he will not imagine that he is doing anything creditable to himself, but that it is the inescapable condition of his having the means of giving. And he will not neglect his property, since it is his desire to come to the aid of others, and his property gives him the means of doing so. But he will not give to any and everybody, in case he should be left without the means of giving to the right persons, and at the right time, and where the object has something fine about it. It is, however, eminently characteristic of the liberal man to give rather too much, and so leave himself too little, for with him it is natural to forget his private interests. But before we call a man liberal we must reckon the extent of his resources, liberality consisting not in the sum-total of what is given but in the disposition of the giver, which is a readiness to give a reasonable proportion of what he has. It may easily be, then, that of two donors the one who gives less may be the more liberal, if the funds at his disposal are less. It is popularly believed that men who have inherited money are more open-handed than those who have made it, because they have never felt the want of it. A man who has grown rich by his own efforts is like a parent or a poet ; he has a special place in his heart for that of whose existence he is the author. But wealth and liberality are uneasy yoke-fellows, for the liberal man has no talent for either getting or keeping money, and spends rather freely, money being valued by him not on its own account but as something to give away. Hence that complaint against fortune, that it is those who deserve wealth most who have it least. Yet this is a perfectly natural result. You won't have money, any more than other things, unless you take trouble to have it.

On the other hand the liberal man will not give to the wrong persons, nor at the wrong time, nor in any wrong way, since, if he did, he would no longer be sustaining his character of liberal man, not to mention that, if he squandered money upon the wrong objects, he would not have any left to spend upon the right. Remember our definition: The liberal man is the man whose expenditure is proportionate to his means and is directed to its fitting objects, the man who exceeds the mean in this respect being what we have called a prodigal. This accounts for the fact that we do not speak of the heads of autocratic governments as prodigal; their wealth is such that one finds it hard to imagine how they can spend or give away too much of it.

It has been shown that liberality consists in the observance of due measure in the getting as well as the giving of wealth. In other words the liberal man will not only give and disburse the right amounts on the right objects, in small and great matters alike, and do it gladly; he will also take, but take the right amounts and from the right quarters. Since it is the virtue of the liberal man to observe the mean, both in giving and in taking, he will give and take in the right way. Right getting is associated with right giving, and wrong getting is incompatible with right giving. It follows that the associated activities are manifested in the same person, while the opposing activities as clearly are not. If the liberal man should find himself in the position of laying out money wrongly and ignobly, no doubt it will give him pain – though in the right way, that is not in an extreme degree – since it is a mark of moral excellence to feel pleasure and pain only in the right objects and in the right manner. And the liberal man is not a hard bargainer; he may easily come off second best, because he thinks there are more important things than money and is more distressed by the suspicion that he has not paid enough than by the thought that he has paid more than he should – the maxim of the worldly wise Simonides is not at all to his liking. The prodigal, on the other hand, follows the wrong course here too. He does not feel pleasure or pain on occasions when he should, nor feel them in the right way, as we shall gradually discover as the argument proceeds.

We have now reached this point. Prodigality and illiberality or meanness are excesses and deficiencies, and this in two respects, giving and getting.* Prodigality is excess in giving and deficiency in getting, meanness is deficiency in giving and excess in getting – not, however, when large sums are in question. Now it is not easy to give to everybody if you get from nobody. For, if you are a private person – and only private persons are thought capable of being prodigal – your property soon gives out if you go on distributing presents. Consequently you do not often find prodigality working both ways in the same individual. I am sure that the man in whom it did would strike us as markedly superior to the illiberal man. Poverty and the passage of the years will soon cure him and make it possible for him to arrive at the mean. For he has the natural bent towards liberality – the instinct to give and to shrink from taking; only he does both in a wrong and morally unsound way. If this error could be rectified, by training or in some other way, he would *be* a liberal man, giving his money to the right persons and not accepting it at the wrong hands. It is this that makes people think him not a bad fellow at heart, for to carry too far the habit of giving without getting may show that you are silly but does not prove you to be a scoundrel or a cad. So the man whose prodigality takes this turn is held to be a much better type than the mean man both for the above-mentioned reasons and because he benefits a number of people, whereas the niggard benefits nobody, not even himself. However, as I remarked, prodigals of this stamp are far from common. The average prodigal both gives wrongly and takes from wrong sources, which has the effect of making him from this point of view actually mean. Such men are prepared to accept these questionable profits, because they are eager to dispense them. But they discover that they cannot be as open-handed as they would like be-

* Expenditure we regard as a form of giving.

cause of the rapidity with which their own resources dry up. The consequence is that they are forced to replenish them from elsewhere. And, having no standard of honourable behaviour, it does not seem to them to matter where their money comes from. What they want to do is to give it away, and they are totally uninterested in the question of how and whence it comes to them. So even their benefactions are not truly liberal; they are ignoble and given for an ignoble purpose and in the wrong spirit; nay, they sometimes enrich people who *ought* to be poor. They never think of giving to persons of good character, but lavish their favours on toadies or anybody who ministers to their pleasures. That is why most prodigals are intemperate as well. Making the money fly, they plunge into dissipation regardless of expense, and having no standard by which to regulate their lives, they fall away into mere sensuality. That is the rake's progress of the prodigal if left to himself, although, if he is taken in hand, he may arrive at that intermediate position between prodigality and meanness which constitutes true liberality.

As for meanness, it is incurable if, as people think, it may be a product of old age and incapacity or feebleness in any of its forms. More deeply than prodigality it is rooted in human nature, for most men are fonder of getting money than of giving it away. It takes many forms and spreads its tentacles far and wide; it is a protean thing. Comprising both deficiency in giving and excess in taking, it does not come in its entirety to everyone, but sometimes divides itself between the two classes of those who take too much and those who give too little. The sort of persons who are variously described as 'cheese-paring', 'close-fisted', 'tight-wads', are all very poor at giving, but do not covet other people's property and have no desire to get it. But this class may be subdivided according to the motives of its members. Some are influenced by a certain regard for virtue and by fear of disgrace. Not uncommonly these are careful of their money – at least so they say and most people take their word for it – simply that they may not be forced to do something discreditable.* Others are scared into keeping their fingers from other people's property by the reflection that this cuts both ways – if you rob other people, you will find it hard to keep other people from robbing you. So they profess themselves content with the plan of neither giving nor taking. The second class consists of those whose excessive desire of getting takes the form of accepting anything from anybody. It includes all who work at disreputable trades, souteneurs and men of that description, as well as usurers lending small sums at extortionate interest. These are all specimens of people who take more than they are entitled to from persons at whose hands they ought not to take it. Their common factor is the love of lucre, for the motive of every one of them is gain, and petty gain at that, for the sake of which they submit to the social stigma incurred thereby. Yet meanness is not the term we apply to those who operate in this way on a grand scale – high and mighty persons, for example, who sack cities and plunder temples. Such we prefer to call wicked or impious and unrighteous. But the dicer, the thief, the footpad may be reckoned among the mean, because their own hope is to turn a dishonest penny. That is why they labour in their vocation regardless of the world's reproach; the thieves running the greatest risk for the sake of the haul, the gamblers skinning their friends, who ought rather to benefit by their connexion. So both sorts are unscrupulous profit-hunters, looking to the main chance in discreditable circumstances. And this criticism applies to all similar ways of making money.

Meanness is naturally spoken of as the opposite of liberality. In itself it is a worse thing, and there is also a greater tendency for men to sin in that way than in the direction of prodigality, as I have described it. ...

* To this set belong the skinflint and anybody of that kidney, the name having been suggested by their extreme reluctance to part with anything to anybody.

Aristotle next speaks of a quality much admired in ancient Greece, but possible only for the rich or well to do. An Athenian who happened to be well off was expected to finance certain public services. So Aristotle, who makes no bones about admitting that the rich have greater opportunities for cultivating the virtues than the poor, thinks it worth while to include among them this of generous, but judicious, spending from a motive of patriotism. 'Magnificence' is about as near as we can get to it in English.

CHAPTER TWO

THE next thing to be considered by us is, I take it, magnificence in spending, which is another virtue that has to do with money. It differs from liberality in being limited to such transactions as result in the expenditure of money, operating on a larger scale than liberality, for, as the word itself implies, magnificence is the suitable expenditure of wealth in large amounts. But in the case of this virtue there is not any fixed measure of quantity. The man who undertakes to fit out a trireme should not have to spend as much as the man who defrays the cost of a State-embassy to a place like Delphi. Therefore we must calculate how much will be a suitable outlay considering (a) the spender, (b) the circumstances, (c) the object of the expenditure. Observe, however, that we do not bestow the epithet of 'magnificent' on a man who rises to the occasion when that is a small one or of no particular importance, such as giving something to an impoverished exile –

The wanderer oft my bounty felt.

No, the magnificent man must make the appropriate gesture on the great occasion, for, though the magnificent man is always liberal, the liberal man is not necessarily magnificent.

For its corresponding extremes magnificence has (a) in the way of deficiency, shabbiness, (b) in the way of excess, vulgarity, bad taste or the like, the excess showing not in the magnitude of the sums disbursed on suitable objects but in ostentatious spending in the wrong direction and the wrong way. Of these faults there will be more to say at a later stage.

The magnificent man is by way of being a connoisseur; he has an eye for the suitable object and a talent for spending on it with taste.* So his outlay will not only be large, it will be suitably directed. This implies that the results of his expenditure also will have appropriateness as well as an impressive size, for that alone will justify the great expense. The result must be worthy of the expense, and the expense worthy of the result, or rather more so. Also the motive of the magnificent man in these expenditures will be fine, such a motive being an essential element in all the virtues. Moreover, he will spend gladly and generously, for there is something paltry about exact book-keeping; he will be more deeply interested in embodying his conception in its most beautiful and appropriate form than to ask himself how much it will cost and the cheapest rate at which it can be done. It follows that the magnificent man must also be liberal. For the liberal man as well as he will spend liberal sums and in a suitable manner, liberality being shown in these sums and in this manner. The magnificent man, doing the same, does it on a great scale, which explains the element *magni* in his name. Again, the magnificent man with no greater outlay will produce a more splendid result than the shabby man or the vulgarian. The explanation lies in the different ways in which we estimate the excellence of something we own and something we have created. We rate a possession – say a quantity of gold – at its money value. But when it is something created by our own efforts we rate it by its grandeur and dignity;† and part of the excellence of a human production lies in its grandeur. Now there are some ways of spending money to which we apply complimentary terms. Such are oblations to the gods, votive offerings, public buildings and sacrifices, and anything to do with religion. Then there

* It should be remembered that, as I said towards the beginning of these lectures, a disposition finds expression in its activities and the objects which it seeks to attain.

† I mean, we look on such a work with admiration, and admiration is due to what is magnificent.

are public benefactions made by aspirants to popular favour. Examples of these are – in states where such things are felt to be incumbent on the rich – dressing a chorus handsomely, or fitting out a warship, or entertaining the whole body of the citizens at a banquet. But, as I said, it is all a matter of proportion; we must take into consideration who the donor is and the extent of his resources, and measure by that the due amount of his expenditure, which ought to correspond to his means and fit not only the product but the producer. This puts it out of the question for a poor man to be magnificent. He has not got the wherewithal to spend large sums in a way to do him credit, and, if he tries it, he will make an exhibition of himself. He is spending beyond his means and in a way he ought not, since his behaviour will be morally right only if he spends in the right way. Those for whom we regard it as right and proper to make such donations are people with suitable incomes derived from property acquired by their own exertions or inherited from their ancestors or relations; or they may be persons of good family or high distinction or otherwise specially qualified. For all these are important advantages and take a high place in the estimation of the public. Now to these requirements the magnificent man answers perfectly, and it is in just such displays of magnificence that this virtue finds scope, as we have noted, these being the grandest and most highly esteemed forms it can take. But magnificence may be displayed also on unique private occasions, such as a marriage or something of that sort which may happen to excite public interest or attract people of importance, or parties to celebrate the arrival or departure of friends from abroad, or the exchange of complimentary presents. For the magnificent man reveals his character in spending not upon himself but on public objects; his gifts are a sort of dedication. It is also like him to furnish his house in a way suitable to his means, for that gives him a kind of distinction. And it is his way to spend more upon things that are made to last than on things that are not, for it is the lasting things that are most beautiful and noble. And when he spends for a particular purpose it will be a sum appropriate to that purpose, for he recognizes that there must be a difference in the amount of what he offers to men from the amount of what he offers to the gods, and between a contribution to a temple and a contribution towards the expenses of a funeral. Three points must be taken into consideration. (1) The amount of the expenditure must be estimated in the light of the particular object for which it was incurred. (2) While the most magnificent expenditure, considered by itself, must be large, and must be laid out on an important object, the most magnificent in any particular case is what is reckoned great in *that* case. (3) Greatness in the result must be distinguished from the amount spent upon producing it.* But if these three conditions obtain, the magnificent man will reveal his character by producing in every kind of expenditure a magnificent result which will set a standard not easily surpassed and will be a fair equivalent of what he spent on it.

Corresponding to the magnificent man on the side of excess is the vulgarian, who spends too much.† He spares no expense in order to make a splash on trifling occasions – dining the members of his club as if they were wedding guests and (if he happens to be financing a comedy) insisting that the chorus be dressed in purple when they first come in – a practice actually followed at Megara – and committing similar *faux pas*. And in all this he will not be fired by any noble aspiration. All he wants to do is to make a display of his opulence, since he imagines that he is admired for that. He spends little where he ought to spend much, and much where but little is called for.

On the other hand a deficiency in all these respects will appear in the shabby man, who, even when he has been led into great expense, will spoil the sheep for a ha'p'orth of tar, shilly-shallying at every point and wondering what is the smallest sum he can pay, and groaning over that, always suspecting that he is doing more than the occasion demands.

* For example, a ball or a scent-bottle, however pretty, costs little or nothing, but it is magnificent as a present to a child.
† See above.

Now both these dispositions are bad, but they cannot be said to bring their owners into disrepute. For they do no harm to neighbours and we are not profoundly shocked by them.

The following chapter treats of a quality called in Greek megalopsuchia *and in Latin* magnanimitas. *It is not magnanimity in the modern sense, but something like 'justifiable pride'. The translator must be allowed a certain freedom in dealing with so intractable a word, but the reader will soon discover for himself what Aristotle means. The picture here presented of the justifiably proud man has been thought partly humorous or even ironical. The reader may judge for himself. But there is this to be said. Aristotle is here speaking of the quality in isolation from other qualities which would in any actual great man tend to soften and humanize his consciousness of superiority to other people.*

CHAPTER THREE

'MAGNANIMITY', or 'greatness of soul', is, as the word itself leads us to infer, concerned with great matters, and before we go further we must try to grasp what sort of matters they are. Not that it will make any difference whether we attend to the quality itself or to the person in whom it is embodied.

Well then, what we mean by a great-souled or superior man is one who claims, and is entitled to claim, high consideration from his fellows. Of course a man who makes such a claim on insufficient grounds is but a silly person, and silliness is not a virtue. The superior man, then, is such as I have described. The man who makes small claims for himself when his merits deserve these and no more shows a wise restraint, but great-souled we must not call him, for that kind of superiority must rest on greatness, just as personal beauty requires that one should be tall; little people may have charm and elegance, but beauty – no. The man who makes lofty but unjustified claims for himself is conceited, but not everybody is conceited who claims more than his due. On the other hand the man who claims less than his due is poor-spirited. It is not a case of claiming much or little or something that is neither too much nor too little. The point is, it must be less than he is entitled to claim. In fact, it is the man who has great deserts that shows the poorest spirit if he does not assert his claim. What would he do if his merits were less? We see, then, that the superior man, while in the extent of his claim going to an extreme, still, by claiming no more than his due, is justified and so avoids both extremes, coming as he does between those who claim too much and those who claim too little – between the vain or conceited and the poor-spirited.

We see, then, that the superior man makes large, even the largest, claims and is entirely justified in doing so. But he must have a particular object in view. What is it? When we say somebody or something has 'worth' or 'value' we are thinking in terms of external goods. The greatest of these we take to be that which we assign to the gods as their due and which is desired by the eminent and awarded as the meed of victory in the most glorious contests, namely, honour. For honour is the greatest of external goods. The superior man, then, has the right attitude to honours and dishonours. Indeed, it goes without saying that he concerns himself with honour; it is what he claims, and claims justly, above all. The small-souled or poor-spirited man errs in the way of deficiency not only by failing to assert his own just claims but also by failing to support the comparison between himself and the superior man in this respect. On the other hand the vain man claims more than his worth.* As for the superior man, since nothing is too good for him, he must be the best of men. For the better a man is, the more he deserves, so that he who deserves most is the best. Therefore the truly superior man must be a good man. Indeed, greatness in all the virtues is surely what stamps him for what he is. For instance, it would be totally out of character for such a man to run away helter-skelter, or to be guilty of cheating. For what motive could a man of his standards have to perform dishonourable

* Not more, however, than the superior man is worth.

actions? Indeed, if we examine his conduct in all its branches, we shall find the absurdity of supposing he could do anything but good. Besides, he would not be worthy of honour if he were bad. For honour is the guerdon of goodness and is awarded to the good. It would be nearer the truth to say that greatness of soul is the beautiful completion of the virtues, for it adds to them its own greatness and is insepar- able from them. And this makes it hard for a man to be truly great in soul; without a fine moral sense it is impossible.

Well, then, the grand objects of the superior man's ambi- tion are honours; by them he will be gratified, if they are distinguished and are bestowed by estimable persons – but gratified only up to a point, because he will feel that he is getting no more than his due, or rather less, for no honour can be enough for perfected virtue. Nevertheless he will ac- cept such honours on the ground that they are the highest those men have it in their power to give. But honour coming from men with no special qualities to recommend them and proffered for trifling reasons he will not consider for a mo- ment; that sort of thing is altogether beneath him. And dis- honour he will treat in the same way; dishonour and he can never be justly associated. But, while it is true, as has been said, that honour is the main theatre of the great man's ac- tivity, still he will also deal in the right spirit with riches, power, every form of good and bad fortune as it may befall him. And when he meets with good fortune he will not be overjoyed, nor will he be excessively depressed when he meets with bad. For even honour does not arouse in him these strong emotions, although it is the chief of external goods. For, while power and riches are desirable, it is for the sake of the honour that surrounds them. At all events the holders of these advantages hope that they may be honoured on account of them. Accordingly the man who sets little store even by honour will set little store by these things. This is the reason why the superior man gives the impression of superciliousness.

No doubt it is a common belief that advantages of fortune do something to confirm the great man's sense of his merits.

People do look on high birth and political power and wealth as proper objects of respect because those who possess them have something more than other people, and that which has the superiority in some good is always more honoured. Therefore such advantages increase the great man's sense of superiority. For he is receiving honour on their account – honour from a certain class of persons. But in truth it is only the good man who is to be honoured. No doubt if a man is prosperous as well as virtuous he wins an accession of honour. But those who possess the advantages I have mentioned without being themselves virtuous cannot fairly make any large claims to respect and are improperly described as superior men – for true superiority complete virtue is a *sine qua non*. The fact of the matter is that those who can boast of these advantages only are apt to be supercilious and overweening, for without virtue it is hard to bear good fortune modestly. Accordingly such persons, unable to support the favours of fortune without presumption and fancying themselves above the rest of mankind, look down on everyone else, although their own behaviour is no better than that of ordinary mortals. They imagine that they are conducting themselves like the superior man despite the fact that there is no real likeness and they can only behave in this way where imitation is possible. They are like the superior man in looking down on other people, but do not like him act in the character of the perfectly good man. And if the superior man does contemn the rest of the world, it is with justice and because he takes a correct view of his relation to it. But of those merely lucky people most have no special reason for putting on such airs at all.

The superior man will not run petty risks, nor indeed risks of any kind if he can help it, because there are so few things he considers worth while. But he rises to meet a crisis and, so long as that lasts, he will put his life in peril for the cause, since he is not the man to purchase life at any price. It is also part of his character to confer benefits. But he hates receiving them. This is because the former action implies superiority, the latter inferiority. When he does repay a service it is with interest, for in this way the original benefactor will become the beneficiary and debtor in his turn. Again, the superior man is suspected of having a better memory for benefits conferred than benefits received – the recipient in such a relation is in the inferior position and the great man covets the superior role – and likes to be reminded of what he gave and not of what he got. That is why the Homeric Thetis says not a word to Zeus about her good offices to him, and why the Spartans said nothing to the Athenians of what they had done for Athens, but mentioned only what the Athenians had done for them. Another mark of the superior man is his refusal or reluctance to ask anyone to help him, while always ready to bring help himself. And he stands on his dignity with those who are high in public esteem or favourites of fortune, but does not assume airs in his dealings with persons of no great distinction, because to maintain one's superiority in the presence of notabilities is not easy and impresses others, so that here a dignified manner is not unbecoming of a gentleman, though in the worst of taste when one is dealing with humble people – as bad as hustling the weak. He will not enter the lists against ordinary competitors for distinction, or where he has no chance of the first prize; and it is his way to make no effort or to hang back, except when some really great honour or achievement is open to him. He will rarely undertake anything or, if he does, it will be something great and glorious. Since it is an indication of fear to conceal one's feelings, the superior man is bound to be open in his likes and dislikes, and to care more for the truth than for what people think, and to be straightforward in word and deed.* He must live his own life uninfluenced by anyone, unless perhaps a friend, since to permit such influence would involve some degree of complaisance.† He is not a gushing person, because nothing

* The poor opinion he has of other people enables him to speak his mind freely, and his language will be sincere, unless when he has recourse to irony, which will be his tone in addressing the generality of men.

† It is this tendency to servility that makes humble people flatterers, and flatterers toadies.

strikes him as a subject of mighty admiration. He does not nurse resentment, for it is not like a superior man to remember things against people, especially the mischief they have tried to do him – he tends to overlook all that. He does not care for personal talk, being indisposed to speak either about himself or anyone else. He is not interested in compliments paid to himself or in uncomplimentary remarks about his neighbours, although this does not mean that he is himself given to paying compliments. For the same reason he is not given to recriminations, even against his ill-wishers, unless he means to be deliberately insulting. In troubles which are unavoidable or of no great consequence he is not pathetic or pressing, for that would be to give them too great consequence. He prefers that his possessions should be beautiful and of no profit to him rather than that they should be profitable and meant for use, because this goes to show that he is sufficient to himself. Add that he never hurries (or so people think) and has a deep voice and a deliberate way of speaking. For the man who believes that there is little or nothing worth getting excited about will not be prone to hurry or be high-strung and as a result shrill in his tones and bustling in his movements.

Such, then, is the great-souled or superior man. To him correspond in one direction the poor-spirited, in the other the vain, man. These, like the vulgar and paltry, are not generally thought of as evil – for they do no evil – but as wanderers from the straight path. The poor-spirited man is one who, though not undeserving, deprives himself of such advantages as he deserves, the effect of his failure to claim his deserts being to convince people that there must be something bad about him. Otherwise why did he not seek the advantages to which he was apparently entitled? It is not that such persons are regarded as fools; rather they appear to suffer from *mauvaise honte*, and a reputation of that kind actually seems to have the effect of making them worse men. For one seeks to get what one is entitled to, and if one holds aloof from honourable actions and pursuits, and at the same time makes no claim to external advantages, it looks as if the reason must be that one is conscious of one's own un-worthiness. Vain men, on the other hand, *are* silly, not reali-zing their own limitations. This comes out in glaring fashion when they take on an important job for which they are not qualified, and are proved incompetent. It is a type which affects showy clothes and a smart manner and that sort of thing. They tell the world what successful men they are, and make that the topic of their conversation, as if that would win respect for them. . . . *

The next virtue of which Aristotle speaks lacked in Greek, as in English, a single particularizing name. 'Proper ambition' is about as near as we can get. Aristotle explains how it differs from the 'magna-nimity' of the superior man.

CHAPTER FOUR

BUT it further appears, as I said at the outset, that there is another virtue which may be shown in our dealing with honour. It might be said to have pretty much the same rela-tion to 'magnanimity' that liberality has to 'magnificence'. It does not, any more than liberality, deal with what is great, but in its separate sphere each enables us to have a right attitude towards what is of small or minor importance. I mean that, just as in the getting and giving of money we may go to extremes of too little or too much, or keep the middle course, so in the matter of honour we may desire it too much or too little, or in the right way and from proper sources. We call a man 'ambitious' when he shows an inordi-nate desire for honour or desires it from an improper source, and 'unambitious' if he does not regard honour as an object to be aimed at even when he has a noble cause. I use both terms in a derogatory sense, but we are not consistent in our use of them, for sometimes we commend the ambitious per-son as 'manly' and 'noble-hearted', and the unambitious as

* Note that poor-spiritedness is more opposed than vanity to great-ness of soul. It is in fact a worse thing and more widespread.

'a quiet sensible fellow.' * The explanation lies on the surface. The expression 'fond of' is used in a variety of ways, so that we do not always apply the word 'fond-of-honour' (or 'ambitious') to the same object. As a compliment it means 'unusually fond of honour,' as a criticism it means 'discreditably fond of honour.' The mean condition between the extremes of 'ambitious' and 'unambitious' has no name, and this leaves a kind of no-man's-land between them. But where you have too much and too little you must have just enough. Now you have men desiring honour too much and men desiring it too little. Therefore it must be possible to desire it in the right measure, and it is this intermediate state in men's dispositions towards honour that, though we have no name for it, we really approve. Place it beside ambition, and it seems to be lack of ambition; contrast it with the latter, and it looks like ambition; in its relation to both it in a manner *is* both. We observe the same phenomenon in the other virtues. In the present case, however, the extremes seem to be left in immediate opposition because the intermediate condition is not distinguished by a name of its own.

Aristotle now discusses the disposition of the good man when he has reason to be angry. 'Gentleness' or 'good temper' is as near as we can get to describing it. But Aristotle's own word (praotes) is not very apt either.

CHAPTER FIVE

'GENTLENESS' is the disposition which observes the mean in anger. It is not a very good name for this disposition, which is really nameless; and this is more or less true also of the extremes. An objection to applying the term 'gentleness' to the mean is that it tends to suggest the corresponding deficiency. That also has not found a name, although the excess may fairly be denominated 'irascibility', the emotion concerned being anger. Anger may be produced by a variety of causes, but, however that may be, it is the man who is

* See above.

angry on the right occasions and with the right people and at the right moment and for the right length of time who wins our commendation. Such a person would be what we mean by a 'gentle' man, if gentleness be regarded as a laudable quality.* The deficiency may be called 'tameness', 'submissiveness', 'meekness' or some such name, and it is blamed by us because we think that a man who does not get angry when he has reason to be angry, or does not get angry in the right way and at the right time and with the right people, is a dolt. It looks like insensibility or want of proper spirit. For if he never gets angry, how can he take his own part? So people think that to swallow an affront, or to let our relatives be insulted, is no conduct for a gentleman. – Then there is the corresponding excess, which is getting angry with the wrong persons, or for the wrong reasons, or too violently, or too quickly, or too long. Still it must not be supposed that the same man is guilty of all these modes of excess. That could not happen, because evil destroys even itself and, when it is unmitigated, cannot be borne.

To take the irascible then first. It is characteristic of these to fly into a passion with the wrong persons and upon wrong grounds and with excessive violence. But their fury is as quickly spent, and this is the best trait in their character. It is made possible by the fact that they do not nurse their wrath but, being hot-tempered, give vent to it openly, and then it is gone. Those who are excessively sensitive to provocation are 'choleric', so called because they lose their tempers at anything and on any occasion. Then there are the 'bitter', who are implacable and nurse their wrath for a long time. Now when a man has given as good as he got he feels that the affair is over, the satisfaction he has received putting a stop to his resentment by instilling pleasure into his breast instead of the painful emotion of rage. Otherwise he con-

---

* When I call a man 'gentle' I must be taken to mean that he is of a calm and equable temper, never getting angry except on justifiable grounds and for a reasonable length of time, though people mostly regard a man of this type as going too far in the direction of meekness because of his tendency to forgive an injury rather than seek redress for it.

tinues to labour under it and, since he does this in secret, he cannot find anyone to argue him out of his resentful mood, and it takes him a long time to digest his spleen. Of all irascible people it is these embittered ones who cause most vexation to themselves and to their closest friends. – Lastly, there are those who lose their tempers on occasions when they should not, and more completely and for longer than they ought, and who refuse to make a quarrel up unless they are allowed to inflict some vengeance or some punishment. These we call 'bad-tempered'.

Of the two extremes it is the excess which we consider most opposite to gentleness. For (a) it is commoner, since human beings are always more disposed to seek revenge than to forgive, and (b) the bad-tempered are harder to live with than the meek. But our present discussion proves the truth of what we said before, that it is not easy to define how and with whom and for what reasons and how long one ought to be angry, or within what limits a man does this rightly or wrongly. To go a little beyond these limits is not regarded as a very wicked thing, whether the transgression is in the direction of the too much or the too little. Sometimes, to be sure, we commend those whose capacity for getting angry is deficient, calling them 'gentle', sometimes the bad-tempered, calling them 'manly' and 'natural leaders'. But it is not easy to give a reasoned account of how, and how far, a man may transgress before incurring censure. For the transgression takes place in particular circumstances, and we decide each case according as we feel about it. So much at least is clear: the intermediate disposition, which leads us to be angry with the people, for the reasons, in the manner and all the rest of it, that we ought, is commendable, while the extreme dispositions, which lead us to be angry too much or too little are blameable, though not all to the same extent – that is to say, not much if there is but a slight deviation from the mean, very much more if the deviation is considerable. Clearly, then, we are bound to lay hold upon the middle state. . . .

Aristotle passes now to problems of social behaviour and the good and bad qualities exhibited in dealing with them.

CHAPTER SIX

IN social intercourse, when people live together and there is interchange of talk and business, we find a set of men who are thought to carry politeness too far. Everything according to them is splendid and delightful; they offer no criticisms and suppose it their duty to avoid giving distress to anyone they meet. But there is another set, just the opposite of these, who raise objections to everything and are totally regardless of any pain they may inflict – they are the people we call 'surly' or 'quarrelsome'. Now I need hardly point out that these dispositions are such as we must condemn. But it is equally obvious that the disposition which comes between them and leads a man to approve of the right things in the right manner is something to be praised; and this remark applies equally well to his disapproval. To this quality no name has been assigned, but it is more like the love of friends than anything else. For the man who embodies it is the sort we mean when we say that so-and-so is 'a likeable fellow', though in that expression there is an extra touch of personal affection. It is the absence of this affection towards the members of our social circle that makes the difference between the middle state we are discussing and the love between friends. For the man who embodies the state is moved to act not by likes and dislikes but simply by being that kind of man. And, being such, he will make no difference in his treatment of strangers and of acquaintances, of those he is used to and of those he is not, except that he will suit his behaviour to the particular society in which he finds himself, since it is quite out of place to show the same consideration, or lack of it, for intimate acquaintances as for strangers.

I have stated, then, the general proposition that such a man will act rightly in society. In less general language he will, in seeking to give pain or pleasure to others, always conform to a certain standard of moral worth and beauty. He will disapprove of pleasures – and it is with pleasures and pains arising in social intercourse that he is concerned – which it is not honourable, or which it is harmful, for him to share; rather than this he will hurt some feelings by declining to be a party to them. He will (provided his antagonism does not give serious pain) even repudiate a pleasure which involves the participant in some notable disgrace or harm. His manner to men occupying important positions and to his intimates will be different from what it is to ordinary people and those who are comparatively little known to him – to mention no other distinctions – in that he will give each class the deference to which it is entitled. As a rule he will prefer contributing to the enjoyment of the company he is in to offending their susceptibilities, and he will be on his guard against that. He will follow the development of the situation; I mean, he will observe in what way the honour and interests of his friends are affected, in case these should be compromised to an extent which would more than counterbalance any pleasure he could contribute. But he will also be prepared to inflict a little pain, if that will ensure much pleasure at some future date. ...

The next chapter explains itself.

CHAPTER SEVEN

WITHIN much the same field operates a virtue which is the mean between boastfulness and another extreme. Like that which we have been discussing this mean has no name. But we shall find it a good plan to examine these nameless qualities too, for it will extend our knowledge of human nature, if we examine each of its qualities in some detail. It will also tend to confirm our belief that the virtues are means,* if we see in one comprehensive view that our belief is justified in every instance.

* i.e. conditions of the soul which dispose it to aim at the mean between extremes in the material of human conduct.

I have already spoken of human behaviour in society so far as it is concerned with pleasure and pain. Our next task must be to discuss such behaviour from the point of view of its truthfulness or falsity in men's words and actions and in their pretensions. In this last respect the boaster or charlatan is regarded as one who pretends to have distinguished qualities which he either does not possess at all or possesses less fully than he would have us believe. At the other extreme is the ironical man, who professes that he does not have, or has in less measure than the world supposes, the good qualities which he does in fact possess. Between these two comes the man who professes to be exactly what he is, and is sincere both in his speech and in his demeanour, frank about his own qualities, making neither too much nor too little of them. A representative of any of these three types may or may not act with some specific end in view. But, if he has such an end, his character declares itself in his words, his doings, and his way of life. Falsehood being by its own nature bad and reprehensible, and truth on the other hand a fine and laudable thing, the boaster and the self-depreciator, equally insincere, come in, particularly the boaster, for censure, while the sincere man, occupying the ground between them, is praised. As we shall have to discuss both the sincere and the insincere types, let us begin with the sincere man. By the 'sincere' man I do not mean one who, when he enters into a contract or agreement, puts all his cards on the table. Nor have I in mind anything that raises the question of its justice, for that belongs to another virtue. I am speaking of cases where no such complication enters, and a man is truthful in word and deed just because truthfulness has become second nature with him. Such a man can hardly fail to be good. For the sincere man, who is truthful even in matters where nothing depends on his veracity, will be still more careful of the truth when something does depend on it. For surely the man who has been consistently on his guard against falsity as such will be on his guard against it when it is morally indefensible. And such a man wins our applause. If he shows a tendency to depart from the strict truth it will take the form of understatement rather than exaggeration. It is the more engaging trait, since there is something annoying about excess.

We come now to the man who pretends that his qualifications are higher than they are. If he has no ulterior object, he is evidently more of a fool than a knave, although he has some resemblance to the latter, for a good man would find no pleasure in false pretences. But, if he has such an object, we must draw a distinction. If glory or honour be his aim, he should not be blamed too much; but if it be money or the means of making money, he is, comparatively speaking, a disreputable character.* (In the same way we may divide liars into two classes: those who lie for lying's sake, and those who lie for reputation or profit.) Well, those who brag in order to win reputation pretend to such qualities and achievements as make people offer their praise and congratulations. Those whose object is material gain claim such qualification as (a) may be profitable to their immediate circle, (b) cannot easily be shown to be non-existent. They may, for instance, pretend to be prophets or philosophers or doctors. Most charlatans pretend to skill in these professions, because these possess the two characteristics I have mentioned.

'Ironical' persons, who depreciate their own merits, give an impression of superior refinement, because we feel that their way of speaking is not dictated by greed of gain but by the desire to avoid showing off. As the boastful claim, so these – Socrates, for example – disclaim the possession of distinguished qualities. If they disclaim merely trifling or commonplace accomplishments, they are called pretentious humbugs and we want to kick them. At times their mock-modesty looks like self-advertisement. The Spartan dress has this effect on us because of its extreme plainness, for there is a measure of ostentation about that, just as there is about

---

* Boastfulness is not measured by the capacity or incapacity of the boaster to make good his boasts, but by the nature of his purpose. In other words, he is a boaster in virtue of his disposition and because he is that kind of man.

over-dressing. But if a man employs irony in moderation and when the subject is not too banal and obvious, he makes a pleasant impression.

The boaster seems to be more directly opposed to the sincere man than is the ironist, for he goes farther in the wrong direction.

What is it that makes a man good or bad 'company'?

CHAPTER EIGHT

WE must not forget, however, that recreation or relaxation has its place in our lives, and that includes entertaining conversation. In this sphere also, it is considered, we ought to show a certain adaptability in the way we address people in society and a certain fitness both in the matter and the manner of what we say to them, though it should be added that it will be a great advantage to us if those who are listening or talking to us have our own code of behaviour. Clearly this is another range of activities in which it is possible to have an excess and a falling short of the mean.

Well, the man who carries fun to all lengths is regarded as an ill-bred buffoon who feels he must be funny come what may and would rather venture on *risqué* jokes and hurt the feelings of his victim than fail to raise a laugh. On the other hand, the man who never cracks a joke himself, and does not care for those who do, is looked upon as a dour and humourless fellow. A man whose pleasantries do not go too far is called a 'wit'; that is to say, he is ready-witted or versatile, a witticism being thought of as the sally of a mobile temperament. (We judge characters or temperaments, as we do bodies, by the movements they make.) As one never has to go far to discover food for laughter, and as most men like fun and ridicule even more than they should, it will happen that even a buffoon is described as 'witty', as if he were someone of real intelligence, though it is clear from what has been said that there is a wide difference between the buffoon and the wit. Then as to the middle state in dealing with the humorous, particularly characteristic of that is social tact or address, which may be defined as the gift of saying just the right things for a gentleman to say and of getting others to say such things to him. For there are things of this kind suitable for such a man to say and have said to him by way of pleasantry, the pleasantry of a man of liberal sentiments differing from that of a man of servile temper, and that of an educated from that of an uneducated person. You can see the difference if you compare the Old with the New Comedy. The masters of the Old Comedy thought obscenity was amusing, the masters of the New prefer innuendo, which is a great improvement from the point of view of decency. Suppose, then, we define propriety in ridicule as the power of saying amusing things that are not unsuitable on the lips of a gentleman and do not wound the feelings of the person who is being made fun of, but perhaps even give him pleasure. Probably, however, it eludes definition. For what one man detests in the way of humour another thinks delightful. The witty man will insist that the things which are said to him shall not fall below the level of the things he says himself, because whatever a man permits to be said about him he would, it is thought, actually do. There are some things, however, which the witty man will not do, and therefore will not suffer to be said about him. For ridicule is a form of abuse or slander, and slander in certain circumstances is prohibited in our codes of law – there is a strong case for prohibiting some forms of ridicule as well. In this matter, then, the gentleman will be a law to himself and regulate his behaviour in the way I have described. Such, then, is the man who keeps the right – that is the middle – course in this matter, whether he be called witty or socially accomplished. On the other hand the buffoon never can resist a joke, sparing neither himself nor anyone else, provided he can raise a laugh, and saying things which a man of taste and intelligence would never dream of saying and sometimes would not even listen to. As for the boor, he is 'impossible', contributing nothing to the conversation and taking offence at anything that is said, forgetting that relaxation and amusement are necessary ingredients of human existence. . . .

Aristotle now discusses a quality for which the Greek word is aidos. *Originally it meant respect for any thing or person towards whom respect is due, including the weak and defenceless. But like the English word 'modesty' it was gradually restricted to the special sense it has in the following chapter.*

CHAPTER NINE

WE must now speak of 'modesty', though strictly speaking it is not a virtue, being more like an emotion than a habit of the soul. It is defined at any rate as a certain fear of disgrace, and it has an effect very like that produced by the fear of danger. The only difference is that we blush when put out of countenance, whereas fear of death induces pallor. So in both cases it is the body which is somehow affected, and that seems to be the result of a feeling or emotion rather than a settled state of mind. It is not an emotion which becomes every stage of life; it is fitting only in youth. We think it becoming in young persons to be easily abashed, because, their life consisting largely in emotion, they are apt to commit blunders, from which they may be saved by modesty. Again, we commend a modest youth, but nobody would commend an older man for being shamefaced, for we think that he should not do things calculated to make him feel like that. Shame in fact is not the emotion of a good man, because it is felt when we do ill. Since ill ought not to be done, the emotion ought not to be felt.* It is a bad man who ought to feel shame, and it comes of his being the sort of man to be guilty of a shameful deed. But it is absurd to think that the merely being so constituted as to feel shame at doing something shameful makes you a good man. An action must be voluntary before you can feel modest about it, and a good man

* It makes no difference whether the things done are really shameful or only thought to be so; they should not be done in either case.

will never voluntarily do anything bad. The goodness of modesty must depend on whether or not it fulfils a certain condition, which is this, that if a man do something shameful he will be ashamed. But no such condition is binding upon *virtue*. Shamelessness – the absence of any feeling that it is dishonourable to do what is dishonourable – is admittedly bad. But this does not go to prove that shame at performing such actions is a virtuous emotion. In the same way temperance is not to be regarded as altogether a virtue; it is partly virtuous and partly not. But the proof of this is reserved for a later discussion. We must now turn to the subject of Justice.

BOOK FIVE

What is Justice?

CHAPTER ONE

IN treating of justice and injustice we have to consider (a) what sort of actions come within their scope? (b) justice being a mean, what is the nature of that mean? (c) what are the extremes between which justice lies? It will be taken for granted that our inquiry is to be conducted on the lines hitherto followed.

Well, then, when people speak of justice we see that they invariably mean a state of mind which disposes them to perform just actions, and behave in a just manner, and desire what is just. In the same way we mean by injustice a state of mind which disposes them to be unjust and desire unjust things. So we may accept this broad statement as something from which we can proceed to a more detailed discussion.

We must, however, distinguish between the various sciences and faculties on the one hand and the dispositions on the other, because they operate differently. We find that one and the same science may deal with things that are the opposites of one another. But a disposition operates with only one set of conditions and not their opposites as well. For instance, a healthy state of mind leads to the performance of healthy actions, but never of unhealthy. Thus when we say a man walks in a healthy way we mean that he walks like a man in good health. We may even sometimes infer the existence of a disposition from the existence of its opposite, and in many cases from the material on which it is working. For example, if we know what is meant by a sound condition of the body, we also know what is meant by an unsound condition. Not only so, but we know what a sound bodily condition is from bodies in that condition, and what bodies are sound from knowing what a sound condition is. Suppose, for instance, that a sound body means firm flesh, an unsound body must mean a loose texture of flesh, and what contributes to physical soundness must go to produce firmness of flesh. Again, supposing we have a group of usually associated words which is given a variety of meanings, it is apt to follow that there is a corresponding group with an equivalent variety of meanings. For example, if the word 'just' is used in more senses than one, so will be 'unjust' and 'injustice'. Now it appears that more than one meaning is attached to the words 'justice' and 'injustice', but since the conceptions here embraced under a single name come very close to one another, we fail to note the differences between them, although these are comparatively clear in the case of things called by the same name which are widely separated in our thoughts of them. Here is an example. The collar-bone in animals and the instrument with which a door is locked are both called in Greek a 'key'. But, since the one could by no possibility be mistaken for the other, we are not misled by their possession of a common name.

Well, then, let us grasp the various senses in which a man may be said to be 'unjust'. In the popular mind the description 'unjust' is held to apply both to the man who takes more than his due and to the man who breaks the law. It follows * that the man who does not break the law and the man who does not take more than he is entitled to will be 'just'. 'Just' therefore means (a) lawful and (b) what is 'equal', that is fair. Moreover, since the unjust man grasps at more than his fair share, his character will come out in his dealings with goods, though these will be only such goods as it is fortunate to have and unfortunate to lack. Now these, although in themselves they are always good, are not always good for the individual. Yet it is the latter that form the objects of men's prayers and pursuit. But it should not be like that. When men choose what is good for themselves they should pray that this should coincide with the absolutely good. The unjust man, however, does not always choose the larger

* From our argument about 'opposites'.

share; of evils that are absolutely evil he in fact chooses the
lesser portion. He is none the less regarded as seeking more
than he deserves because his fault is seeking more than his
due share of what is *good*, and the lesser of two evils is
thought to be in a manner good. Let us call him 'unfair', for
that is a comprehensive description which covers the grasping man in both his aspects. Again, it is clear that, since the
lawless man is, as we saw, unjust and the law-abiding man
just, all lawful things may be regarded as just, where by
'lawful' we mean what is plainly prescribed by the legislative power.* The different laws, whatever the subject of
them, are drawn up so as to aim at the good of the community as a whole or of a select class to whom power is en-
trusted on the ground of higher qualifications or some such
reason. So here we have one meaning of the word 'just'. It is
applied to whatever creates or conserves for a political association its happiness or the happiness of some part thereof.
Besides this the law imposes certain regulations about the
way a man should behave. For instance, he must prove his
courage by refusing to leave his post in battle or run away or
discard his accoutrements; prove his continence by refraining from adultery, outrage, etc.; prove his gentleness by (for
example) not wounding others by words or blows. And so
with the rest of the virtues and vices – law deals with all of
them, enjoining the former, prohibiting the latter. If it has
been rightly enacted, it will do this rightly; not so rightly, if
it is a hastily devised expedient.

Now justice in this sense of the word is complete virtue –
not justice unqualified, but as it appears between one party
and another. Hence we often find it regarded as the sovran
virtue, 'more wonderful than evening or morning star,' and
we have a proverb:

> All virtue is summed up in dealing justly.

Justice *is* perfect virtue because it *practises* perfect virtue. But
it is perfect in a special way, because the man who possesses
justice is capable of practising it towards a second party and

* We imply that these ordinances are every one of them 'just'.

not merely in his own case. I say this because there are plenty of people who can behave uprightly in their own affairs, but not when they come to deal with others. So the saying of Bias, 'Office will prove the man,' has found favour with the world. For to accept office is to enter into relations with others and to become one member of an association. And for just this reason – that a relation is established with others – justice is the only virtue which is regarded as benefiting someone else than its possessor. For it does what is to the advantage of another, whether he is in authority or just a partner. As it is the extreme of wickedness to practise villainy towards one's friends, as well as to debauch oneself, so the highest virtue is shown not by the man who practises it in his own case but by the man who performs the difficult task of practising it towards another. Thus righteousness or justice, so understood, is not a part but the whole of virtue, while injustice, its opposite, is not a part but the whole of vice.*

We pass now from justice in its general aspect – righteousness – to justice (and injustice) in its special sense.

CHAPTER TWO

I T is, however, the justice that forms a *part* of virtue that we are at present investigating, since it is my contention that such a form of justice exists. In like manner we are to investigate that form of injustice which is part of injustice as a whole. Certain considerations induce one to believe in the existence of this limited justice. For instance, when a man behaves ill in other ways – as playing the coward by throwing away his shield, or showing a nasty temper by abusing other people, or his illiberality by refusing to contribute any-

---

* What makes the difference between justice in this sense and virtue transpires from what we have already observed; they are the same except for one essential distinction, which may be expressed by saying that, while virtue is an unqualified disposition of the soul, justice is qualified by its relation to others.

thing to the relief of a friend in financial straits – he is of course not behaving well, but he is not grasping more than his fair share of anything. When he is guilty of such grasping he is often uninfluenced by any, not to say all, of these other faults of character, though *some* bad quality must be impelling him,* and this bad quality is injustice. That proves that there is an injustice different from and part of general injustice, and that a thing may be described as unjust which is part of the unjust in general, meaning by that all that is contrary to law. Or take the case of two men guilty of adultery. One of them commits it for money or some advantage he gets out of it, the other because he wants the woman and is prepared to pay the penalty. The second man would be regarded as a sensualist, not as a covetous fellow; the first as a wrongdoer, but not a sensualist. From this it appears that what constitutes the injustice of the act is its being done for gain. Lastly, all other bad activities, wherever they happen, are ascribed to some particular vice – adultery to incontinence, abandoning one's comrades in battle to cowardice, physical violence to anger. But suppose a man has profited by an offence, that offence is considered the result of injustice and of no other vice whatsoever. – It is clear, then, that there exists side by side with universal injustice another kind which forms part of that. They have the same name, because their definition places them in the same genus, for both find their significance in their relation to someone not themselves. But they are differentiated in this way. Particular injustice is interested in honours, money, security – or all three if we can find a single name to cover them – with the one purpose of deriving pleasure from the advantage they yield. Universal injustice, however, occupies the same ground as perfect virtue.

We may now take it as proved that there is more than one kind of justice, and that there is a form of it distinguishable from virtue as a whole. We must therefore try to understand what this form is and what qualities we must attribute to it. Now we have seen that there are two ways in which the

* That it must be bad is shown by the fact that we condemn it.

word 'injustice' is used. In one it means 'contrary to law', but it has another meaning, namely, 'contrary to fairness' or 'to equality'. What is thus unfair or unequal is distinguished from what is unlawful as part from whole, everything that is unfair being unlawful, but not everything unlawful being unfair. In the same way the unjust and injustice, viewed as parts of injustice as a whole, are distinguishable from injustice as a whole. Injustice in the former sense is a part of universal injustice. Similarly the justice I now propose to discuss is a part of justice viewed as a whole. That is to say, we are to discuss justice and injustice, the just and the unjust, in the sense which we attach to these words when they stand for *parts* of universal justice and injustice. Let us dismiss, then, further consideration of the justice which corresponds to, and practises, universal virtue in its dealings with others, and of the injustice which practises universal vice in such dealings. Another point which has become clear is how we must define the just and the unjust as they are related to justice and injustice. For, broadly speaking, what we do as a result of practising virtue in general are those very actions which conform to law. For behaviour in accordance with this or that particular virtue is enjoined on us, and behaviour in accordance with the particular vices forbidden, by the law. Again, the things that tend to produce virtue as a whole have the same effect on a man as the rules prescribed by law for education in social relations. As for the education of the individual, by which I mean the education that makes him simply good, it will be for us in a later examination to decide whether it falls within the province of political or some other science. For of course it is not always the same thing to be a good man and a good citizen.

There are two kinds of particular justice, distributive *and* corrective.

To return to particular justice and that form of the just which corresponds to it, we find two kinds. (*a*) One is shown

in the distribution of honour or money or such other possessions of the community as can be divided among its members.* (*b*) The other kind is shown in private transactions or
business deals, where it serves the purpose of correcting any
unfairness that may arise. This corrective justice itself consists of two parts. For private transactions or agreements,
being divisible into voluntary and involuntary, require an
appropriate form of justice to deal with each division. By
'voluntary' transactions are meant such operations as buying, selling, loaning money at interest or without interest,
pledging, depositing, hiring out.† As for 'involuntary' transactions, they may be divided into (*a*) *secret* – e.g. theft,
adultery, poisoning, procuring, alienating of slaves, killing
by stealth, perjury; and (*b*) *violent* – e.g. assault and battery,
casting people into prison, homicide, robbery, mutilation,
insulting language, insulting treatment of others.

Distributive justice more particularly described.

CHAPTER THREE

SINCE the unjust man is a man who is not content to have
an equal share with others, and since the unjust thing is the
unequal thing, it is obvious that there must be a mean between the greater and the less inequality. This is the equal.
In whatever action we find a greater and a less there must
be an equal. If then the unjust is the unequal, the just is the
equal; everyone accepts this conclusion without demanding
a reason for it. But, since the equal is the mean, the just
must also be a mean. Now equality cannot be stated in less
than two terms. From this certain consequences naturally
flow. *First*, the just is both a mean and an equal. *Second*, in
its character as mean it must have extremes between which

---

* Note: The division need not be *equal*.

† They are described as voluntary because the first step in the bargaining is voluntary.

it lies.* *Third*, in its character of equal its equality must be expressed in two equal parts of what is shared. *Fourth*, in its character of just there must be certain persons to whom it is just. Here then is a minimum of four terms in which justice finds expression – two *persons* and two *shares*. And the equality of the second pair will be reflected in the equality of the first. The ratio will be the same in the one case as in the other, because, if the persons are not equal, their shares will not be equal. As a matter of fact when quarrels and complaints arise, it is when people who are equal have not got equal shares, or *vice versa*.

We see the same result when we look at the practice followed in awarding shares according to merit. It is admitted on all hands that in distributing shares justice must take some account of merit. By 'merit', however, people do not all mean the same thing. Men of democratic sympathies measure degrees of merit by degrees of freedom, oligarchs by degrees of wealth, others judge by good birth, those who believe in the rule of the 'best' go by moral and intellectual qualifications. Justice, then, is the expression of a proportion. For proportion is not merely a property of numerical quantity, but of quantity as such. It is in fact an equality of ratios. And, as we saw, it involves four terms at least.† If you look at the diagram before you, you will see the equation. As the line representing the first term (1) is to the line representing the second (2), so is (2) to the line representing the third term (3). Thus (2) is mentioned twice. Therefore, if it is counted in twice, there will be four proportionals.

The just, then, like the equal, requires a minimum of four terms for its complete expression. Also the ratio between the two sets of terms is the same. Here is another diagram. Observe that the line representing the persons is divided in the same proportion as the line representing the shares. Then, as the first term is to the second, so is the third to the fourth.

* The greater, namely, and the less.

† It is open to inspection that a discrete – that is a discontinuous – proportion is in four terms. But this is equally true of a continuous proportion, for it treats one term as two by repeating it.

Hence by alternation as the first is to the third, so is the second to the fourth. Therefore as the first term is to the second, so is the sum of the first and third to the sum of the second and fourth. This is the combination which is produced in a fair division, and the combination is fair if sharers and shared are connected in this way. In this manner we get 'distributive' justice, which results from the conjunction of the first term of a proportion with the third, and of the second with the fourth; and such justice is a mean between the two extremes of more and less of what is fair. In a word the just is the proportionate.*

We see, then, that the just, by which is here meant the expression of distributive justice, can be stated as a proportion, and the unjust in this sense is a violation of proportion. What is unjust, therefore, is what is either too much or too little. One sees this happen. When some good is at stake the man who acts unjustly is the man who takes too much; the man who suffers the injustice gets too little. The position is reversed when the matter at stake is an evil. In that case the lesser evil is reckoned as a good in comparison with the greater, because of two evils the lesser is more desirable than the greater, and the desirable is good, the degree of goodness being measured by its desirability.

* This is the kind of proportion which Greek mathematicians call 'geometrical', being one in which the sum of the first and third terms is in the same ratio to the sum of the second and fourth as one term to the other in either of the two pairs. On the other hand distributive justice is not a continuous proportion, the reason being that its second and third terms, consisting as they do in a sharer and a share, do not make a single term.

The next chapter treats of corrective justice. This does not involve a 'geometrical' but only an 'arithmetical' proportion, as it does not take into account the parties to a transaction but only the transaction itself. The business of the judge here is to find or restore the mean between the too much and the too little.

CHAPTER FOUR

WE come now to the remaining kind of justice, the 'corrective' or 'emendatory'. We get this in private transactions, voluntary and involuntary. As a form of justice it belongs to a different kind from that which we have just been discussing. For where common property has to be shared the justice we call 'distributive' is always reducible to a proportion of the nature we have described.* The injustice which is the opposite of distributive justice is a violation of that proportion. On the other hand in private transactions the just, though it may be fairly represented as an equal,† is not the equal according to geometrical, but according to arithmetical, proportion. For in corrective justice it is all one whether a good man has cheated a bad or a bad man a good, whether a good man has committed adultery or a bad. The law never looks beyond the question, 'What damage was done?' and it treats the parties involved as equals. All it asks is whether an injustice has been done or an injury inflicted by one party on the other. Consequently what the judge seeks to do is to redress the inequality, which in this kind of justice is identified with injustice. Thus in a case of assault or homicide the action and the consequence of the action may be represented as a line divided into unequal parts, as in the diagram I now show you. What the judge aims at doing is to make the parts equal by the penalty he imposes, whereby he takes

---

* The distribution, if made from a common stock, will be made on the basis of a ratio identical with that between the separate contributions to the stock.

† And the unjust, it may be added, as an unequal.

from the aggressor any gain he may have secured.* The equal, then, is a mean between the more and the less. But gain and loss are each of them more and less in opposite ways, more good and less evil being gain, and more evil and less good being loss. The equal, which we hold to be just, is now seen to be intermediate between them. Hence we conclude that corrective justice must be the mean between loss and gain. This explains why the disputants have recourse to a judge; for to go to a judge is to go to justice. The judge aims at being as it were the incarnation of justice. Then, what men seek in a judge is a middle term – in some societies the judges are actually called 'mediators'. People think that, if they get the mean, they will get the just. Thus the just is in its way a mean, the judge being, as we have seen, a mediating factor between the disputing parties. What the judge does is to restore equality. Suppose we illustrate what happens by means of a diagram. A line is divided into two unequal segments. From the greater of these the judge takes away that part by which it exceeds one-half of the whole line, and this he adds to the lesser segment. The whole is now divided equally – that is in half – and when this happens and the parties have got their equal shares, they have 'their own', as people say. This is how the word 'just' gets its name, *dikaion*, so called from *dicha*, 'in half', *dichaion* being changed in pronunciation to *dikaion*. In the same way *dikastes*, 'judge', is *dichastes*, 'divider'. In arithmetical proportion the equal is a mean between the greater and the less. Suppose you have two equals. Take a part from one of these and add it to the other. Then that other will exceed the former by twice the part taken away. For, if it had been taken from the one and not added to the other, the other would exceed its equal by no more than the part taken away. Therefore it will exceed

* In such cases the word 'gain' is used in a general sense, even if, as sometimes happens, it is inappropriate. It is, for example, an inappropriate word to use in connexion with a man who has struck another, just as 'penalty' or 'loss' is an unsuitable description of what happens to the man who has been struck. Still, the words serve well enough when it comes to measuring the extent of the damage done.

the mean by the part only, and the mean will exceed that from which the part was taken by the part only. By this method, then, we shall discover what must be taken from the party who has too much and added to the party who has too little. That is to say, we must add to the party who has too little the amount by which the mean exceeds what he has, and take away from the party who has too much the amount by which the mean is exceeded by what he has.

At this point Aristotle refers to another diagram, which would resemble what follows when English letters are substituted for Greek.

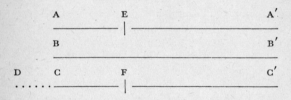

It is to be understood that AE = DC = CF.

Let AA', BB' and CC' be three equal lines. Let the segment AE be taken from AA', and the segment CD be added to CC', so that the whole line DCC' exceeds the line EA' by CD + CF. Then DCC' will exceed BB' by CD.*

* A note on terminology. The expressions 'gain' and 'loss' are borrowed from the process of voluntary exchange. In that process to have more than one's fair share of the bargain is called 'gaining', to come out of it with less than one's fair share is 'losing'. They are the words used, for example, in buying and selling and all other exchanges permitted by the law, although, when the transaction is concluded with neither party having too much or too little, but exactly what they had before they started bargaining, they do not speak of gaining or losing, but say that each party 'has his own'. It follows that in non-voluntary transactions justice will be a mean between gain and loss, if we like to put it in that way. It is to have as much after as one had before the transaction.

Continuing his discussion of corrective justice, Aristotle next considers the nature of reciprocity in dealings between man and man.

CHAPTER FIVE

THERE are some who think that justice is nothing more or less than reciprocity. This was maintained, for example, by the Pythagoreans, who actually defined the just as simply 'to have done to one what one has done to another.' But simple reciprocity cannot be squared either with distributive or corrective justice, though people would like to say it was the latter, quoting the judgement of Rhadamanthus:

> If he that did has had done unto him
> That which he did, then justice will be wrought.

But they cannot be identified – there are many points of difference. For example, if a man in authority strikes somebody under him, it is wrong for the latter to return the blow. But if *he* strikes his superior officer, it is not enough that he should be struck back; he should receive some extra punishment. Again, it makes a world of difference whether consent entered into an act or not. It is true that in the give and take of mutual services this kind of justice – reciprocity of treatment – forms the bond between the parts of the process. But the *ground* of it is not equality but a proportion. It is just the feeling that, as one does, so one will be done by, that keeps a political association in being. For men regard it as their right to return evil for evil – and, if they cannot, feel they have lost their liberty – or good for good. Without some such understanding no exchange can be effected, and the link formed by the exchange is what holds the members of the association together. That is why a temple of the Graces is set up in a place where it cannot fail to be seen and remind men to repay a kindness. To make such a return is the distinguishing mark of grace, for it is our duty not merely to repay a service done, but to do one ourselves on another occasion.

This process of give and take according to the right proportion is carried out by 'diagonal conjunction'. Let me give you an illustration. A is a builder, B a shoemaker, C a house, D a shoe. It is required that the builder shall receive from the shoemaker some part of what the latter produces, giving him at the same time some part of what he produces himself. Now if they achieve, first, proportionate equality, secondly fair give and take, they will find the problem we have stated solved. But if they fail to achieve this, there will not be equality, nor will there be fairness in their dealing, and it cannot continue. For nothing prevents the product of one of the parties from being better value than that of the other, and this requires a process of reducing them to equality. It is the same with all the other arts and crafts. They would never have survived unless the active element – the producer – produced and received the same quantity and quality of products as the passive element – the recipient – gets. Each party must have something different to offer. Two doctors cannot associate for the purpose of exchanging what they have to give, but a doctor and a farmer can, and so, generally, can different types of people. Where there is not an original equality between them it has to be created. This implies that all products exchanged must be somehow comparable. It is this that has led to the introduction of money, which may be regarded as a medium of exchange, since it is a measure of everything, and so a measure of the more and the less than the mean in value, informing us, for example, how many shoes are worth one house or a fixed quantity of food. In this way we arrive at the formula: As a builder is to a shoemaker, so are x shoes to a house. Unless it be carried out in accordance with this formula, there can be no true exchange or association, and such reciprocity will be found impossible, if the things exchanged are not somehow reduced to equal value. To repeat what I said before, there must be one standard by which all commodities are to be measured. This standard is in fact demand; in every situation of the kind demand is the unifying factor. For if people should have different wants from what they do have, or no wants at all, there would be a different kind of exchange or none at all. By a convention which has come to be accepted, demand is expressed in the form of money, which is the reason why money is called 'currency'. For it is not a natural thing, but exists by current custom, while at the same time it is in our power to change or destroy its value.

After the products have been equalized reciprocal proportion will come into operation, so as to produce an equation: As farmer to shoemaker, so the product of the shoemaker to the product of the farmer. When they exchange their products they must reduce them to the form of a proportion, because, if they fail to do this, one or other of the two, having more than he ought, will have the advantage both in this respect and in the equivalent loss suffered by the other party to the exchange. When on the other hand they 'have their own' they are equal and can enter into an association with one another, because their case admits of such equality.* But if reciprocal proportion could not be arrived at in this way, there could be no association between the parties. That it is demand, forming as it does a single standard, that holds such associations together, comes out clearly in the circumstance that, where there is no demand for an exchange of services from one or both the parties, they do not enter into association. ... This possibility makes it necessary to introduce some means of producing equality.

The function of money in exchange of commodities.

Now what money does for us is to act as a sort of pledge or guarantee that a prospective exchange of commodities will in fact take place if the necessity arises, though in the meantime the necessity is not immediate. For if we proffer the money it should be possible for us to get the goods. No doubt money is subject to the vagaries of the market just like other commodities, for its purchasing power keeps rising and fall-

* A = farmer, C = food, B = shoemaker, shoemaker's product = D (equalized).

ing. Still, it is pretty constant. For this reason everything should be rated at a fixed value in money, for that will always make exchange possible and, if exchange, association for the purpose of exchange. So money acts as a measure which, by making things commensurable, renders it possible to make them equal. Without exchange there could be no association, without equality there could be no exchange, without commensurability there could be no equality. Strictly speaking no doubt things so widely different can never become commensurable. Still in demand we have a common measure which will be found to work pretty well. Some one standard there must be, and it must be accepted by a general agreement or understanding.* Such a standard has the effect of making all things commensurable, since they can all be measured by money. Suppose A is a house, B ten pounds, C a bed. Then (supposing the house to be worth five pounds and a bed one) $A = \dfrac{B}{2}$ and $C = \dfrac{B}{10}$. Now we see how many beds are equal to a house, namely, five. It is obvious that in times when money did not yet exist exchange must have been effected on this principle. For – putting convenience on one side – it makes no difference whether you pay five beds for a house or the value of five beds.

We are now in a position to say what justice is.

Thus we have arrived at the definition of the just and the unjust. But when the terms of it have been stated we see that just behaviour is a mean between doing injustice and suffering it. For to do injustice is to have more than one ought, and to suffer it is to have less than one ought. And justice may be regarded as a mean, though not the same kind of mean as the other virtues, for it is not, like them and like injustice, related to the extremes, but is a permanent attitude of the soul towards the mean. Or we may describe it as the disposition in virtue of which a just man is said to choose de-

* Hence 'currency'.

liberately to do what is just. When he has to apportion goods between himself and someone else, or someone else and another, such a man will not administer the property so as to award too much of the desirable portion to himself and too little to his neighbour, while reversing the process when it comes to apportioning what may be harmful. What he will do is to give each his proportionately equal share, whether he is himself one of the parties or not. Injustice bears the same relation to the unjust. For the unjust is an excess of the harmful and a deficiency of the beneficial, contrary to the rule of fair apportionment. Thus injustice turns out to be excess and deficiency in the sense that it is productive of these. I mean – where the unjust man is himself concerned – the result is his having an excess of what is, generally, beneficial and a deficiency in what may be regarded as similarly injurious. Where the distribution is made to others than the distributor the result will be the same as a whole, but the disproportion may take the form of too much or too little, according to the circumstances. . . .*

At this point the Greek text contains a passage, the relevance of which to its context is not clear. But we need not doubt that it comes from Aristotle himself.

<h3>CHAPTER SIX</h3>

A MAN may commit an unjust or bad action without having become bad. We must therefore ask ourselves what is the nature of those offences the commission of which makes a man definitely bad in that form of badness. What makes him a confirmed thief or adulterer or bandit? But this may be putting the question in a form which leaves out the decisive point of *motive*. For instance, a man may lie with a woman in full knowledge of what he is doing but with his will in abeyance, because he is under the sway of passion. Of course he

* Note that when an injustice is done, the smaller part of it is in suffering, the greater part in doing, the wrong.

is acting badly, but he is not a bad man. A man is not necessarily a thief because he has stolen something, or an adulterer because he has committed adultery, or a brigand because of some act of brigandage. ...

Aristotle now passes to a discussion of what he calls 'political' justice.

But we must not forget that our subject is not only justice in the abstract but also political or social justice. Political justice is manifested between persons who share a common way of life which has for its object a state of affairs in which they will have all that they need for an independent existence as free and equal * members of the society. Between persons who do not enjoy such freedom and equality there can be no political justice but only a simulacrum of it. The reason is that justice can exist only among those whose relations to one another are governed by law, and law exists only among those who may be guilty of injustice. This is so because it is the business of the law to decide between the just and the unjust. Now people between whom injustice is possible are capable of acting unjustly towards one another.† (Acting unjustly is assigning oneself too much of unmixed good and too little of unmixed evil.) That is why we will not have a man to rule over us, for a man rules with an eye to his own interest and becomes a tyrant. We will have the law for our ruler, for we consider that the function of a ruler is to be the guardian of justice and, if of justice, of equality. It is agreed that a just ruler does not consider his own interest.‡ He must then have his reward in some other form, namely, honour and dignity. Some rulers, however, are not satisfied with such rewards, and it is of these that tyrants are made.

* Actually or proportionally.
† We noted, however, that a man may act unjustly without being an unjust man.
‡ That is to say he does not assign to himself a larger share of what is purely good than is proportionate to his merits, so that his labours are altruistic. Hence the saying, already quoted, that justice is the good of others.

Domestic Justice.

There is another form of justice which is not the same as, though it is analogous to, the forms we have already discussed. This is justice between master and slave, and between father and child. The distinction lies here, that injustice towards what is one's own cannot be absolute but only relative. Now a slave, or a child before it has reached a certain age and acquired an independent status, is in a manner of speaking a part of oneself. Since nobody deliberately injures himself, he cannot be guilty of injustice towards them. This means that there can be nothing in their relations which is politically just or unjust. For political justice and injustice are, as we saw, defined by the law and in communities where the rule of law is naturally accepted, namely, those whose members rule and are ruled on terms of equality. Hence justice between husband and wife comes nearer true justice than does that between master and slaves or that between the father and his family. It is in fact justice between husband and wife that is the true form of domestic justice, although it too must be distinguished from 'political' justice.

Political Justice.

CHAPTER SEVEN

Now of political justice. There are two forms of it, the natural and the conventional. It is natural when it has the same validity everywhere and is unaffected by any view we may take about the justice of it. It is conventional when there is no original reason why it should take one form rather than another and the rule it imposes is reached by agreement, after which it holds good. It might, for instance, be agreed that the ransom of a prisoner of war shall be fixed at one pound, that the sacrifice in a certain ritual be one goat and not two sheep. Such are the rules prescribed by law in particular cases – I might instance the ritual observed in the worship of Brasidas – and details calling for special legislation. Some philosophers are of opinion that justice is conventional in all its branches, arguing that a law of nature admits of no variation and operates in exactly the same way everywhere – thus fire *burns* here and in Persia – while rules of justice keep changing before our eyes. This last statement, however, needs qualification. (It can hardly be true of justice among the gods.) But in this world of ours, while natural justice undoubtedly exists, the rules under which justice is administered are everywhere being modified. Thus a man's right hand is naturally defter than his left, yet he can always make himself as clever with the one as with the other. And it will be found that a distinction of this kind can always be made. It is not obvious what rules of justice are natural, and what are legal and conventional, in cases where variation is possible and equally possible. Yet it remains true that there is such a thing as natural, as well as conventional, justice.

Rules of justice established by convention and on grounds of convenience may be compared to standard measures. Thus the measures in general use in the wine and corn trade are not invariably the same, being larger in the wholesale and smaller in the retail business. The same is true of purely man-made laws. They are not the same everywhere, because forms of government are not the same. This does not alter the fact that there is only one natural form of government, namely, that which is best.

The rules of law and justice are in each case related to the actions performed in conformity with them as is universal to particular, for the actions are many, the law governing them only one, being universal.

Aristotle adds a note on the differences between certain cognate terms.

We must note the difference between *adikema*, 'unjust behaviour', and *to adikon*, 'the unjust'; and again between *dikaioma*, 'just behaviour', and *to dikaion*, 'the just'. A thing is unjust because nature or a generally accepted principle makes it so. Only when the thing is done is it an unjust *act*. And so with just conduct, which we call *dikaioma*, though a better word for the general conception is *dikaiopragema*, since the former strictly means the reparation of an injustice. ...

Actions must be voluntary before the agent can be regarded as responsible.

CHAPTER EIGHT

WE have now discussed just and unjust actions. It remains to observe that it is only when they are voluntary that they have the character of just or unjust. When a man acts involuntarily his action cannot be called just or unjust in itself, though it may come about that circumstances make it have the effect of a just or unjust action. Therefore the injustice of an unjust, and the justice of a just, act are determined by its voluntariness. It is when the act is voluntary that the moral issue presents itself. We blame the doer and, with that, his deed becomes an unjust act. But suppose the voluntary element does not enter; then you may have an act which has an unjust *effect* without having itself an unjust *quality*. By a voluntary action, let me repeat, I mean one which (*a*) it was in the agent's power to do or not to do, (*b*) he performs not in ignorance but with full knowledge of the person affected by his action, the instrument he is using, the object he seeks to attain,* (*c*) in no particular is determined by accident or *force majeure*. Thus if a man were to seize the hand of another and with it strike a third party, the second man would not be a voluntary agent, for he could not help himself. A man strikes his father without knowing that it is his father, yet aware that he is striking a man and aware perhaps that his father is one of the company. In such an action we have ignorance of the person affected. But the ignorance may be of

* For example, if he strikes anyone he must know whom, with what, and why.

the result and the general circumstances surrounding the action, so that our definition of 'ignorant' should be extended along these lines. An involuntary act, then, is an act performed in ignorance or, if not in ignorance, without ability on the agent's part to prevent it, or else under compulsion. There are many such things we have to do or suffer in the course of nature, none of them either voluntary or involuntary, though we are fully conscious of them. Growing old is one of them, dying is another.

Again, an action may be rendered just or unjust by the circumstances in which it is done. Suppose a man returns a sum of money deposited with him, but reluctantly and from fear of the consequences. We must not say, then, that he is behaving justly, though we may say that he is doing the right thing by accident. By parity of reasoning we must admit that a man who is only prevented by fear from restoring a deposit is not behaving unjustly except by accident.

When we act voluntarily it is sometimes by deliberate choice, and sometimes not.

When a number of persons form an association a member may be injured in any one of three ways. Injuries inflicted in ignorance – that is, when the offender did not realize who it was he was injuring, or what instrument he was using, or what would be the upshot – are to be regarded as mistakes. (Thus when an associate had been hit by a missile the offender could plead that he had no intention of hitting anybody, or not the associate, or not with that missile, nor with that purpose; only the result was different from what he expected,* or the person or the missile was different.) However that may be, when the injury is inflicted contrary to reasonable expectation it is a *mishap*. When the injury is such as could reasonably have been expected but was inflicted without evil intent, it is a *blunder*.† When it is done knowingly but without premeditation, it is an *offence* or unjust act. Under

---

* e.g. he may have meant only to give the other a prick, not a wound.

† The blunder is made when the cause of the agent's ignorance originates in himself; when it is outside him we can only speak of a misadventure or mishap.

this third heading come such injuries as are done out of anger or any other of the unavoidable and natural passions that are incident to humanity. A man guilty of such injuries and errors is in the wrong, and his action is an offence. But that does not make him an unjust or wicked man; for the harm he did was not suggested by wickedness. It is when a man wills the harm he does that he is unjust and wicked. This gives us ground for thinking that acts inspired by an outburst of anger do not belong to the class of premeditated offences. It is not the man who does something in a rage, but the man who has put him in a rage that takes the first step in the process that leads to the action. In such a case it has further to be considered that it is not the fact that is in question but the justification for it, since what makes a man angry is the *belief* that he has been injured. (It is otherwise in disputes about a contract. There the issue *is* one of fact, and one of the parties to the dispute must be a rogue, unless the explanation is to be found in a lapse of memory.) Here the fact is admitted by both sides, and the only question is which side is to blame, one man being convinced that he has not had fair play, the other denying this. As for the man who does an injury of set purpose, he is guilty of an offence of the kind that makes the offender an unjust man when his action is a breach of proportion or equality.* In the same way a man is just when he acts justly as the result of a settled purpose, though this is possible only if his actions are voluntary.

Involuntary actions may be divided into the pardonable and the unpardonable. When mistakes are made not merely *in* but *as the result of* ignorance, they are venial. When made in ignorance but not as the result of it, but of unnatural and brutish passion, they are not to be forgiven.

* The man who has planned an offence is not acting in ignorance.

*But doubts may linger. It may be asked, Can a man be wronged
voluntarily? Can a man wrong himself? Is it in our own power to be
just, and is it as easy as people think? Aristotle suggests answers to
these questions.*

CHAPTER NINE

A DOUBT may remain whether the question of doing and
suffering wrong has been quite cleared up. To begin with, is
there a degree of truth in the paradoxical lines of Euripides:

> 'I slew my mother' – four words tell the tale.
> 'Willingly both or both unwillingly?'

When a wrong is done it is never without the consent of the
wrongdoer. Is it then really possible for a man to have injustice done to him without the consent of the wrongdoer, or
does that never happen? Secondly, is suffering wrong always
voluntary, always involuntary, or sometimes the one and
sometimes the other? The same problem arises in the matter
of just treatment.* It is then reasonable to believe that just
and unjust treatment are severally opposed to just and unjust behaviour in the same way – both are voluntary or both
involuntary. Yet it would be thought a very odd position to
take if one maintained even in the case of just treatment that
it was experienced with the consent of the person so treated;
surely in some cases people receive fair treatment without
asking for it. One might indeed raise another point. Is the
man who has experienced a piece of injustice in every case
an unjustly treated person? Or may we say that what may
be true in the case of doing an injustice may equally be true
in the case of suffering it? One may surely be an object, as
well as a promoter, of a just action in a purely incidental
way. The same may be said without fear of contradiction
about unjust or wrong actions. To do wrong things is not the
same as to be a wrongdoer, and to suffer wrongs is not the
same as to be a wrongly treated person. And we may argue

*. It does not arise in the case of just *behaviour*, which is always voluntary.

in this way about doing right and being rightly done by. For it is not possible for a man to suffer a wrong unless another inflicts it, or to be rightly done by unless the other does rightly by him. But if to wrong a man is nothing else than to injure him intentionally, where 'intentionally' means with knowledge of the person injured, the instrument and the manner of the injury – and if it is also true that the morally weak man voluntarily hurts himself – then such a man must suffer wrong voluntarily. It also follows that a man may wrong himself.* It may also happen that through moral weakness a man may submit to injustice at the hands of another, which further implies the possibility of being injured with one's own consent. However, this can hardly be an accurate definition of what is meant by acting wrongly or unjustly towards another, and the words 'to harm, knowing the person harmed, the instrument, and the manner in which the harm is done' must be further qualified by the words 'against the will of the person.' For, granted that a man may have an injury or injustice done him voluntarily, he cannot voluntarily suffer injustice. Nobody *wishes* to be wronged, not even the weakling, whose wish is contradicted by his action, for a man cannot wish for something that he does not think is good; and what the morally weak man does is something which he thinks that he ought not to do. The man that, like Glaucus, who, according to Homer, gave Diomede

Gold arms for bronze, a hundred oxen's price for price of nine,

insists on giving away his own property is not the victim of an injustice. For a man can give something away if he likes, but he cannot suffer injustice if he likes – there must be somebody else to do him the injustice.

There remain two of the problems we set ourselves to consider. (*a*) When an injustice is done, is it always the person who receives an unduly large proportion of what is distributed that is the guilty party? May it not sometimes be the distributor? (*b*) Can a man wrong, or act unjustly towards, himself?

* Whether this be so is another of the debated points.

If (*a*) can be answered in the affirmative, and it is possible that the guilty party may be the giver and not the receiver of too large a share, then a man who should knowingly and deliberately apportion a larger share to another than to himself is acting unjustly towards himself. (This kind of renunciation is held to be characteristic of the gentleman, whose instinct is to take less than he is entitled to.) But here again there is evidently some over-simplification. For it might happen that the man who gave himself that smaller share got the lion's share of some other good thing – say, reputation or moral dignity in its purest form. But the difficulty involved in the unqualified statement admits of another solution, this time on the lines of our definition of unjust behaviour. For our seeming altruist suffers nothing against his will, and so escapes our definition. The conclusion must be that he does not suffer wrong in getting the smaller share; if he suffers at all, it is only a modicum of damage. It further emerges that it is not always the man who gets too much that is guilty of injustice; it may be the man who gives it. For the guilty person is not he who merely does the wrong, but he who does it intentionally – which is another way of saying he with whom the action originates. Now here the action originates with the giver, not the recipient.

We may further note that the word 'do' has a variety of meanings. Thus we may speak of a murder being 'done' by some inanimate object, or the killer's arm, or a slave at the command of his master. But in such cases, though a crime is committed, there is no criminal. Again, if a judge has given a wrong decision in ignorance, he is not guilty of injustice, nor is his decision wrong in law.* But if he gave his decision knowing it to be wrong, then he is guilty of taking more – it may be of favour or it may be of revenge – than belongs to him. We may even say that the judge who is induced by such motives to give a wrong decision is in his grasping spirit just as bad as if he took his share in the profits of the crime. For, if he does not do this literally, a judge who, for instance,

* No doubt it is wrong from the point of view of absolute justice, which is not identical with legal justice.

assigns a piece of land on that understanding gets money even if he gets no land.

Men cherish the notion that, since it lies in their own power to do a right or a wrong thing, it must be easy to be righteous. That is a mistake. It is easy enough to go to bed with your neighbour's wife, or hit the man next you, or grease the palm of some personage – that sort of thing any-one can do. But to do it as the result of a certain disposition is not easy and is not within the power of everybody. In like manner it is easy to perform a good action, but not easy to acquire a settled habit of performing such actions. So again people are under the impression that there can be no diffi-culty in understanding what is explicitly mentioned in the laws. But what the law prescribes, though just, is so only in an acquired or accidental way. It does not answer the vital question *how* actions are to be performed and distributions to be made in order to be just. To know that is harder than to know how to keep well. Even in medicine it is easy to have some knowledge of honey and hellebore, of cautery and sur-gery. But when it comes to knowing *how* and *to whom* and *when* to apply these remedies we have to be trained doctors for that. And for the very reason that it is (in their opinion) in everyone's power to do a wrong people suppose that the just man may as readily behave unjustly as justly. For (the argument runs) the just man is as, nay better, able to do any particular injustice. It is not out of his power to commit adultery or assault, just as the brave man *can* discard his shield, turn left or right as may be, and run away. But to be a coward is not the same thing as to commit an act of cowardice, and to be an unjust person is not the same as to do an unjust thing, except so far as an accident may give it the appearance of injustice. No, to be a bad man one must do such things out of a bad disposition, just as being a com-petent doctor does not consist in using surgery or drugs, but in using them in a particular way.

Claims for just treatment arise between persons who are entitled to a share in things which in their general character are good, and for whom that share can be too great or too small. No doubt there are some – the gods for instance – to whom one could not assign too much of these goods, just as there are some – the incurably vicious – who are benefited by no portion of them and get nothing but hurt from any of them. Yet there are others who do benefit from them up to a point, and these are in fact the majority of ordinary men and women.

Aristotle now discusses the nature of Equity.

CHAPTER TEN

WE must next say something about equity, and about the fair and equitable. What is the relation of equity to justice, and of the equitable to the just? When we look into the matter we find that justice and equity are not absolutely identical, yet cannot be classified as different. Actually we sometimes commend the equitable and the equitable man to the extent of applying the epithet as a term of approbation to other things as if it were equivalent to 'good' and saying that a thing is 'more equitable' when all we mean is that it is better. At other times, however, when we follow the train of our reflections, it does seem odd that the equitable, if it differs from justice, should yet be thought worthy of commendation. If this difference exists, then of two things, one: either the just or the equitable is not good. Conversely, if both are good the difference does not exist, and justice and equity are identical. That is roughly the difficulty which presents itself when we consider the equitable from this point of view. Yet, sound as the objections are, there is no real inconsistency. Equity, though a higher thing than one form of justice, is itself just and is not generically different from justice. Thus, so far as both are good, they coincide, though equity is to be preferred. What puzzles people is the fact that equity, though just, is not the justice of the law courts but a method of restoring the balance of justice when it has been tilted by the law. The need for such a rectification arises from the circumstance that law can do no more than generalize, and there are cases which cannot be settled by a general statement. So in matters where it is necessary to make a general statement, and yet that statement cannot exclude the possibility of error, the law takes no account of particular cases, though well aware that this is not a strictly correct proceeding. Yet that does not make it a bad law, the error lying not in the law or the lawgiver but in the nature of the case; the *data* of human behaviour simply will not be reduced to uniformity. So when a case arises where the law states a general rule, but there is an exception to the rule, it is then right when the lawgiver owing to the generality of his language left a loophole for error to creep in, to fill the gap by such a modified statement as the lawgiver himself would make, if he was present at the time, and such an enactment as he would have made, if he had known the special circumstances. So, while it is true that equity is just and in some circumstances better than justice, it is not better than absolute justice. All we can say is that it is better than the error which is generated by the unqualified language in which absolute justice must be stated. And equity essentially is just this rectification of the law, where the law has to be amplified because of the general terms in which it has to be couched. This in fact is the reason why everything is not regulated by law; it is because there are cases which no law can be framed to cover and which can only be met by a special regulation. It is useless to apply a definite yardstick to something indefinite; we must be like the Lesbian architects and employ a leaden rule. Just as that rule is flexible and can be bent to take the shape of the stone, so a special decree or regulation can be made to fit the peculiar conditions.

We now see what equity is, and that it is just and superior to one kind of justice. And this lets us also see clearly the nature of the equitable man. He is one who by deliberate choice has taught himself the habit of doing equitable things, who is not a stickler for his rights to the disadvantage of others but refrains from pressing his claims even when he has the law on his side. It is a disposition of this kind which finds its expression in equity – equity which we have just shown to be a species of justice and not a disposition of a different genus altogether.

We are now in a better position to answer the questions whether a man can wrong himself, or suffer wrong, willingly.

CHAPTER ELEVEN

ALL this sheds light upon the question, Can a man wrong himself? Take suicide. Whereas there are some virtuous actions, definable as just, which are enjoined by the law, there are others not so prescribed, and one of these is suicide. Now what the law does not prescribe it forbids. When a man voluntarily – that is, knowing who is being attacked and with what weapon – does an injury (not by way of retaliation) to some person contrary to the law, he is guilty of injustice. But the man who cuts his throat in a fit of temper is voluntarily doing an injury which the law does not allow.* It follows that the suicide commits an injustice. But against whom? Is it not the State rather than himself? For he suffers of his own volition, and nobody suffers injustice voluntarily. It is for this reason that the State attaches a penalty, which takes the form of a stigma put on one who has destroyed himself, on the ground that he is guilty of an offence against the State.

A further observation may be made. It is not possible for a man to do injustice to himself, if by 'injustice' we mean unjust behaviour and nothing more on the part of a man who is not absolutely wicked.† It is not possible because, if it

* Such an injury violates the principle which rightly governs our behaviour in such a case.

† The distinction is necessary because in this case the 'unjust' man is bad only in a limited sense and not as embodying the whole of badness. One may compare the case of the coward. This being so, we have to prove that a man cannot wrong himself in this restricted sense either.

were, it would then be possible for the same thing to have been subtracted from and added to the same thing at the same time; and that is impossible. Justice and injustice cannot co-exist in one and the same person. Again, an act of injustice must be (*a*) voluntary, (*b*) unprovoked. (A man is not considered to be acting unjustly if he merely pays back an injury in the same coin.) But when it comes to injuring himself, then a man both does and suffers the same thing at the same time. Thirdly, if it were possible for a man to act unjustly towards himself, it would be possible for him to suffer injustice of his own volition. Fourthly, a man is not guilty of injustice unless he commits particular acts of injustice. Yet in some instances it is impossible for a man to commit an injustice. He cannot commit adultery with his own wife, or break into his own house, or steal his own property.

Finally, a general solution of the question whether a man can act unjustly towards himself may be given on the lines of the definite answer we found to that other question, whether a man can be wronged with his own consent. (Another point which emerges clearly from our discussion is this. To suffer wrong and to do it are both evils, for the former is to have less, and the latter to have more, than the mean.* Yet doing it is the greater evil. For not only is it censurable in itself, but it implies wickedness in the wrongdoer, wickedness complete and absolute or nearly so, because not every wrong intentionally committed implies a vicious disposition. On the other hand to suffer injustice does not *ipso facto* involve the vice of injustice in the sufferer. Thus in itself it is the lesser evil, though some conjunction of circumstances may make it the greater. That, however, is a consideration which science does not take into account. Thus medical science pronounces pleurisy to be a more serious disturbance of health than a sprain, regardless of the fact

---

* In medicine the mean appears in the form of whatever it is that produces health, while in the training of athletes it takes the form of whatever it is that conduces to their being in condition.

that in certain circumstances the sprain may happen to be more dangerous than the pleurisy.*)

It is possible, however, by a figure of speech – metaphor or analogy – to speak of justice not towards oneself but between certain parts of our moral being. It is not of course justice in the full sense but something like what constitutes just dealing between a master and his slaves, or between the head of a household and his family. It is necessary to say that, because in the discourses which treat of this topic a clean cut is made between the rational and irrational parts of the soul. Those whose attention is fixed on this division actually come to believe that there is such a thing as injustice towards oneself, because it is possible for these parts to thwart, and be thwarted in, one another's desires. In such an event a certain kind of justice may be supposed to exist between them similar to that which exists between ruler and ruled. . . .

---

* The sprain might cause you to fall, with the result that the enemy caught and killed you.

BOOK SIX

Aristotle now approaches the intellectual virtues. He is at once involved in the question of what is meant by the right principle (logos), *which in the definition of virtue is said to determine the mean.*

CHAPTER ONE

I HAVE already said that, to be good, we must choose the mean, avoiding both the too much and the too little. I have also said that the mean is such as 'the right principle' makes it out to be. It is this concept we are now to analyse.

In all the moral habits or dispositions of which I have spoken, as well as the others of which I have had no occasion to speak, there is a certain mark or target for us to aim at. On this the man who is in possession of the right principle in his endeavours fastens his eyes, tightening or slackening his string as fits his purpose. There is also a certain limitation or standard applicable to those mean states which according to us lie between the two extremes of excess and deficiency; and this is what is meant when we say that the means are 'in accordance with right principle.' True, but not very illuminating. In the sciences generally it is no doubt correct to say that the student's application to his subject should not be exerted or relaxed too much or too little but only intensified to the degree requisite for avoiding these extremes and in the way indicated by the right principle. But, if that is all he knows, he will be none the wiser. Suppose he wants to take medicine. He will not know what to take merely because somebody tells him to take what medical science or the profession prescribes. This shows the need in the domain of mental and moral habits too of having something more than the generalization I stated accurately expressed. We need a definition of 'the right principle' and the standard whereby it is determined.

Now the virtues we have divided into two classes, the

moral and the intellectual. The former we have already discussed, and it remains to discuss the latter. But first we must say something about that of which these are the virtues – namely, the soul.

Aristotle now makes some observations on the psyche *or 'soul', which for a Greek meant that part of us with which we think as well as feel.*

It has already been observed that the soul consists of two parts, a rational and an irrational. Let us go on to subdivide the rational part into two faculties – one which enables us to speculate about those things whose first principles admit of no variation, the other whereby we deliberate about those which do admit of change. For, if it be granted for the sake of argument that things are known because of some similarity or kinship between them and that which knows them, it follows that the parts of the soul which are able to know things of different kinds must themselves be different in kind. Let us call these faculties the 'scientific' and the 'calculative' respectively, using the latter term because we may identify calculation with deliberation, which is never exercised upon invariable things. This justifies us in regarding the calculative faculty as a separate part of the rational element in the soul.

Our task, then, is to get a clear notion of what is the best disposition of each of these two faculties, for this disposition will be the virtue of each.

CHAPTER TWO

To ascertain the virtue of a faculty we must see the faculty in relation to its peculiar function. Now there are in the soul three things which determine or influence action and the discovery of truth: sensation, the reasoning power, desire or appetition. Of these, sensation is never the source of considered action, as may be seen from the fact that the lower animals have sensations, but exhibit no trace of such action.

In desire pursuit and avoidance play the same part as is played in our intellectual processes by affirmation and negation. We have seen that moral virtue is a habit of making the right choice in conduct, and that such choice is a reasoned desire. That being so, the inference is clear. If our choice is to be such as a good man would make, our guiding principle must be true and our desire right. To this we must add that what the principle affirms as true must be the object of our desire. Observe, however, that we are here speaking of thought and truth in *conduct* – speculative thought is not in question. Speculative thought has nothing to do with action or production, and it performs its function well or ill according as it succeeds in reaching a true or a false conclusion. To be sure, ascertaining the truth is the function of any part of the intellect. But what the *practical* intellect does is to reach that kind of truth which answers to right desire.

Now the cause * of action is will or deliberate choice, and the cause of choice is desire and a reasoned conception of the end we are seeking to attain. Choice therefore entails the exercise of reason or thought as well as a disposition of character. But thought, if it is to have some practical result – for of itself it can set nothing in motion – must have an object. This purposive kind of thought gives rise also to productive activity. For when a man makes a thing it is always to serve some purpose; the process of making it is not an end in itself but only the means to an end and is subordinate to something else. But an action – a piece of human conduct – is an end in itself. For 'doing well' is here the end, and the end which desire seeks to attain. Thus we view choice either as thought wedded to desire or desire wedded to thought. In man, the originating cause of action, the two elements work in combination.† Thus both the intellectual parts of

---

* The efficient, not the final, cause.

† The past is outside the range of choice; nobody can *choose* to have been the sacker of Troy. Neither can one deliberate about the past, but only about the future and the may-be. What is done cannot be undone. Agathon is right:

> 'One power has Fate to God himself denied –
> To make undone the thing that has been done.'

the soul exercise their function in the search for truth. It follows that the special virtue of each will consist in that disposition which will most effectually enable it to attain the truth.

CHAPTER THREE

LET us now, but in a more thoroughgoing fashion, take up again the subject of these virtues. And let us begin by postulating the existence of five modes or expressions in which the soul may arrive at the truth in what it affirms or denies; art, science, practical wisdom, speculative wisdom, pure intelligence. Conception and opinion are not included, because they are liable to fall into error.

What is meant by Science.

What is meant by science, in the strict sense of the word and disregarding extensions of it on similar lines, may be rendered clear by this consideration. We all see that scientific knowledge is of things that are never other than they are; for as to things that do admit of variation we cannot, if they are outside the field of our observation, discover whether they exist or not. So anything that science knows scientifically must exist by an unalterable necessity. It must therefore be eternal, because anything which exists by this absolute kind of necessity must be eternal.* Again, the view has found acceptance that all scientific knowledge can be imparted by teaching and that what is known in this way can be learned. But, as I say in my treatise on logic, all teaching starts from what we know already, and this is equally true whether the teacher uses the method of induction or deduction. What induction does is to furnish us with a first principle or 'universal', while deduction starts from universals. This means that there must be first principles – the first principles from which deduction starts – which cannot be proved by deduc-

* What is eternal cannot be brought into or put out of existence.

tion and must therefore be reached by the method of induction. Science, then, may be defined as a habit of mind with an aptitude for demonstration, though to this definition we must add the qualifications made explicit in my logical writings. They may be stated thus. A man has scientific knowledge when (*a*) he is satisfied in his own mind that he has it as the result of the process described in these writings, and (*b*) the first principles on which his conviction rests are known to him with certainty. This second condition is necessary because, unless his first principles are more certainly known to him than the conclusion he draws from them, the knowledge he will acquire will not be scientific in the full sense of the word.

What is meant by Art?

CHAPTER FOUR

AMONG things liable to change we count (*a*) articles manufactured, (*b*) actions done. Making and doing are quite different activities. (On this point I am in full agreement with what has been stated elsewhere.) Consequently the rational faculty exercised in doing is quite distinct from that which is exercised in making. Moreover, they are mutually exclusive, for doing never takes the form of making, nor making of doing. Take architecture. It is an art, that is a rational faculty exercised in making something. In fact there is no art which cannot be so described, nor is there any faculty of the kind that is not an art. It follows that an art is nothing more or less than a productive quality exercised in combination with true reason. The business of every art is to bring something into existence, and the practice of an art involves the study of how to bring into existence something which is capable of having such an existence and has its efficient cause in the maker and not in itself. This condition must be present, because the arts are not concerned with things that exist or come into existence from necessity or according to Nature, such things having their efficient cause in themselves. Then, since making is not the same as doing, it follows that art, being a kind of making, cannot be a kind of doing. We may even say that in a manner art and chance work in the same field or – as Agathon puts it –

> Art is in love with luck, and luck with art.

We have seen what art is. Its opposite, which can only be called absence of art, is a rational quality exercised in making when associated with *false* reasoning.

What is meant by Phronesis *or Practical Wisdom?*

CHAPTER FIVE

IT will help us to comprehend the nature of *phronesis*, if we first consider what sort of persons we call 'prudent' or 'sagacious'. A sagacious man is supposed to be characterized by his ability to reach sound conclusions in his deliberations about what is good for himself and advantageous to him, and this not in one department of life – in what concerns his health, for example, or his physical strength – but what conduces to the good life as a whole. We also speak of a man as sagacious or prudent in a particular way when he calculates well for the attainment of a particular end of a fine sort; * and this is good evidence that the man who is sagacious in every department of life will be one who deliberates in general to good purpose. No one, however, deliberates about things which cannot be changed or do not admit of being done by him. Now we saw there can be no science without demonstration, whereas in the case of things whose fundamental assumptions allow of change or modification there can be no demonstrative proof, since in every respect change is possible. We have also seen that there can be no deliberation about things the existence of which is determined by an absolute necessity. In view of these two facts

* Of course it must not be an artistic end.

we must admit that practical wisdom is not the same as science. Nor, we must admit, as art. It is not science, because conduct is variable, and it is not art, because doing and making are different in kind, since the maker of a thing has a different end in view than just making it, whereas in doing something the end can only be the doing of it well. We are left then with our definition: Practical wisdom is a rational faculty exercised for the attainment of truth in things that are humanly good and bad. This accounts for the reputation of Pericles and other men of like practical genius. Such men have the power of seeing what is good for themselves and for humanity; and we assign that character also to men who display an aptitude for governing a household or a state. . . . *

We must consider, too, that while there is such a thing as excellence in the quality of a work of art, there cannot be excellence or virtue belonging to practical wisdom, which *is* a virtue. In the arts, again, a deliberate mistake is not so bad as an undesigned one, whereas in matters to which practical wisdom is applicable it is the other way round. Clearly, then, prudence is a virtue and not an art. It must be the virtue of one of the two parts of the soul which have reason, and this must be the calculative or 'opining' part. For opinion is concerned with a variable subject matter, and so is prudence. Yet it would not be correct to describe prudence as a purely rational quality. That it is not is shown by the fact that such a quality can be forgotten, whereas to forget prudence or common sense is worse than such an inability to remember.

* A note on *sophrosyne* or 'temperance'. The word comes from *sozein*, 'to preserve', and *phronesis*, 'prudence', and means 'that which preserves prudence.' Now it is true that temperance does preserve a belief of this prudential sort. We must not imagine that pleasure and pain destroy or distort every belief – such a belief, for instance, as that the sum of the angles of a triangle is equal to two right angles – but only beliefs about what men do or have done. The first principle of an action is the end to which the action is directed. But a man corrupted by the love of pleasure or the fear of pain cannot see this at all – he cannot see that everything he chooses and does must be chosen and done as a means to this end and for its own sake. For vice produces a kind of moral blindness to the principle to which all our conduct must ultimately be referred.

What is meant by Intelligence or Scientific Insight?

CHAPTER SIX

SCIENCE is the coming to conclusions about universals and necessary truths. Now all science (for science involves a process of reasoning) and all facts scientifically proved depend ultimately upon certain first principles. When we see this we perceive that the first principles upon which all scientific results depend cannot be apprehended by science itself; nor, we may add, by art or common sense. The body of scientific knowledge is the product of logical deduction from premises which are eternally valid; but art and practical wisdom deal with matters susceptible of change. Nor can we say that speculative wisdom is merely a knowledge of first principles. For there are some truths which the philosopher can learn only from demonstration. Now if the qualities by means of which we reach the truth and are never led to what is false in matters variable and invariable are science, prudence, wisdom and the intelligence which apprehends the truth in reasoning; if, moreover, this mental endowment by means of which we are enabled to grasp first principles cannot be either prudence, science, or wisdom, we are left to conclude that what grasps them is 'intelligence'.

What is meant by Wisdom?

CHAPTER SEVEN

'WISDOM' is a word we use both in a particular and in a general sense. Thus, in the fine arts we attach the epithet of 'wise' to the masters – Phidias, for instance, as sculptor and Polyclitus as statuary. Here all that we mean by 'wisdom' is excellence in an art. But we also think of some people as wise not in any one of the human aptitudes but in all of them –

not 'wise in some other things' or (as Homer puts it in his *Margites*):

> Neither a delver nor a ploughman he,
> Nor other wisdom had the gods bestowed.

This makes it evident that of all kinds of knowledge wisdom comes next to perfection. The wise man, you see, must not only know all that can be deduced from his first principles but he must understand their true meaning. So we conclude that wisdom must be a combination of science and reason or intelligence, being in fact the highest form of that knowledge whose objects are of transcendent value. I find it strange that anyone should regard political science or *practical* wisdom as the noblest of studies, for that is to assume that man is what is best in the world. But just as 'wholesome' and 'good' mean one thing to men and another to fish, whereas 'white' and 'straight' have always but one meaning, so 'wise', as men use the word, would always have the same significa-tion, while 'prudent' would not. For every human creature says in effect, 'Whoever considers what is to my particular advantage is prudent and to him will I entrust myself.' And this leads people to maintain that some even of the lower animals have prudence, namely, those which evidently pos-sess the ability to foresee what will be needed for their con-tinued existence.

Another point that emerges clearly is that wisdom cannot be identified with political science. If men are to give the name of wisdom to the knowledge of what is to their own advantage, there will be more than one form of wisdom as there is more than one species of animal. You cannot have a single wisdom contriving the good of all living beings any more than an art of medicine consulting the health of every-body and everything. It is all very well to say that man is the noblest of the animals. There are creatures far more divine by nature than man, for instance – to take what stares us in the face – those luminaries of which the starry heavens are composed.

Enough has been said to show that wisdom is exact knowledge or science combined with the intelligence that grasps the truth of first principles when this combination is employed upon the grandest subjects of contemplation. The rareness of it leads many to say that men like Thales and Anaxagoras are no doubt wise but lack common sense. They say this when they observe such men at sea about their private interests. They allow that their knowledge is 'exceptional', 'wonderful', 'deep', 'superhuman', but they aver that it is useless because it is not the good of humanity that they explore. Common sense or prudence, however, does concern itself with human affairs and such matters as may form the subject of deliberation. To deliberate well – that, people say, is the special business of the practically wise man.*

Observe, too, that prudence is something more than a knowledge of general principles. It must acquire familiarity with particulars also, for conduct deals with particular circumstances, and prudence is a matter of conduct. This accounts for the fact that men who know nothing of the theory of their subject sometimes practise it with greater success than others who know it. Let me make my meaning clearer by an illustration. A man is aware that light meats are easily digested and beneficial to health but does not know what meats are light. Such a man is not so likely to make you well as one who only knows that chicken is good for you. It is in fact experience rather than theory that normally gets results. Practical wisdom being concerned with action, we need both kinds of knowledge; nay, we need the knowledge of particular facts more than general principles. But here, too, there must be a faculty – political science – in which the ultimate authority is vested.

* We must not forget that no man deliberates about things that cannot be otherwise than as they are, or about things which, while admitting of variation, are not a means to some end, and that end a good that can be realized in action. Broadly speaking, a man good at deliberation is one who by careful calculation is able to make a good shot at some attainable advantage.

The quality of phronesis *reconsidered.*

CHAPTER EIGHT

ACTUALLY political science is an aspect of practical wisdom, though in essence they are different. Of political science one branch, regarded as sovran over the other, is legislative science; the other, dealing with the details of administration, is called political science, although that is also the name for both branches together. Political science in the narrower sense – politics in fact – is a matter of action and deliberation or policy.* This explains why it is only administrators who are described as practical politicians, because it is they alone who *do* things. They bear the same relation to the lawgiver as workmen to the master-craftsman. In the popular mind prudence is more particularly associated with the self and the individual – a usurpation of the title of prudence, which actually belongs to all the forms and kinds, including those designated as domestic economy, constitution-building, the art of the lawgiver, and political science, which again is subdivided into deliberative and juridical science. Now, knowing one's own interest would no doubt be one species of prudence, but there is a wide difference between it and the other species. Anyhow, the man who understands and minds his own business has the reputation of sagacity, while the practical politician is apt to be regarded as an interfering nuisance. Hence, Euripides was moved to represent a character as saying:

> I *prudent?* I, that might have lived unvexed
> By public cares, one man of many men,
> And with the wisest shared the common lot.
> Yet do we rather honour the proud fool
> Pestered for ever with a thousand cares.

Of course people do seek their own good and consider it their duty to do so, and it is the belief that this is so which

* A decree of the executive in a democratic government, embodying the result of a deliberative process, is an instrument for action.

has given rise to the notion that it is the self-regarding man who is prudent. Yet who can doubt that it is impossible for a man to secure his own interest without the aid of domestic economy, nay, without the aid of politics? Not to mention that even the best way of pursuing one's own interest is an obscure point and calls for investigation.

The truth of what I have said gets confirmation from another quarter. It is notorious that young persons are capable of becoming excellent geometricians and mathematicians and accomplished students in subjects of that nature. Yet the public is not easily persuaded that a young man can be prudent. The reason is that prudence involves a detailed knowledge which comes only from practical experience, and practical experience is what the young man lacks – it comes only after many years.* Moreover, a man who deliberates may go astray either in the principle he applies or in the particular *data* to which he applies it. Thus, in a study of water he may labour under the mistaken notion that (*a*) all heavy water is bad, or (*b*) that a particular specimen of water is heavy.

In one respect, then, prudence is the exact opposite of intuitive intelligence. Intelligence apprehends the truth of definitions which cannot be proved by argument, while prudence involves knowledge of the ultimate particular thing, which cannot be attained by science but only by 'perception'. By this I mean not perception by any one of the special senses but the power of perceiving such a truth as that the irreducible figure in mathematics is the triangle, beyond which we cannot carry our analysis. Yet this mathematical perception deserves the name better than does prudence, which perceives a certain kind of truth by a process of a different order.

* The further question may be asked why a lad may become an expert mathematician, but not a metaphysician or a natural philosopher. The answer, it may be suggested, is this. The mathematician deals with abstractions, the metaphysician and the philosophic naturalist with first principles derived from observation and experience. A young man will have their principles on his lips, but he has no conviction of their truth. On the other hand the fundamental assumptions of mathematics are evidently true.

Our next task is to discover in what deliberative excellence consists.

CHAPTER NINE

WE ought also to ascertain the nature of that quality which enables a man to deliberate well, and we must try to discover whether it involves true knowledge, or opinion, or conjecture, or something else that differs from these in kind.

Well, it is not knowledge. Men do not investigate what they know already, whereas to deliberate well is a form of deliberation, and deliberation involves some investigation or calculation. Yet we must not identify deliberation with investigation in general but only when investigation is restricted to a particular field, namely, human behaviour. Nor must we say that it is clever guessing, for that gives the answer in a flash without the guesser's being able to render a reason for it. Deliberation, however, is a slow process; as the proverb says, *Act quickly, think slowly.* Nor is it mental alertness, for that is just an aspect of the ability to guess or conjecture with success. Finally, excellence in deliberation has nothing to do with opinion.

Seeing that a man who deliberates badly is in error, while he who deliberates well is right, it is clear that excellence in deliberation is a form of rightness or correctness, though not in knowledge or belief. One can no more speak of 'correctness' than of 'error' in knowledge, which is not knowledge, if it is not correct. On the other hand correctness of opinion is truth. Besides, one cannot have an opinion except about something which has already a definite meaning.* Opinion or belief has got beyond the stage of investigation and must be regarded as having become a form of affirmation. On the other hand a man who is engaged in deliberating – whether well or ill makes no difference here – is at the same time investigating and reasoning or calculating. But wise delibera-

* It may be added that wise deliberation is impossible without reasoning. It remains therefore that it is a correctness in thinking or deliberating – thinking being only on the way to affirmation.

tion is a kind of correctness in deliberating or (as we called it) thinking. It is plain, however, that not every kind of correctness – for the word in this context admits of more than one meaning – is exhibited in wise deliberation. A weak or bad man may make a calculation which will enable him to do what he sets before himself as something which he ought to do. In that event he will have deliberated correctly, though the end he has achieved may be something very wicked or injurious. Yet to have deliberated well is, people feel sure, a good thing. We conclude that it is the sort of correctness in deliberation which ensures a good result that constitutes deliberative excellence. Such a result, however, may actually be achieved by fallacious reasoning. That is to say, one may reach the right conclusion by way of a wrong argument, the fallacy lying in the middle term. A procedure of this kind, then, by which one reaches the right conclusion but on the wrong grounds falls short like the other of the quality under discussion.

Another point arises. One man may deliberate too long, another not long enough. Here again we have not yet got the quality in its completeness. For that quality is correctness of deliberation, on the subject of what is advantageous, arriving at the right conclusion not only in the right manner but at the right time. Again, a man may have deliberated well towards achieving a particular end, or he may be good at deliberation as such. This general excellence in counsel is what secures the correct approach to the general end, while correctness of deliberation applied to a particular end is a particular exercise of good counsel. I conclude: If wise deliberation reveals a prudent man, it must be correct deliberation about what serves an end. Prudence consists in a true conception of what serves that end.

What is meant by Understanding or the faculty in respect of which a man is said to be 'intelligent'?

CHAPTER TEN

UNDERSTANDING – that is sound understanding – the quality in virtue of which we say that certain persons are 'men of understanding' or 'of sound understanding' is not to be confused with knowledge in the sense of knowing what is always true, nor is it any one of the specialized sciences like medicine, which is concerned only with health, or geometry, which is concerned only with magnitudes.* Understanding is not employed upon the things that are eternal and unchangeable, nor upon anything that is brought into being. It is limited to things which admit of doubt and deliberation. That is to say, it is concerned with the same matters as prudence. Yet it is not the same as prudence. Prudence is imperative, understanding only judicial. (I mean that, whereas prudence gives orders, its end being a declaration of what we must or must not do, understanding is content to pass judgement.) Thus, understanding is neither the having nor the getting of prudence. What it is may be gathered from an analogy. When we learn a thing by using the faculty of knowing we are said to 'understand' it. Similarly, when we use our power of forming opinions to judge the truth of what somebody else says about matters on which prudence is qualified to speak we are said to 'understand'.† Our analogy in fact is something more, for the use of 'understanding' as a name for the quality in virtue of which men become 'of sound understanding' comes from the use of it as applied to the process of learning. For in our language 'learn' often means 'understand'.

* It need hardly be said that it is not the same as opinion; if it were, we should all be men of sound understanding!

† To 'judge' in this context means to judge rightly, a right judgement being equivalent to a sound understanding.

What is meant by Gnome, *the quality which takes things into consideration or treats people with consideration.*

CHAPTER ELEVEN

THE quality in virtue of which we describe some men as persons of good feeling or as having fellow-feeling for others is an aptness to form a correct judgement of what is equitable. This is shown by our habit of saying that the equitable man is especially prone to have sympathy or a fellow-feeling for others, and that it is equitable to have sympathy in certain cases. But sympathy involves a correct judgement of what is equitable, which comes to the same thing as saying a judgement of what is *truly* equitable.

Reflection will show that all these qualities have the same reference; we attribute right feeling, understanding, prudence, and intelligence to the same persons. This is what we do when we say of one who has reached years of discretion that he has got right feeling, intelligence, prudence, understanding. For all these faculties are engaged upon ultimate and particular things. Thus a man has (*a*) understanding and (*b*) good feeling or fellow-feeling, if he shows himself a good judge of the things in dealing with which (*c*) prudence is shown, equitable conduct being uniformly a mark of the morally good man in his relations to his fellow-men. On the other hand all conduct addresses itself to particular and ultimate things – since the prudent man is bound to take cognizance of such – and understanding and good feeling are involved in conduct, and that means particulars. Also, (*d*) intelligence apprehends the ultimates at both ends of the scale. (It is intelligence, not reasoning, that sees the truth both of the definitions from which reasoning starts and of the particulars in which it ends.) When it is a case of proving something, intelligence apprehends the immutable definitions *above* which we cannot go; in what we may call practical inferences it apprehends the contingent fact *below* which we cannot go. It also grasps at once the truth of the minor premise in the kind of syllogism which such a 'practical inference' presumes.* It is these particular instances – since it is upon them that generalizations are based – which enable us to reach the first principles from which the end is deduced. All this would be impossible without the immediate apprehension of particulars, which apprehension is what we mean by 'intelligence'. It is some inkling of this which has produced the common belief that the qualities we have just been discussing are natural endowments. No man, it is thought, is born wise, but good feeling and understanding and intelligence come by nature. It is an indication of this that we think of them as going with certain periods of life. We say, for example, 'Here is a man old enough to have intelligence and good feeling,' implying thereby that both are gifts of Nature. And so we ought to pay no less attention to the unproved assertions and opinions of elderly people and men of experience than to those which they seek to prove. They have an 'eye' for the truth, and this can only come of experience. ...

The intellectual virtues and happiness.

CHAPTER TWELVE

THE question may be posed: What is the use of the intellectual virtues? To begin with wisdom, it does not contemplate the means by which a man shall become happy, for any process of becoming is beyond its purview. What then of prudence? No doubt prudence does not regard itself as thus limited; but what do we need prudence for? What it studies is the just and the noble and what is good for man, things which a virtuous person does by the very law of his being. Knowing what they are does not make us any better at putting them into practice, because the virtues are ingrained in character. It is just the same with our knowledge of what constitutes bodily health and fitness.† We are not

* In a syllogism of this kind the major as well as the minor premise is a statement about particulars.

† Not what *conduces* to health and fitness, but these conditions themselves when they are completely established.

rendered any more capable of healthy and athletic activities by any knowledge we may have of medicine and physical training. If, however, we are to say that prudence is useful by enabling us – not to be but – to become good men, what use can it be to those who are good already? Then what of those who have not yet achieved goodness? It is of no use to them either, because they will get just as much good out of listening to those who possess prudence as they would if they possessed it themselves. We may be satisfied to adopt the same attitude to prudence as we do to our health. We should all like to be healthy, but we do not all learn to be doctors.

Think, too, how strange it would seem if prudence, which cannot be ranked so high as wisdom, is nevertheless to have the greater authority. We must consider if this is possible, because the talent which creates a thing in every case commands and directs it; and prudence may be said, in a sense, to create wisdom.

We must therefore now discuss these difficulties; so far we have only stated them.

Let us begin, then, with the following proposition. Wisdom and prudence – this, the virtue of one part of the intellect, that, of the other – are of necessity desirable in themselves, even if neither of them produces any concrete result. Yet a result they do produce. Wisdom produces happiness, not as the doctor's art produces health – where the doctor or his art is the efficient cause – but as a healthy state of the body produces it. For wisdom is part of virtue as a whole, thus making its possessor happy by its exercise if not by its mere possession. Again, it is prudence and moral goodness that make possible the full performance of the function of a man. It is due to virtue that the end we aim at is right, and it is due to prudence that the means we employ to that end are right.*

But we must go a little more deeply into the suggestion

* The fourth part of the soul – for we have already dealt with the scientific, calculative and appetitive parts – is the nutritive faculty. But this possesses no virtue, such as prudence has, which could help a man to perform his function, for it is not in its power to act or not to act.

that prudence does not make us any better at doing the fine and the just thing. As a starting-point let us consider the following proposition. While it is true, as we contend, that some men perform just actions without being (as yet) just men,* yet evidently there is a certain feeling or state of mind which leads the man who has it to do these particular things, so that he must be regarded as already a good man – that is of course when he does them by an act of choice or will and for the sake of the things themselves. It is moral goodness that makes us choose our end aright – true – but doing the things which by their nature are such as must be done if we are to attain our chosen end – that falls outside the range of *moral* goodness and within that of quite another faculty.

The rôle of cleverness or talent.

To make the matter clearer we must give it further consideration. There is a certain faculty called 'cleverness' or 'talent', which is the ability to do the things of which we have been speaking as contributory to the end we have set before us, and so to achieve that end. Now, if the clever man's aim is high, his talent must win our approbation; if it is low, we call him an astute rascal. But we do call him clever just as much as we call the prudent man clever. That is an ambiguity we must try to avoid. Cleverness is not the same as prudence, though prudence contains an element of cleverness. On the other hand that 'eye' of the soul to which we referred cannot acquire prudence or sagacity unless it has first acquired virtue, an obvious point which we have made before. If we apply deductive logic to the material of ethics, it is always necessary to have a major premise of the form 'Since the end (or supreme good) is such and such ' – what-

* The sort of people I have in mind are those who carry out the requirements of the law but do this unwillingly, or in ignorance, or with some ulterior purpose and not with a view to obeying the law, although in fact they are doing what is right and all that a good man is bound to do.

ever it may be, let it be anything you like for the sake of the argument. Now the supreme good appears such only to the good man, for vice gives a twist to our minds, making us hold false opinions about the principles of ethics. It is therefore obvious that a man cannot be prudent unless he be good.

Aristotle sums up.

CHAPTER THIRTEEN

THIS means that we must reconsider the nature of virtue. We shall find that virtue exhibits a relation very like that which prudence bears to cleverness – not one of identity but of similarity. This is the relation between natural and true virtue; that is to say, between the good qualities we share with the lower animals and those which belong only to man. It is the universal belief that in some sense the moral qualities are each and all the gift of Nature; if we have a disposition to justice, to temperance, to courage, and the other virtues, we have it from birth. For all that we look to find that true goodness is something more than this, and that the good qualities that are in the full sense of the word good have their origin elsewhere. For the natural dispositions, which even children and wild animals possess, are demonstrably capable, if undirected by intelligence, of doing harm. Thus much at any rate anyone, I presume, can see for himself. A powerfully built man who has been blinded trips and falls heavily as he moves about, because he is unable to see. Well, it happens like that in morals; if we don't have a guide, we stumble. But if a man who possesses the natural disposition to goodness acquires good sense as well, then he behaves in the best way, and the disposition which *resembled* will now *be* true virtue. So just as we found when treating of the calculative or opining faculty that there are two qualities involved – cleverness and prudence – so also in our moral nature there are two qualities, namely natural and true virtue. Now true virtue cannot exist without prudence any more than prudence without virtue. This has suggested the view held in some quarters that all the virtues are forms of prudence or practical wisdom. In particular it was the view of Socrates, who adopted it in his inquiries. In this he was partly right and partly wrong. He was wrong in thinking that the virtues are forms of sagacity, right in saying that they cannot exist without sagacity. In proof of this we may observe that every philosopher even at the present day seeking to define virtue, after saying what disposition it is and enumerating its objects, adds that it is a disposition in accordance with the right principle. Now the right principle is that which concurs with sagacity. So it appears that everybody feels instinctively in some way that virtue is a disposition of this kind; that is, brought into conformity with prudence or sagacity. We must, however, go a little beyond this formula. For virtue is not merely a disposition in *conformity* with the right principle but a disposition in *collaboration* with the principle, which in human conduct is prudence. So, while Socrates thought that the virtues *are* principles,* we say that they work along with a principle. So we see from these arguments that it is not possible to be good in the true sense of the word without prudence, or to be prudent without virtue.†

Lastly, we have to meet the objection that we seem to be erecting prudence into a position of greater authority than wisdom. Now, in fact it is not true that prudence exercises authority over wisdom or the nobler part of our intellectual being any more than the art of medicine has authority over

* What he said was that they are all forms of knowledge.

† It may be added that this might enable us to meet the dialectical argument that could be produced in support of the view that it is possible for the virtues to exist independently of one another, the argument being that no man is equally well endowed by nature in respect of them all, so that he may have acquired one of the virtues before he has acquired another. So far as the natural virtues go, this is possible. But it is not possible when the virtues concerned are those which constitute a man's title to be called good without qualification. For let a man have the one virtue of practical wisdom, all the moral virtues will be added unto him.

health. The doctor's business is not to take our health into his hands but to give it a chance. Accordingly his orders are not given *to* but *for* health. To use another illustration, it would be like saying that political science is sovran over the gods, because it issues regulations about everything in the state, including what is due to them.

BOOK SEVEN

In the main this book is an analysis of 'incontinence', the opposite of the characteristic Greek virtue of enkrateia. *But it is introduced by a short account of the states intermediate between virtue and vice.*

CHAPTER ONE

WE must now embark upon a new division of our subject, namely, those qualities of character which are to be avoided. They may be taken as three in number, and we shall call them 'vice', 'incontinence', and 'brutishness' or 'bestiality'. There is no doubt as to what are the opposite dispositions to two of these three: opposed to vice is virtue, opposed to incontinence is continence. But the opposite of bestiality? One may with propriety call it 'superhuman virtue' – moral goodness on the heroic or godlike scale. One thinks of the words which Homer has put into the mouth of Priam respecting Hector, of whom, because Hector was preeminently brave, he says:

> Nor seeméd he to be
> Son of a mortal sire, but of a god.

So, if what men say is true, that mortals become gods by sheer nobility of character, the disposition opposed to bestiality will clearly be of this transcendent order. For virtue does not belong to a god any more than vice or virtue to a beast; the goodness of a god transcends our virtue, while the badness of a beast is different in kind from our vice. And on the same grounds as make it a rare thing for a man to be 'divine' in the sense in which that epithet is commonly applied by the Spartans when they wish to express the highest admiration,* so a bestial person is a *rara avis* among men. The type is commonest among the non-Greek races, but individual cases are found, produced by disease or arrested

* Their pronunciation of the word is slightly different.

development. We also sometimes go as far as to describe exceptionally vicious men as 'bestial' in order to express our loathing of them. But to this bestial disposition we shall have to devote some attention later, while of vice I have said something already. I cannot, however, omit here some account of incontinence and softness or luxuriousness, as well as of continence and fortitude or endurance. We should not think of either of those dispositions – the good and the bad – as identical with virtue and vice respectively. Neither must we think of them as different in kind.

The true method for us to follow, here and elsewhere, is to set forth the views which are held on the subject and then, after discussing the problems involved in these, to indicate what truth lies in all or – if that proves impossible – in the greatest in number and importance of the beliefs generally entertained about these states of mind. I am convinced that, if the difficulties can be resolved and we are left with certain of these beliefs – those, namely, which have stood our test – we shall have reached as satisfactory a conclusion as is possible in cases of the kind. In the present case the general beliefs are these. (*a*) Continence and endurance are good and commendable qualities, whereas their opposites, incontinence and softness, are bad and blameworthy. (*b*) The continent man has the characteristic of sticking by the conclusions he has been led to draw, whereas the incontinent man tends to give his up. (*c*) The incontinent or morally weak man does wrong, knowing it to be wrong, because he cannot control his passions, whereas the continent man, knowing that his lusts are evil, refuses to follow them, because his principles forbid it. (*d*) The temperate man is always continent and enduring, though whether the continent man is always temperate is an open question, some asserting and others denying that it is so, the former distinguishing between the intemperate and the incontinent man, the latter confounding all distinctions between them. (*e*) It is sometimes maintained that it is impossible for the prudent man to be incontinent, sometimes that *some* prudent and clever men are guilty of incontinence. (*f*) Some men are described as 'incontinent' in their anger and in their pursuit of honour or gain. – Such are the views that have found expression.

These views involve certain difficulties.

CHAPTER TWO

Now for the difficulties that may be raised. To take the third (*c*) of our opinions first, how can a man be said to show incontinence, if he has a correct apprehension of the fact that he is acting wrongly? Some thinkers maintain that he cannot, if he has full knowledge that the action is wrong. It is, as Socrates thought, hard to believe that, if a man really *knows*, and has this knowledge in his soul, it should be mastered by something else which, in Plato's phrase, 'hauls it about like a slave.' Socrates to be sure was out and out opposed to the view we are now criticizing, on the ground that there is no such thing as this moral weakness we call 'incontinence'. For, said he, nobody acts in opposition to what is best – and the best is the goal of all our endeavours – if he has a clear idea of what he is doing. He can only go wrong out of ignorance. This reasoning, however, is in glaring contrast with notorious facts; and that obliges us to look more closely into the frame of mind on which it is based. Conceding that ignorance is the cause of moral weakness, let us consider what form of ignorance. For it is clear that the man who succumbs to temptation is not ignorant of the wrongness of his action *before* he is involved in the temptation. There is, however, an amended form of the doctrine which is accepted by some. They agree that nothing can exert its superiority over knowledge, but they do not agree that nobody acts against what he believes was the better course. For this reason they maintain that, when the incontinent man is unable to resist the temptations of pleasure, he is not in possession of knowledge but only of belief. And yet if it is really belief and not knowledge – not a conviction that holds out against opposition but a mere suspension of disbelief such as we find among people who cannot make up their minds – one does not like to be too hard upon the man who cannot stick to his opinion when strong desires are pulling the other way. But vice we do condemn; that and any other culpable quality. And here we may take up that point about the continence of the prudent man. Is it when there is a struggle between prudence and desire that we blame a man for yielding? He ought not, it is thought, to succumb in such conditions, for prudence is a very strong thing. But this lands us in a paradox. If it were true, one could be at the same time both prudent and incontinent. But could any one maintain that the prudent man has it in his character to do the basest actions voluntarily? Besides, it has already been shown that the prudent man exhibits his prudence in conduct (which means dealing with ultimate particulars) and possesses all the other virtues as well. To proceed with the question (d) of continence. If the exercise of this virtue demands the possession of strong and evil desires, the temperate man cannot be continent, nor the continent man temperate. For the temperate man does not have these desires, but a continent man must have them. For, if a man's desires are good, the disposition which will not let him indulge them can only be bad. From which it follows that continence will not always be good. On the other hand, if his desires are weak but not evil, it is no proud achievement to resist them. Even if they are evil as well as weak, resistance to them is nothing to boast of.

Coming now to the first (a) and second (b) of the six views I stated, we may object that, if continence has the effect of making a man stick to *all* his opinions, it may be a bad thing – in the event, that is to say, of its making him stick to a false one. Also, if incontinence disposes him to give up *any* opinion, that will create the possibility of a good incontinence. Neoptolemus in the *Philoctetes* of Sophocles is an illustration of this. He does not persevere in the course to which he had been persuaded by Odysseus, because it distresses him to persist in a lie; and we applaud him. Here incontinence, in the form of inconsistency, is *good*.

Again – and this involves the first (*a*) and third (*c*) view – there is the difficulty stated in the argument which the Sophists are fond of adducing.* This is that argument of theirs which leads to the conclusion that folly *plus* incontinence is a virtue. For (they argue) a man who is both foolish and incontinent is led by his incontinence to do the opposite of what he believes that he ought to do; but he believes that good things are bad and that he ought not to do them; *ergo* he will do good and not bad things. And another sophistic argument might be developed from the second (*b*) and fourth (*d*) of the six views. It is this. A man who does or pursues what is pleasurable as the result of conviction and because he deliberately chooses that course might be regarded as a better man than he who acts in the same way, not because he has reasoned himself into doing this, but because he cannot master his love of pleasure. It seems a plausible argument, because the deliberate voluptuary is more likely to be cured, since there is a chance of persuading him to alter his point of view. But as for the incontinent man, our byword applies to him – 'When water chokes you, what are you to drink on top of it?' He already has all the conviction he can get down. Otherwise a change in the conviction that he was right might have stopped him. As it is, he is convinced that he ought to do one thing, and does another all the same.

Lastly, with respect to the sixth (*f*) view, if a man can show continence and incontinence about anything what is meant by calling one just 'incontinent'? Nobody can be incontinent in *every* direction, yet we speak of some people as incontinent without adding any qualification.

These, roughly, are the difficulties that may be raised in a discussion of the six views. Some points in them we should remove from our path once for all; others we must leave un-

* In order to impress people with their cleverness, the Sophists try to make them swallow a paradox. When they succeed in this the deduction which can be logically drawn from the admission ends in puzzling their auditors completely; the mind is in bonds, at once unwilling to stand still, because it hates the conclusion to which it has been drawn, and unable to go forward, because it can't untie the knot of the argument.

settled, while not forgetting that the solution of a difficulty in some problem leads to the discovery of the truth about that problem.

Some other points arise which call for discussion.

CHAPTER THREE

WE have then to consider these points. (1) When men show moral weakness (or incontinence) do they or do they not know the wrongness of their actions? If they know it, in what sense do they know it? (2) What are we to posit as the objects to which continence and incontinence are directed? I mean, are they concerned with every kind of pleasures and pains or only with a special division of them? (3) Is continence the same or not the same as endurance? (4) Other questions germane to the subject.

We may begin our inquiry by asking whether it is the objects or the dispositions of the continent and incontinent man that enter into the definition of these types as their differentiating qualities. Put it this way. Is a man to be described as incontinent merely because he cannot restrain his desires for certain things, or is it because he has a certain disposition, or do both causes operate? Here is a second question. Can incontinence and continence be exercised towards everything? Yes or no? One is aware that when a man is described as 'incontinent' without further qualification it is not implied that he is incontinent in everything, but only in those things in which a man can show intemperance; nor is it implied merely that he is concerned with those things,* but that he is concerned with them in a certain way. The intemperate man deliberately chooses to follow in the train of his lusts from a belief that he ought always to pursue the pleasure of the moment. The incontinent man pursues it too, but has no such belief.

* For if that were so, incontinence would be identical with intemperance.

(1) The theory that when men behave incontinently they are not acting against knowledge but against true opinion contributes nothing of value to our discussion. It never occurs to some people to question the truth of their opinions; indeed, they do not regard them as opinions but as ascertained truths. Consequently, if we base an argument on lack of conviction in some men, and say that this is the reason why those who shall be found to act against their conception of what is right must be said to have an opinion rather than knowledge, the difference between opinion and knowledge will vanish. For some men are just as sure of the truth of their opinions as are others of what they know. Heraclitus alone proves that. And if we say a man 'knows' something, we may be using the word in one of two senses. We may mean that he has the knowledge and acts upon it, or that he has the knowledge but makes no use of it. This being so, it will make a difference whether a man who is doing wrong knows that what he is doing is wrong but has this knowledge only in a latent or subconscious form, or whether, having the knowledge, he has it in an active form. If the latter, his doing wrong may well surprise us; but it will not, if his knowledge is not fully realized.

(2) When logical reasoning is applied to actions, the premises will assume two forms.* Now a man who is acting against knowledge may very well know both premises, yet put into practice only his knowledge of the universal or major premise and not his knowledge of the particular or minor premise. Yet it is this minor premise that is decisive for action, because acts are particulars. We have also to note that in reasoning about actions there are two universals involved. One is predicated of the *man*, the other of the *thing*. For example, he may know, and be in a position to act on the knowledge, that (*a*) dry food is good for all men,† and (*b*) he is himself a man. But he may not know, or may not be prepared to act on his knowledge, whether the particular

---

* In other words the application of a 'practical syllogism' involves two syllogisms.

† He may even know that such and such a food is dry.

food before him is that sort of food. It will be found then that there is an immeasurable distance between these two ways of knowing, so that we cannot think it odd that the incontinent man should know in one and not the other. The truly strange thing would be if he *did* know in the other.

(3) Moreover, it is possible for men to have knowledge – I use the word without prejudice – in another way besides those described. We have noted the distinction between actual and potential knowledge. But even in the second case, which is a condition of having knowledge without allowing it to operate, we can see a distinction. For there is a sense in which a man can both have and not have knowledge – he might, for instance, be asleep or out of his mind, or drunk. And what better are people when their feelings are too much for them? Doesn't everybody know that rage and lust and some other passions actually produce physiological changes, in some cases even insanity? It is evident then that, if we must say that the incontinent have knowledge, it can only be like that possessed by the persons to whom I have referred. The moral weakling may *say* he has knowledge, but that is no proof that he has it. People suffering from the disabilities I have mentioned will repeat to you the proof of some problem in geometry or a passage from Empedocles. In the same way people who have begun the study of a subject reel off a string of propositions which they do not as yet understand. For knowledge must be worked into the living texture of the mind, and this takes time. So we should think of incontinent men as like actors – mouthpieces of the sentiments of other people.

(4) It is also possible to study the cause of incontinence from the point of view of the scientist. This involves what we call the practical syllogism. In this the major premise is an opinion, while the minor premise is a statement about particulars, the objects of sense-perception. When the two premises are combined to form the syllogism, we have a result analogous to what we have in pure ratiocination. As in the latter the mind is forced to *affirm* the conclusion, so in the practical syllogism we are forced straightway to *do* it. Sup-

pose you have these premises: 'All sweet things ought to be tasted,' and 'That thing is sweet.'* When these premises are brought into relation you are bound, if nothing prevents you and you can do it, to go and taste the thing. Now there may be simultaneously present in the mind two universal judgements, one saying, 'You must not taste,' the other, 'Every sweet thing is pleasant.' When this happens, and then the minor premise, 'That thing is sweet,' presents itself,† while at the same time desire is present, then in spite of the fact that the first universal bids you avoid the thing in question, the desire leads you to it.‡ It is therefore, we conclude, to some extent an intellectual principle or opinion which influences the incontinent man to behave as he does – an opinion not in itself contradictory of the right principle but only opposed to it by an accidental conjunction of circumstances.§ This is the reason why the lower animals are not incontinent. They are incapable of understanding a generalization; all they have is mental images and the memory of particular objects.

We may ask how the ignorance of the incontinent man is overcome and knowledge restored to him. The explanation which accounts for the so-called knowledge of the drunk or sleeping man will serve in this case also; it applies to more than continence. But on this point it is for the physiologist to instruct us.

There are then these points to be considered. (*a*) The last – that is the minor – premise, that which can influence action, is an opinion which is related to some object of sense-perception. (*b*) This opinion the incontinent man, when he abandons himself to his emotions, does not possess or possesses only in such a way as does not entitle it to be regarded

* Here the minor premise is a particular instance of the class of things about which the major premise makes a general statement.

† Remember that it is the minor premise that introduces the possibility of action.

‡ This is because only desire can set the various limbs in motion – the body corresponding to the potential major premise, and the desire to the active minor.

§ It is the desire, not the opinion, that is the true opposite.

as knowledge, but only enables him to quote its tenor as a drunk man quotes Empedocles. (c) The ultimate term – that is, the particular proposition which forms the minor premise – is not a universal and is not regarded as an object of knowledge in the way that a universal judgement is. Since these three statements are evidently true, it does appear that our conclusion must be that which Socrates directed his questions to prove. For the knowledge which accompanies the collapse of moral resistance is not what is thought to be knowledge properly speaking. Neither is it true knowledge that is dragged about by passion, but only such as can be supplied by the senses. ...

Continence (and incontinence) concerned with the bodily pleasures.

CHAPTER FOUR

THE next question to be discussed by us is this. Is there such a thing as absolute incontinence, or must the incontinent man in every case show his incontinence in particular actions? If the second alternative is true, what is the nature of these actions? Now it is clear that the matters in which men show continence or incontinence, endurance or softness, are pleasures and pains. Of the things that give pleasure there are two kinds, some being what may be called 'necessary', others desirable in themselves but capable of being indulged in to excess. The necessary sources of pleasure are those connected with the body.* The other pleasure-giving things are not in this sense necessary, but are desirable in themselves.† Now those who indulge to excess in this second class of pleasures contrary to the right principle within them are not described as just 'incontinent'. We qualify the bare word

* I mean things like eating and drinking and venery, in short the bodily functions, which we found reason to regard as the theatre in which men show their temperance or lack of it.

† Things like victory, honour, riches, and the other things that may be described as good and pleasant.

'incontinent' by adding 'in the matter of money' or 'gain' or 'honour' or 'anger.' This we do because we regard them as distinguishable from the absolutely incontinent and as only called incontinent because of the analogy between them. (You will recollect the example I used to quote: 'Man, the Olympic victor.' There is little difference between the definition of the individual named Man and the general definition of *a* man. Still, the difference between him and men in general exists.)* But it is not so with those who indulge to excess in fleshly delights, which are what give occasion for our calling a man temperate or intemperate according as he deals with them. In this sphere the man who pursues excessive pleasure, and seeks to avoid extreme hunger and thirst and heat and cold and every painful experience of touch and taste, and does this not from deliberate choice but against it, and against the more intellectual part of his nature, is described as incontinent without any qualification such as we add in the case of a man who is incontinent in anger. He is just incontinent.† This is our reason for putting the incontinent man in the same class as the intemperate,‡ because incontinence and intemperance are exercised in the same matter of pleasures and pains.§ We must observe, however, that while they are concerned with the same things, they are not concerned with them in the same way, since the intemperate man acts deliberately and the incontinent does not. It would therefore be more appropriate to give the description of intemperate to a man who pursues excessive pleasures

* The view that those who cannot resist the temptations of money, honour, and so on are only called incontinent by analogy seems to be proved by the following observation. A man of that type is not blamed as a vicious person, but we do regard incontinence pure and simple as well as incontinence in the indulgence of bodily pleasures not merely as an error but as a vice.

† A proof that incontinence (understood without qualification) means the inability to control our physical pains and pleasures is afforded by linguistic usage. We apply the term 'soft' to men who yield to these bodily sensations, but not to those who give way to emotions like anger.

‡ And the continent in the same class as the temperate.

§ Those who succumb to anger and emotions of that kind we do not admit to this class.

and shuns even moderate pains – and that though feeling little or no desire – than to a man who is impelled to this course by the force of his appetites. For what would the former do if he were assailed by the boiling passions of youth, and by violent pain when denied the satisfaction of his bodily desires?

I will now assume the truth of these propositions. (*a*) Some desires and pleasures are concerned with things that are fine and good in kind.* Examples of such things are money, gain, victory, honour. (*b*) Men are not blamed for liking or desiring or for their susceptibility to all these neutral or naturally desirable things, but for doing this in a particular way, namely, to excess.† Well then, those two propositions being granted, we must also grant that there cannot be any vice or utter wickedness in this field because, as has been stated, every one of these things is naturally desirable in itself, though an extravagant absorption in them is bad and to be avoided. Similarly, there cannot be incontinence either, for incontinence is not only a thing to be avoided but a thing that calls for moral reprobation. No doubt people use the *word* 'incontinence' for the emotional state which is generated in dealing with anger or profit or the like, because this state does resemble absolute incontinence. But in every case they add a qualification expressing in what the incontinence is found. In the same way we call somebody a 'bad doctor', or a 'bad actor', although we should never think of calling him simply 'bad'. So, just as we do not call them bad, be-

* I am led to distinguish this class by the fact that some pleasant things are naturally desirable, others the opposite, while others again are neutral – a classification on the lines of that which we made before.

† So, while we look with indulgence on those who, contrary to the principle that should guide them, pursue or fall under the sway of some naturally fine and good thing – those, for example, who care too much for honour or for their children or parents (for children and parents are good things, and those who show devotion to them win our commendation) – still it is possible even in their case to go too far. Thus it would be going too far to enter into rivalry with the very gods, like Niobe boasting of her children, or to behave like Satyrus, who was nicknamed 'Filial Love' because he was thought to carry his devotion to his father beyond all reasonable bounds.

cause being a bad doctor or actor is not a vice, though it looks somewhat like it, we must observe the same distinction in the case of continence and incontinence. For clearly it is only the continence and incontinence that are shown in the same things as those with which temperance and intemperance deal that should be considered as continence and incontinence properly speaking – terms which are applied to anger only by analogy, so that we add a qualification, saying 'incontinent *in anger*,' just as we say 'incontinent *in the pursuit of distinction* or *profit*.'

A chapter on the pathology of pleasure.

CHAPTER FIVE

SOME things are naturally pleasant, and of these some are pleasant in any case, while others give pleasure only to particular races or species of men or animals. But there are other things which are not naturally pleasant but come to give pleasure from some pathological cause, such as arrested development or vicious instincts, or as the result of bad habits. Consequently it is possible to see, corresponding to each of these unnatural pleasures, certain abnormal qualities of character which may be described as 'bestial'. Examples of such bestiality are the female who is said to rip up the bellies of pregnant women and devour the unborn children, and some of the savages by the shores of the Black Sea, who are cannibals, or have a taste for raw flesh, and others among them who supply in rotation a child for the tribal feast, or the notorious behaviour of Phalaris. All this may be called bestiality, but there are other perversions. Some are the product of disease, which may be mental,* others the product of habit, such as plucking out hairs, biting one's nails, eating charcoal or loam, homosexuality among men. Practices of this nature are sometimes the result of congenital

---

* e.g. the madman who literally sacrificed his mother and made a ritual meal of her, or the slave who ate his fellow's liver.

tendencies, sometimes of habit, as in the case of those who have been subjected to gross indignities since childhood. Where Nature is the cause, no one would charge the sufferers with incontinence any more than one would apply the term to women on the ground that their part in sexual intercourse is passive. Nor should we apply it even to those who are in a morbid condition as the result of forming a bad habit. The possession of these morbid dispositions cannot in any single case be brought under the definition of a vice; and the same is true of bestiality. To be mastered by them is not incontinence in its strict sense but in its analogical use, as when we say of a man who cannot control his temper that he is 'incontinent in anger' – we must not say just 'incontinent'.* A man so constituted that he is scared by anything, even the squeak of a mouse, is barely human in his cowardice; the man who was afraid of the house-ferret had a phobia, and was therefore in a pathological state. But what has been said is equally true of folly, which becomes bestial in some, who are congenitally incapable of reasoning and live a life of pure sensation, like certain wild tribes on the borders of the civilized world, or morbid in those who lose their reason from the effects of some malady like epilepsy or from an attack of insanity. Occasionally a man may have one of these proclivities without giving way to it. I mean it is conceivable that Phalaris might have longed to eat a baby or indulge in some abnormal form of sexual intercourse, and yet have resisted the craving. But of course it is also possible both to have the propensity and to yield to it. Well, just as vice – natural vice – is called vice and nothing more, whereas the unnatural kind is not called simply 'vice' but has the epithet 'bestial' or 'morbid' attached to it, so with incontinence. Clearly there are two kinds, one incontinence in the strict sense of the word, the other incontinence in the secondary or borrowed sense. To the latter belongs bestial and morbid incontinence, to the former only that which covers the same ground as human or natural intemperance. . . .

* It may be noted that folly, cowardice, intemperance, cantankerousness, carried to excess, invariably issue in a morbid or bestial condition.

*There follows a parenthetical chapter on the question whether inconti-
nence in anger is less blameable than incontinence in desire, that is,
incontinence in general.*

CHAPTER SIX

WE have now to consider the view that incontinence in
anger is less disgraceful than incontinence in our desires.

The trouble about anger would seem to be that, while it
does to some extent listen to reason, it does not hear it aright.
It is like an over-hasty servant who scuttles out of a room before he has heard the whole of his instructions, which he then
proceeds to bungle; or like a dog that barks at nothing more
than an approaching footstep before finding out if it is a
friend's or not. So anger, which is of a hot and impulsive
nature, listening to a suggestion instead of to its orders,
rushes off to get its revenge. His reason or his imagination
suggests to a man that an insult or a slight has been offered
him, and instantly he flares up. Yet the process is not entirely irrational, for he has argued in his own mind upon the
assumption that a man ought actively to resent an insult.
But the senses have only to hint that something is desirable,
when off he rushes to enjoy it. That is to say, anger is
amenable to reason up to a point, but desire is not. We conclude that it is more disgraceful to yield to desire than to
anger. For he who cannot master his anger is in a way subject to reason, but the man who cannot master his desires is
subject to them and not to reason. There is the further consideration that it is thought more excusable to follow the
natural impulses, which all men feel, than those which are
peculiar to certain persons. For we feel like that even about
the desires; we are more indulgent to those which are common to all men, and indulgent to the extent to which they
are common. Now anger and bad temper are commoner
human frailties than desire for excessive and unnecessary
pleasures. I am reminded of the story of the man who was
answering the charge of beating his father. 'Well,' said he,

'my father there, who is prosecuting me, used to beat *his* father, and this little fellow' – pointing to his small son – 'will beat me when he grows up. It runs in the family.' Then there is the man who, when his son was going to kick him out of doors, used to cry, when they had got to the threshold, 'Stop! This is as far as I dragged *my* father.'

Again, the craftier a man is, the worse he is. Now, the choleric man is not crafty but open and above-board, and so is the passion that fills him. Desire, however, is crafty, like Aphrodite herself, of whom the poets say that she, the 'Cyprus-born', is 'weaver of wiles', while Homer, describing her 'embroidered zone', says that it had, inwoven in it,

> Beguiling speech, that steals the hearts of wisest men.

Therefore, since incontinence in desire is a worse as well as a more disgraceful thing than incontinence in anger, incontinence in desire is incontinence as such, and we should not be far out in calling it just 'vice'.

Again, an offence against the person is the opposite of painful to the perpetrator, but a man acting in a rage is always in a state of painful emotion. So, if the wrongness of an act is to be measured by the righteousness of the indignation felt by its victim, incontinence in desire is worse than incontinence in anger, for there is nothing brutally insulting about anger.

We have seen that it is upon bodily desires and pleasures that true continence and incontinence are exercised. But there are certain differences between these desires and pleasures which we must try to apprehend. As I said when we began to discuss this topic, some are human and natural both in kind and in degree, some bestial, some produced by a stunted or diseased organization. The natural, and they alone, are the material with which temperance and intemperance deal. That is why we do not speak of the lower animals as temperate or intemperate; if we do, we are speaking metaphorically. In that case we may apply the words to certain species markedly distinguishable from other animals by their extreme libidinousness or destructiveness or omnivorousness. The lower animals, being irrational, must be regarded as, like the insane, aberrations from Nature. As for bestiality, it is a lesser evil than vice, though it startles us more. For in a beast the reason or intellect, which is the noblest faculty, is not corrupted as it is in a wicked man, for the beast does not have it to corrupt. And the bestial man has come to be like that. So we might as well compare an inanimate thing with a living being, to see which is the worst of the two. The badness of a thing which has no originating principle – and intelligence is such a principle – is always less capable of doing harm than that which is alive and intelligent.* A bad man can do a million times more harm than a beast.

Aristotle continues his account of the moral struggle in the field of pleasures and pains, and enumerates the types of character which emerge in the course of the struggle.

CHAPTER SEVEN

N o w about the pleasures and pains of touch and taste, and the feelings which make us want to enjoy the pleasures and avoid the pains. We have already defined these bodily pleasures and pains as the special province of temperance and intemperance. But we may now observe that men's characters or dispositions vary in such a way that, while one man succumbs to those temptations to which most people rise superior, others have the mastery over those to which the majority of men succumb. The first type shows incontinence in his pleasures and softness in bearing pain; the second displays continence in his pleasure and fortitude in his pains. But the disposition of the great majority ranges between these extremes, though their tendency is to move in the direction of the bad extremes.

* It is like comparing injustice with the unjust man. In one way injustice is worse, for no one can be absolutely unjust; but in another way the unjust man is worse, since it is he who *does* the mischief.

We have remarked that certain pleasures are unnecessary, while others are necessary, though with this limitation that excessive indulgence in them has nothing necessary about it.* The same remark applies *mutatis mutandis* to desires and to feelings of frustration. In view of this we may say that the man who pursues excessive pleasures, or pursues necessary things to excess, and does this by his own choice for their own sake and not with a view to some less immediate result, is intemperate and incontinent. Such we are bound to call him, for a man of this character is little disposed to repent of his excesses, so that he is incurable. For the unrepentant man is incurable, which is another way of saying incorrigible or intemperate. On the other hand the man who is deficient in the capacity for enjoying pleasure is the opposite of the intemperate man, while the temperate comes between these two. By the same token the man who shuns bodily pains not because he cannot bear them but because he chooses to shun them is intemperate.† Of these dispositions that which chooses to avoid pain is a form of softness, that which deliberately seeks pleasure is intemperance pure and simple.

Opposed to incontinence is continence, opposed to softness is hardness or endurance. The difference between endurance and continence is this. Endurance consists in holding out, continence in preserving mastery. They are two very different things, as different as the avoidance of defeat from victory. We are bound therefore to prefer continence. A man

---

* It is, of course, equally 'unnecessary' to take too little of the necessary pleasures.

† When the yielding is not from choice there are two types of person who yield: (1) the man who follows the dictates of passion and (2) the man whose motive is to avoid the pain of unsatisfied desire. We see therefore that there is a difference according as a man yields with or without his own deliberate choice. Everybody must believe that the man who commits a disgraceful action though he feels little or no temptation to do it is a worse man than he who feels the temptation strongly, and that he who coolly strikes another is worse than the man who strikes him in a passion. For what, we ask ourselves, would so cool an assailant have done, if his blood had been up? From this we infer that the intemperate is worse than the incontinent man.

who fails to withstand such pains as most people can and do support is soft or luxury-loving; for luxury is a kind of softness. He is the sort of man to let his cloak trail on the ground rather than have the bother of lifting it, or to affect the languor of sickness without reflecting that an assumed distress is a real distress. It is much the same with continence and incontinence. If a man gives way to violent or excessive pleasure or pain, that can surprise nobody. Indeed, he may be forgiven for succumbing, if he does not do it without a struggle. One thinks of Philoctetes when he is bitten by the viper in the play of Theodectes, or of Cercyon in the *Alope* of Carcinus. Or – to take an example of resistance to pleasure – think of a man trying his best to hold in a laugh who bursts out at last into a stentorian guffaw.* But it does surprise us to see a man give way to pleasures and pains which most of us are capable of withstanding. It is different of course if his weakness is due to disease or some hereditary taint, such as the congenital impotence of the Scythian royal family, or the less hardy constitution of the female, as compared with the male, sex.

It is a popular notion that a love of amusement is a sign of intemperance. In reality it is a sign of softness. For amusement is a way of enjoying one's leisure by relaxation. You may say, then, that the devotee of amusement indulges too much in relaxation. But relaxation is not pleasure, and it is the man who is insatiable in his pursuit of pleasure that is intemperate.

Incontinence is found in two forms, which we may call (*a*) impulsiveness and (*b*) weakness. The weak do form a resolution, but they are prevented by their sensibilities from keeping to it. The impulsive or headstrong are carried away by their feelings, because they have not thought about the matter that excites them at all. If they had, their behaviour might be different. For some people can hold out against strong emotion, whether painful or pleasurable, if they feel or see it coming and have time to rouse themselves – by which I mean their reasoning faculty – beforehand, just as

* This actually happened to Xenophantus.

a man can't tickle you if you have tickled him first. It is high-strung and excitable people who are most prone to the impulsive form of incontinence. The high-strung are too hasty, and the excitable too vehement, to wait for reason, since they instinctively follow the suggestions of their own imaginations.

Aristotle now pursues other differences between the intemperate and the incontinent man.

CHAPTER EIGHT

IT is different with the intemperate man, who, as I said, does not repent or feel remorse, since he abides by his choice. The incontinent man on the other hand is always capable of remorse. Consequently the objection we mentioned – that the intemperate man might be cured – is refuted by the fact. It is just the intemperate man who is incurable; the incontinent man is not. Vice such as is shown by the intemperate man is like dropsy or tuberculosis, whereas incontinence is like epilepsy. For vice is a chronic, incontinence an intermittent, ill. More than that, vice and incontinence are totally different in kind. The vicious man does not realize that he is vicious, but the incontinent man is aware of his incontinence.

With regard to the incontinent themselves, the impulsive among them are morally superior to the weak, who are in possession of the right principle but do not hold fast to it. These are worse, because they yield to a feebler impulse and after deliberation. Such men resemble dipsomaniacs, who get drunk quickly and on a small amount of wine or less than most people. It is obvious in fact that incontinence is not a vice, at least in the strict sense of that word. For vice is deliberate, and incontinence is not. Yet there is a similarity in the actions which result from them. Something of the kind is noted in the epigram of Demodocus upon the citizens of Miletus.

Milesians are no fools, you'd swear,
And yet they act as if they were.

To parody Demodocus: The incontinent are not bad, but they act badly.

To resume. While pursuing bodily pleasures of an excessive kind and contrary to right principle, the incontinent man is so constituted that he pursues them without the conviction that he is right, whereas the intemperate man has this conviction, which he has come to feel because it is now second nature with him to seek these gratifications. Hence the incontinent man can readily be persuaded to change his mode of behaviour – but not the other. For virtue preserves, while vice destroys, that intuitive perception of the true end of life which is the starting point in conduct. We may compare the propositions which the geometer sets out to prove and which are *his* starting-point. In moral as in mathematical science the knowledge of its first principles is not reached by a process of reasoning. The good man has it in virtue of his goodness, whether innate or acquired by the habit of thinking rightly about the first principle. Such a man is temperate, while the man who does not know the primary assumptions of all ethics is intemperate. But there is another type – the man who is driven from his considered course of action by a flood of emotion contrary to right principle. He is prevented by overmastering passion from acting in accordance with that principle, yet not so completely as to make him the kind of man to believe that it is right to abandon himself to such pleasures as he seeks. Such is the incontinent man. He is morally superior to the intemperate man and is not to be called bad without qualification, for he preserves his noblest element – that conviction on which all morality is founded. Different and at the opposite pole from him is the man who having made his choice holds fast by that, unshaken by the storms of passion. These considerations prove that continence is a good, and incontinence a bad, quality.

When a man may excusably change his mind.

CHAPTER NINE

ARE we then to say that a man is continent if he holds firmly to *any* principle or *any* choice, or must it be the right one? Conversely, is a man incontinent if he fails to stick to any principle or choice, irrespective of whether it is sound or not? (You will remember we raised the point before.) The answer must be this. The principle or choice, by which the continent man holds and the incontinent does not, may be of any kind; but that does not affect the real issue. *Essentially* it is the true principle and the right choice that the one holds and the other fails to hold, though *accidentally* it may be any. If a man chooses or pursues one thing as means to another, essentially he is choosing or pursuing the latter, only accidentally the former. 'Essentially' or 'absolutely' – it does not matter which word we use. Therefore, although in a manner of speaking the belief which the one holds fast and the other lets slip may be any sort of belief, absolutely speaking it must be the true belief.

Among those who cling to their opinion are some who are called 'obstinate', being people on whom argument is more or less wasted. They bear a general resemblance to the incontinent such as the reckless spender bears to the liberal man, and the hotheaded to the brave. But at several points they differ. The continent man is not driven from his position by passion and desire; he will on occasion prove open to conviction. The obstinate man, however, is not influenced by argument. Yet he is ready enough to conceive desires, and pleasure often has him on a lead. The obstinate may be subdivided into the 'opinionated', the 'unimpressionable', the 'boorish'. The motives of the opinionated are pleasure and pain. They like to feel that they have got the better of you in argument if you fail to make them change their minds, while they are annoyed if their pronouncements are treated as of none effect like legislation that has been declared null and void. Thus they actually resemble the incontinent more than the continent.

There are some, however, who change their minds under the influence of some other motive than incontinence. Typical of this class is Neoptolemus in the *Philoctetes* of Sophocles. No doubt his motive in changing his mind was pleasure; he had been persuaded by Odysseus to lie, and to such a man it was a pleasure to tell the truth. Yet, though a pleasure, it was a noble one. In truth not every one who does something for the pleasure it gives him is intemperate or vicious or incontinent. Only if the pleasure is a base one can we so describe him.

There is another type – the man who takes less pleasure than he should in what belongs to the body, and in this way does not abide by the right principle. The continent therefore must be placed between this type and the incontinent. The incontinent man is false to his principle because he enjoys the pleasures of the body too much, the insensitive type because he enjoys them too little. The continent man on the other hand holds fast to his principle and is not swayed by the one tendency or the other. And, continence being a good thing, it necessarily follows that the two dispositions opposed to it are bad – that indeed is fairly obvious. But in consequence of the fact that one of them rarely manifests itself, and then only in a few individuals, people conclude that incontinence is the only disposition opposed to continence, just as they believe that temperance has no opposite except intemperance.

Now language is often used figuratively, and this explains why we have come to speak, by analogy and metaphorically, of the 'continence' of the temperate man. The reason is that the temperate, like the continent, man is so constituted that the bodily pleasures never make him do anything against his principle. But there is this difference, that the incontinent man has desires, and bad ones, whereas the temperate man has no such desires. It is not in him to take delight in things which are contrary to his principle, while the continent man is so made that he finds pleasure in such things, though he will not let himself be drawn from his principle by them. There is also a resemblance between the incontinent and the intemperate man in that both pursue bodily pleasures. But the intemperate man thinks it right to do so, while the incontinent does not. And this makes a vast difference between them.

Some further distinctions in respect of incontinence.

CHAPTER TEN

OBSERVE too that one and the same person is incapable of being both incontinent and prudent, for it has been shown that the man of practical wisdom must at the same time be morally good. Besides, just knowing what is right does not make a sagacious man. He must also do it, whereas the incontinent man does not do it.* Why, the incontinent man does not even *know* the right consciously and effectually, but only as a man asleep or drunk can be said to know something. Another point is that, while he does not sin against his will – for in a way he does know what he is doing and why – he is not a wicked man. His *choice* is morally sound, so that he is only half wicked. Nor is he unjust, for he does not plot against people, since, as we saw, of the two types of the incontinent one does not keep to the result of his deliberation, while the excitable type does not deliberate at all. In fact the incontinent man may be compared to a city which votes in favour of all the right proposals and has excellent laws, but never carries any of them into effect. It reminds one of that biting line in Anaxandrides:

So willed the city where they laugh at law.

* On the other hand there is nothing to prevent the incontinent man from being clever – that is why some people occasionally give the impression of being both sagacious and incontinent – because cleverness differs from sagacity or prudence in the way I explained in a previous lecture. So far as they both have a rational basis, they are close to one another. But they differ in this, that of the two the prudent man alone makes a deliberate choice.

On the other hand the wicked man may be likened to a city which does put its laws into operation; only, the laws are bad.

Both continence and incontinence go farther than the character of most of us permits us to go, the continent man showing more, and the incontinent less, power of moral resistance than the generality of mankind possesses.

The form of incontinence shown by the excitable man is more amenable to cure than the form shown by those who deliberate but do not keep to the resolutions to which their deliberations have led them. Similarly those whose incontinence is the result of habit are more easily cured than those who are born incontinent. For it is harder to change nature than a habit. Yet it is difficult to change a habit, too, for the very reason that habit is a second nature. As Evenus puts it,

> Habit, my friend, is practice long pursued,
> That at the last becomes the man himself.

The rest of the book is a discussion – resumed in the tenth book, chapters one to five – of the nature of pleasure.

CHAPTER ELEVEN

WHAT is the nature of pleasure and pain? The problem is one which must be studied by the political philosopher, whose business it is as the master-craftsman to set up an end, this end being the standard by reference to which we are enabled to say whether anything is absolutely good or bad. Such a study is equally essential in ethics, for we settled that virtue and vice are concerned with pains and pleasures, while most people maintain that happiness – the *summum bonum* – must be accompanied by pleasure.*

However, more than one view is held upon the subject. First, there is a school of thought which holds that no plea-

* This explains the word *makarios*, 'supremely happy'; it is derived from *mala*, 'very', and *chairein*, 'to rejoice'.

sure is a good thing, whether in its essence or accidentally. Their argument is that goodness and pleasure are different things. A second view is that some pleasures are good, though most are bad. A third view is that, even if we allow that all pleasures are good, pleasure cannot be the supreme good.

Let us now consider the arguments adduced in favour of these three views, beginning with the first. (1) To prove that pleasure is not a good at all it is argued that (a) every pleasure is a process – a process of which we are conscious – to a natural or normal state. But a process can never belong to the same class of things as the end of the process. For example, the process of building a house can never be brought into the same class of things as the house. (b) The temperate man shuns pleasures. (c) The prudent man seeks, not pleasure, but freedom from pain. (d) The pleasures are a clog upon serious reflection; and the sweeter they are, the heavier the clog. I may instance the pleasure received from the erotic act; nobody could think to any purpose in the middle of that. (e) There exists no art of pleasure; yet every good thing has an art which produces it. (f) Pleasure is sought by irrational beings like children and animals. (2) To prove that not all pleasures are good it is argued that: (a) Some pleasures are disgraceful and the practice of them brings men into ill repute. (b) Some pleasures are harmful, as is proved by the fact that some pleasant things are dangerous to health. (3) To prove that pleasure cannot be the chief good it is pointed out that a process is not an end. – These are, roughly speaking, the opinions of the schools on this subject.

CHAPTER TWELVE

But that these arguments do not succeed in proving either that pleasure is never a good or that it is not the highest good will appear from the following considerations. In the first place the word 'good' can be applied either to what is good absolutely and in itself or to what is good for a particular person – what we call 'relatively' good. That being so, there will be and there is the same ambiguity about the meaning of 'good' when the word is applied to men's natures and dispositions, and consequently when it is applied to movements and processes. And then what of 'bad' processes? Sometimes, though they are bad absolutely, they will not be bad relatively; nay, for a particular person they will be positively desirable. And some processes, not even desirable for him generally, are desirable for an individual on occasion and for a time, though not absolutely. Yet some of these processes towards a normal state, though felt as pleasures, are not really pleasurable. Of such are the painful processes which accompany medical treatment.

A second objection may be founded on the distinction between the good that is an activity and the good that is a state. The pleasures which restore us to a normal state are pleasant only accidentally. But what about our *active* desires? Their activity is that of the state which has remained normal and which alone can desire the process of restoration to itself. If it comes to that, there are pleasures which are not accompanied by any pain or desire,* because in their case the normal state remains unimpaired. There is something which seems to prove that the pleasurable sensations of transition to a normal state are only accidentally pleasant. It is this. We are not gratified by the same things when our natural state is being restored to its normal condition as we are when the restoration is complete. It is only in the normal state that we enjoy the things that are really pleasant. In the process of re-establishing that state we find pleasure even in things that are the opposite of what are really pleasant, such as sour or bitter things, none of which is naturally or unconditionally pleasant. Since this is so, the pleasure we derive from them cannot be absolutely pleasant any more than *they* are. For the distinction between one pleasant thing and another is reflected in the pleasures derived from them.

There is another point. The argument of some that there must be something better than pleasure, because the end is

* e.g. the pleasure of philosophic reflection.

better than the process which leads to it – and pleasure is a process – is not conclusive. The fact of the matter is that pleasures are *not* processes, nor are they all connected with a process. They are forms of activity and, as such, an end. Nor is it the process by which we arrive at the possession of our powers that makes them possible; it is our use of these powers. Nor have all of them some other end than themselves. Indeed it is only those which are involved in our advance to the completion of our nature that do not find their end in themselves. It is therefore a bad definition of pleasure to call it an 'experienced process'. For 'process' we ought to say 'activity' – the activity of our natural state – and for 'experienced' we ought to say 'unimpeded'. Some indeed are of opinion that pleasure must be a process because it is good in the full meaning of that word. But this involves a confusion of ideas. For these thinkers suppose that an activity – and they regard pleasure as such – is a process. Yet it is nothing of the kind. – As for the argument (2) (*b*) that pleasures are bad because some things which are pleasant are injurious to health, one might as well argue that health is bad because some healthy things make a hole in one's pocket. We may infer that in a relative way both pleasant things and healthy things can be bad; but that does not make them bad in themselves. Even the study of a scientific or philosophical problem sometimes hurts the student's health. – To the argument (1) (*d*) that pleasures hinder prudence it may be replied that neither prudence nor any other quality is hampered by *its own* pleasure, though pleasures from another quarter may have this effect. Indeed, the pleasure we feel in studying and learning will rather help than hinder us in our pursuit of them. – Again (1) (*e*), that there should be no art employed upon the production of any pleasure is just what we should expect. An art never produces an activity but only the conditions which make that activity possible. Even so most people would accept the description of the arts of the perfumer and the chef as arts in the production of pleasure. – As for the argument (1) (*b*) that the temperate man shuns pleasure, and the argument

(1) (c) that what the prudent man seeks is freedom from pain, and (1) (f) that pleasure is sought by children and animals, all these can be deprived of their force by one and the same observation. It has been explained how some pleasures are good without qualification, and how not all pleasures are thus good in themselves. Now what animals and children pursue are those pleasures which are not absolutely good, and it is freedom from the pain of being denied these pleasures that the prudent man seeks – the pleasures, that is to say, which are attended by desire and pain; in other words, the bodily pleasures. One ought perhaps to say the excessive forms they take, for it is in dealing with these that the intemperate man reveals his intemperance. That is why the temperate man avoids them; for even he has his bodily pleasures.

CHAPTER THIRTEEN

LET us carry the discussion a stage farther. Since pain is always either (a) an unqualified evil or (b) evil as being in some way an impediment to activity, we must admit that it is to be avoided. Now the opposite of a thing to be avoided – opposite, that is, in so far as that thing is to be avoided and therefore bad – must be good. We are bound to conclude that pleasure is a good. It is true that Speusippus used to employ an argument designed to break the chain of this reasoning. Briefly it ran like this. The greater is opposed not only to the less but also to the equal. In the same way pleasure is opposed not only to pain but also to the neutral feeling which lies between pleasure and pain. But this argument will not hold water, for Speusippus would not say that pleasure as such is evil.

As for the argument (2) that some pleasures are bad, it would not even if true prove (3) that some particular pleasure cannot be the supreme good, just as the fact that some forms of knowledge are bad does not prevent some one form of it from being the supreme good. The correct inference would seem to be that – assuming as we do that there is such a thing as an unimpeded exercise of every faculty – the exercise or activity of all the faculties or of one of them (for our happiness consists in the exercise of all or of one) must when unimpeded be the supremely desirable thing. Now the unimpeded exercise of a faculty is a pleasure. Therefore (the argument might proceed) the supreme good must be a definite pleasure, even if we allow that most pleasures are bad and (if you like) even absolutely bad. And so everybody thinks that the happy life must be sweet, and weaves pleasure into his dream of happiness. And with every justification. For an impeded activity can never be a perfect activity, whereas happiness, to be happiness, must be perfect. This is why a man, if he is to be happy, must have in addition to his other advantages the physical advantages too, as well as external goods and the blessings of fortune – his activity must not be impeded through lack of these things.* But, because happiness has this additional need, some believe that happiness *is* good fortune. That this is an error is proved by the fact that excessively good fortune is itself a check on activity and ought probably to lose its claim to be *good* fortune at all. For any definition of good fortune must express its relation to happiness.

Again, the fact that pleasure is sought by all men and animals is an indication that pleasure must somehow be the highest good. For

> The rumour that from man to man through all the people flies,
> Behold, it is a thing divine, and never wholly dies.

Yes, but they do not all pursue the *same* pleasure, for the natural (or best) state is not, nor is thought by them to be, the same for all of them. Yet it remains true that they all pursue pleasure. Indeed it is not impossible that they do after all pursue the same pleasure and not that which they think and would assure us they do. For there is in all things

---

* People who maintain that, if only a man be good, he will be happy even on the rack or when he is involved in some black disaster are talking nonsense; whether they know it or not.

a divine element which they more or less instinctively obey. In man this is intelligence. But, since it is the pleasures of the body with which men are most frequently brought into contact and can all be supplied, these pleasures have usurped the name, as if they were its sole legatees. The result is that people imagine they are the only pleasures, because they are the only pleasures they know.

There is another obvious point. If pleasure is not a good, and activity is not pleasure, then the life of the happy man is not bound to be pleasant. For if pleasure is not a good, why should he need it? It is in fact quite possible that his life may be a painful one. For if pleasure is neither good nor bad, then pain is not good or bad either. Why then should he shun it? And if the good man's activities are not more pleasant than other people's, then his life cannot be more pleasant than theirs.

CHAPTER FOURTEEN

Our next question must relate to the position or status of the bodily pleasures. There is a theory that some pleasures, generally described as the 'higher' pleasures, are exceptionally desirable, while the bodily pleasures (which give the intemperate man his opportunity) are not. We have to ask ourselves the meaning of this theory. And we may begin by asking why, if the theory is true, are the pains which are opposed to the bodily pleasures bad. Bad is the opposite of *good*. The explanation no doubt is this. The necessary (or bodily) pleasures are good in the sense that what is not bad is good. Or we may express the point by saying that they are good in their degree. There are states and movements of the soul which cannot be in excess of what is good, and states and movements which can. You cannot have excessive pleasure from the former, but from the latter you may. Now you can have an excess of bodily goods. It is the pursuit of this *excess*, not the simple pursuit of the necessary or bodily pleasures, that makes the bad man. Everybody likes rich food and wine and, within limits, the erotic act, although it is not every-body who can observe these limits. With pain it is just the opposite. It is not merely that we shun pain; we shun it through all its degrees. As for that pain which is the opposite and the product of excessive pleasures, that is no pain at all to the good man, who does not pursue any pleasure to ex-cess. But of course it is a pain to the man who does pursue excessive pleasures.

We are bound, however, not merely to state the true ex-planation but to account for the false. (Such a procedure is a contribution to the establishment of truth. When we have discovered a rational explanation of why something which is not true appears to be true, the effect is to increase our confidence that we have found the true solution.) Therefore we must now give our reasons for the fact that bodily plea-sures have the appearance of being more desirable than the other kinds. And the first reason is that pleasure drives out pain. Extreme pain has the effect of making the sufferer go in for excessive pleasure, and bodily pleasure generally, be-cause he feels within himself that he will find an anodyne in these. They are intense – which brings out the contrast with pain – and so he pursues them.* The second reason is that bodily pleasures, just because they are intense, have an irre-sistible attraction for those who can find no pleasure in any other kind. (Think of the people who actually give them-selves an artificial thirst.) Not that there is any objection to the pursuit of pleasures when they are harmless; but when they are not, we must call it bad. To be sure there are per-sons to whom nothing but sensual gratification gives any pleasure, and there are many who find a neutral state of

* The theory that pleasure is not a good is suggested, as has been said, by two circumstances. (1) Some pleasures are concrete indications of a bad nature, whether congenitally bad like that of the lower animals or rendered bad by habit, as we see in the case of bad men. (2) Other pleasures, if they are restorative, can only be restorative of something that needs to be restored. But that is a process of becoming, and to *be* in a natural state is better than to be on the way to it. The truth is that the 'restorative' pleasures are incidental to a process of reaching completion – in technical language they are good *per accidens*.

feeling positively painful – they are made that way.* In like manner the young are permanently in a state resembling intoxication; for youth is sweet and they are growing. Then there are individuals whose constitution inclines them to emotional outbursts. These are constantly craving a remedy for the pain of their wants, because their body is kept by their temperament in a state of chronic irritation, and they are always passionately longing for something. Now any pleasure, whether it happens to be the contrary of the pain involved or not, has the effect, provided it be strong enough, of driving out that pain. These are the causes of men's becoming intemperate and vicious.

On the other hand the pleasures which are derived from objects pleasant by nature and not *per accidens*, and therefore unaccompanied by pain, do not admit of excess. By things pleasant *per accidens* I mean things taken as anodynes or restoratives. That they have this restorative power is due to some effect produced by that part of our bodies which has remained in a healthy condition. And, because it is a movement to a healthy condition, the curative process itself gives us a pleasant sensation. But the things which are really pleasant are those which stimulate a given nature to activity.

Nevertheless it is not possible that the same thing should always give us pleasure, because man's nature is not of a piece but contains a material element the effect of which is to make us perishable beings. Consequently when one of these elements, the material or the intellectual, is active it is acting in opposition to the nature of the other. When they are exactly balanced the result is something which is not felt as either painful or pleasurable. In a simple nature the same activity would always give the greatest amount of pleasure. So God, whose nature is one, enjoys one simple pleasure for ever. For there is an activity not only of movement but of immobility, like that of thought, and there is in rest a more real pleasure than in motion. Yet, as the poet says, 'in all

---

* According to the biologists an animal organism is always in some degree of pain. Seeing and hearing they say are painful, but we are so used to them that we have ceased to be conscious of this.

things change is sweet.' It is sweet to us because of some badness in us. For a nature that needs change is bad, just as a changeable person is bad. And it is bad because it is not simple or good. ...

BOOK EIGHT

The subject of the eighth and ninth books is Philia, *the feeling which friends have for one another. Since this may run through the whole gamut of emotions between love and liking, it cannot be translated by any English word, though in general 'friendship' will serve. Surprise has often been expressed that so large a portion of a treatise on ethics should be devoted to the subject of friendship, and reasons have been sought to account for this. But we may be content to reflect that without this discussion of* Philia *the* Ethics *would have nothing to say on the subject of love, and that would indeed appear a surprising omission. The ancient Greeks looked on the physical attraction of sex for sex as a biological phenomenon, which did not admit of moralization any more than hunger or thirst. So Aristotle does not discuss it. On the other hand the love between friends played a much larger part and reached a far greater intensity among the Greeks than it normally does among us. For that reason Aristotle devotes a great deal of attention to its psychological manifestations and moral values.*

He begins by saying that Philia *is a sort of virtue. Also it is a necessary ingredient in our life as social beings, as well as morally fine in itself.*

CHAPTER ONE

OUR next subject must be friendship. This is necessary because such love has somewhat the character of a virtue, or at any rate involves virtue. Besides, it is one of the things which life can least afford to be without. No one would choose a friendless existence on condition of having all the other good things in the world. So true is this, that the rich and men in positions of authority and power are believed to stand, more than other people, in need of friends. For what would they get out of their prosperity if they were deprived of the chance of performing those offices of kindness for which their friends supply them with the greatest and most laudable opportunities? Or how could their prosperity be guarded and preserved, if they had no friends? For the greater prosperity is, the more precarious. In poverty also and all the other misfortunes of life the thoughts of men turn to their friends as their one refuge. Truly friends are an aid – to the young in keeping them from making mistakes; to the old in supplying their wants and doing for them what in the failure of their physical powers they cannot do for themselves; to those in the prime of life by making it possible for them to get fine achievements brought to accomplishment. Two are better than one, or (as Homer puts it)

> When two upon a journey go, one sees before the other.

For indeed two are better able to 'see' a thing and to do it than is one.

Then the feeling, which we find not only among men but among birds and most animals, of parent towards offspring, and offspring towards parent, seems to have been implanted by nature. We must say the same of the feeling between creatures of the same species, more particularly the human species. Friendship then, being a necessity of human nature, is a good thing and a precious. So we praise those who love their fellow-men. And one notices in one's travels how everybody feels that everybody else is his friend and brother man. Again, it is pretty clear that those who frame the constitutions of states set more store by this feeling than by justice itself. For their two prime objectives are to expel faction, which is inspired by hate, and to produce concord – concord being like friendship. Between friends there is no need of justice, though men can be just and yet lacking in friendly feeling, which some go so far as to think an element in the highest form of justice, which we saw to be equity. It is not only that friendship is necessary to the good life, it is in itself a good and beautiful thing. We praise a man for loving his friends, and the possession of many has always been considered one of the things that ennoble existence. Nay, some even believe that to be a friend you must also be a good man.

But what is friendship? Opinions differ. Some say the attraction comes from similarity, others say it comes from dissimilarity, between the friends.

There are, however, a good many divergent views as to what friendship is. Some aver that it is a matter of similarity – that we love those who are like ourselves. Hence those proverbial sayings, *Like to like*, *Birds of a feather*, etc. Others maintain just the contrary, saying that those who resemble each other are always at loggerheads. So Hesiod:

> Potter is wroth with potter, wright with wright.

Others dig deeper and seek for the causes of friendship in natural philosophy, Euripides saying:

> Earth like a lover longs for rain,

when it is parched; and again:

> The holy firmament, his body filled
> With rain as seed, yearns on the earth to fall.

And Heraclitus says, 'Strife is Concord' and 'Out of the Different cometh Harmony in her fairest form' and 'All things are born in Contention.' But others assert the contrary, and in particular Empedocles, who says, 'The desire of Like is for Like.'

But speculations of this kind belong to natural rather than moral philosophy, and may be dismissed as irrelevant to our present inquiry. Let us look at the human side of the question – all those parts of it which have a bearing on conduct and the emotions. Such is the problem whether all men are capable of friendship or only the good, and whether there is only one kind of friendship or more than one. Those who think there is only one, adducing the argument that friendship admits of degrees, have pinned their faith to something that cannot stand examination. For different kinds also admit of variation in the degrees of their intensity.

Before we can answer these questions we must satisfy ourselves on the point of what are the objects of friendship. They evidently are these: the good, the pleasant, the useful.

CHAPTER TWO

PERHAPS the solution of these problems will present itself when we have got our own minds clear on the subject of what it is that *awakens* friendship. For evidently not everything does. The general opinion is that the object of friendship must be *good* or *pleasant* or *useful*. It is possible, however, to take the view that useful means nothing more than productive of some pleasure or some good, so that there would be only two objects of friendship which can be regarded as ends, namely the good and the pleasant. But this gives rise to another question. Is it the good in itself that men love or only what is good *for them?* For sometimes the two cannot be reconciled. The same reasoning will apply also to the pleasant. Now it would appear that what everyone loves is that which is good *for him*, and that, while it is only the absolutely good that is absolutely lovable, the individual finds that lovable which is good for him individually. Yet we must take account of the fact that it is not what is absolutely good for oneself that each of us loves but what *seems* to each to be good. Still, for the purpose of the present argument, I shall treat 'lovable' throughout as meaning 'what appears to be lovable', so that the distinction will not obtrude itself.

Let us consider then these three grounds or motives for loving. – And observe first that in the case of inanimate objects we do not speak of a friendship with them, and that for two reasons. (*a*) Our affection cannot be returned. (*b*) We cannot wish for the good of such objects.* But when a friend is concerned everybody says that we ought to wish him well

---

* It would, for example, be absurd for a man to wish his wine well. If he has any wish in the matter, it is that the wine may keep, so that he can taste the joys of possession.

for his own sake. Goodwill or benevolence, however, must be reciprocated if it is to become friendship; where it is not reciprocated we can only say that one of the parties is well disposed towards the other. And not only must the feeling between friends be reciprocated; the friends, I suggest, must be alive to this. For many a man has kindly feelings towards someone he has never seen but whom he believes to be distinguished by his goodness or usefulness. And it may happen that the object of these feelings may have the same regard for the man who entertains them. Here then we have two people clearly well-disposed to one another, yet who cannot be friends because they are unaware how each feels towards the other. To be friends then men must have (*a*) mutual goodwill, taking the form of each party's wishing the good of the other, (*b*) knowledge of the existence of this feeling. It should be added that their mutual goodwill must originate in one of the causes I have named as capable of producing friendship.

There are three varieties or species of friendship corresponding to its three objects.

CHAPTER THREE

THESE causes of friendship differing in kind, the liking or loving they occasion will also admit differences in kind. Consequently we find that, just as there are three lovable qualities inducing friendship, so there are three kinds of it. For mutual regard mutually known to the persons concerned is possible under each of the three causes, and it is possible for one of them to show that wish for the good of the other which characterizes friends in any of the three relations which form the basis of friendship. Thus friends who have been brought together by a feeling that they will profit by their association do not love one another for their personal qualities, but only so far as they are useful to one another. It is much the same with those whose friendship is inspired by the pleasure they have in each other's society.

Thus the company of witty persons is agreeable, not because of what they are in themselves, but because it is agreeable to us. This means that, when a friendship is founded on the expectation of some advantage to be received, what the friends are thinking of is their own good; when it is based on the expectation of pleasure, they are thinking of what is pleasant to themselves. Their affection is not for the object of their affection as such. These two forms of friendship then are grounded on an inessential factor – an 'accident' – because in them the friend is not loved for being what he is in himself but as the source, perhaps of some pleasure, perhaps of some advantage. So parties are ready enough to dissolve their association when they themselves are changed. For if they are no longer agreeable or useful to one another, love dies a natural death. And as for utility, it is an impermanent and protean quality. So with the disappearance of the motive, the friendship itself disappears, for it had no other *raison d'être*.

It is between the elderly that friendships of the utilitarian sort appear to be most frequently formed, the reason being that in old age people are more disposed to seek profit than pleasure. But they are also to be found among those in youth and the prime of life who devote themselves to the pursuit of gain. Such persons do not as a rule live together; sometimes they do not even like one another, in which case they feel no need of such close association.* The sum of their pleasure in each other's company is measured by their hopes of some advantage to themselves. And among these utilitarian friendships we put a man's foreign connexions.

But when it is young people who form a friendship, the object of it, we all think, is the pleasure they get from it. This seems natural, when we reflect that the life of the young is one emotion after another, their grand object being to amuse themselves and catch the moments as they fly. And as they grow older the things that please them change too, so that they both make and drop friends quickly. (Their affections change with the source of their pleasures, and their

* That is, if there is no advantage to be got out of it.

tastes change rapidly.) Also the young are much subject to the passion of love, which for the most part is a longing for delight working upon the emotions. And so it comes about that they fall in and out of love quickly, often passing from one stage to the other before the day is out. But of course the young desire to pass the hours in the society of their friends. For that is what friendship means to them, and that is what they get.

But it is only between those who are good, and resemble one another in their goodness, that friendship is perfect. Such friends are both good in themselves and, so far as they are good, desire the good of one another. But it is those who desire the good of their friends for their friends' sake who are most completely friends, since each loves the other for what the other is in himself and not for something he has about him which he need not have. Accordingly, the friendship of such men lasts as long as they keep their goodness – and goodness is a lasting quality. And when two such men are friends each is good not only absolutely but in relation to the other, the good being both good in themselves and profitable to one another. So this kind of friendship *includes* the utilitarian kind. But it also includes the kind which has pleasure for its motive. For each of these friends is pleasant in both ways, since the good are pleasant both in themselves and to each other. For every man is pleased with his own behaviour and, as a consequence, with behaviour that resembles his own. But all good men behave in the same or much the same way.* That friendships of this quality should

* A friendship of this nature may reasonably be expected to last, combining as it does within itself all that is necessary for friends. We have seen that every friendship has some good or pleasurable object – absolutely good or pleasant, or relatively good or pleasant to the percipient, who feels some likeness between himself and his friend. But the friendship of good men has all those qualities which belong to them as their essential attributes. For the friends are alike (and all the rest of it) absolutely and in themselves. Moreover the absolutely good is also absolutely pleasant. Now the absolutely good and pleasant are what most engage our love or liking. So we may conclude that it is between good men that love and liking find their fullest realization.

be rare is only what was to be expected, for men of that quality are rare. And besides goodness they need time and intimacy to establish perfect friendship. As the proverb has it, you cannot learn to know a man until you have eaten a peck of salt with him. Just so, before one man can be admitted to the friendship of another and be his friend, he must prove to the other that he is deserving of his friendship and can be trusted. Those who 'make friends' quickly have the desire to be friends; but they cannot really be friends unless they are worthy to be such and both parties know it. Wishing to be friends is quick work, but friendship is a slow-ripening fruit.

CHAPTER FOUR

THIS, then, is the perfect form of friendship both on account of the time it lasts and because it has all the other good points in a friendship. In every way each friend – as between friends is only proper – receives from the other the same or like advantages.

The two inferior kinds of friendship have less permanence.

The kind of friendship that is sought for the sake of the pleasure it affords has a resemblance to the perfect friendship between good men, for such find pleasure in each other's society. But we can say the same of utilitarian friendship, for good men are useful to one another. We may add that the friendship between them lasts longer when each friend receives from the other the same good gift – pleasure for example – and moreover receives it from the same source, as happens when there is a friendship between two witty people, and as does not happen when the friends are lovers, because these do not have their delight in the same things. The lover finds his pleasure in looking on the beloved, and the beloved in the attentions of his lover. And sometimes when the lad's beauty wanes the friendship wanes also. For the lover is no longer delighted by the sight of the loved one, who for his part is no longer gratified by the attentions of his friend. Yet many do remain friends if, being alike in character, their intimacy has taught them to love each other's character. But when it is not pleasure that passes between lovers but material gain, then the affection between them is less deep and lasting. If all they seek is some mutual advantage, they part as soon as the profit goes. They were not friends for friendship's sake, but to get something out of it.

Neither are the inferior friendships confined to the good.

Thus we may say that both friendship which has pleasure for its object and friendship of which utility is the motive may exist between (*a*) two bad men, (*b*) one bad and one good man, (*c*) one neither good nor bad and one good or bad or neither. But clearly it is only the good who can be friends for love's sake only. For the bad take no pleasure in each other if there be no prospect of any advantage accruing to themselves from the association. Moreover it is only the friendship of the good that is proof against evil tongues; hardly will a man be brought to believe anything discreditable about the friend whose loyalty has been proved by himself through many a year and never been found wanting. Such friends have perfect trust in one another and are incapable of doing each other wrong, and have all the qualities that are confidently expected in true friendship. But in the less genuine kind the calumnious whisper may easily prove fatal. – For all that, people give the name of 'friends' to those whose attachment is based on considerations of utility * or pleasure, as when children 'make friends' with one another. So we too, no doubt, must call those who form such connexions 'friends'. This implies the existence of more than one kind of friendship, that which exists between absolutely good men being friendship in the true and primary sense of the word. The other kinds are friendships only by a

* In the same way we speak of 'friendly' states, though we all know that political alliances are formed on calculations of expediency.

sort of analogy or metaphor justified by the fact that there is a kind of goodness in them, pleasure being a good thing in the eyes of the pleasure-loving. And of course there is a sort of goodness in utility. But these so-called friendships are not apt to coincide; when utility is a motive, the love of pleasure is not likely to be a motive too. For accidental qualities are not as a rule found together.

If we look at these kinds into which friendship has been divided, we shall be disposed to say that it is the ignoble sort who will make friends with an eye to their pleasure or profit, supposing similar motives to animate both parties; but that good men will be friends because each likes the other for himself and his goodness. Such will be friends *simpliciter*, the others only *per accidens* and on the ground of a certain resemblance.

Although friendship is a permanent disposition, it is realized in friendly activities.

CHAPTER FIVE

WHEN we speak of 'good' men we may be thinking of them as in possession of a virtuous disposition or as exerting that disposition in action. The same distinction may be observed in friendship. When friends pass their time together they communicate the pleasure and profit of their society. But if they are asleep, or in different parts of the world, they cannot express their mutual affection in deeds, though retaining the disposition to do so. For separation in space does not kill friendship outright, it only makes its active exercise impossible. Yet, if the absence is prolonged, it does seem to dim the memory of the friendship itself. Hence the poet's words:

How oft, alas, from sight and speech remov'd,
The *Friendship* passes with the *Friend* we lov'd!

Old men and persons whose tempers have been soured evidently do not care to make friends. There is not much pleasure to be got by them out of friends, and nobody can live day in and day out with somebody who gets upon his nerves or is displeasing to him. Avoiding what is painful and seeking what is pleasant is notoriously one of the strongest instincts of human nature. Besides, you may like a man's company without wishing to have it all the time.* Nothing is so characteristic of friends as their fondness for each other's society. If a man is in want he craves help from his friend, and even if he is rich he craves the company of his friend.† But it is impossible for people to live together if they are not agreeable to one another and have different tastes. It is the possession of similar tastes that seems to be the essence of the club spirit.

Well then, to repeat what I have said more than once already, it is friendship between the good that best deserves the name of friendship. We have seen that what is absolutely good and pleasant is to the fullest extent worthy of our love and preference, while that which is good and pleasant for an individual is to be loved and preferred in that relation alone. But when one good man loves another he does it both absolutely and relatively.

Liking has the character of an emotion, friendship of a confirmed disposition. Thus liking can be felt even for sense-less objects; but that reciprocated liking which we call friendship involves deliberate choice, and such choice involves the action of a disposition. Now in wishing the good of their friends for the sake of those friends men are influenced not by an emotion but by a disposition – a settled state of mind. And to love one's friends is to love one's own good. For the good man by the very act of becoming the friend of another becomes that other's good. It may therefore be said that each of the friends loves his own good and makes the balance equal by wishing the good of the other and pleasing him. There is a saying, *Like, and be like*, and the best proof of its truth is found in the friendship of good men.

* The feeling here, however, is rather friendliness than friendship.

† When one comes to think of it **a** solitary existence is what suits the rich least of all.

Kinds and qualities of friendship.

CHAPTER SIX

THE ability of grim and elderly persons to make friends is limited by the fact that they tend to be cross-grained and take small pleasure in society; for it is qualities just the opposite of these that are most amiable and most apt to win friendship. Hence the young strike up friendships quickly, but not the old, for one does not make friends with people whose company gives us no satisfaction. And much the same may be said of morose persons. True, the old and the morose may be inclined to like each other, since they may wish one another well, or even supply each other's needs. But friends in the full sense they are not, as they do not seek to remain in the society of each other or find pleasure in that, although these are regarded as the best evidences of the love between friends.

But to have many friends in the way of perfect friendship is no more possible than to be in love with many at the same time.* It is not even easy for a man to have at the same time a large circle of agreeable acquaintances, and indeed it may be doubted if good men are so common. When you do find such a man you must become intimate with him and learn to know him before you make him your friend, and nothing is harder than that. On the other hand it is perfectly possible to have a *liking* for quite a number of people at the same time for the pleasure and profit one gets out of them. There are plenty of people capable of providing us with either, and it does not take long to furnish ourselves with the advantages they offer.

Of the secondary forms of friendship that which has pleasure for its object is nearer than the other to true friendship, for in it the contribution of both friends is the same. That is to say, they have common tastes and like to be together.

* Sexual love involves an excess of emotion, such as can be naturally felt only towards one person.

The friendships of the young are like that. In them one finds a more generous spirit than in utilitarian friendships, such as are affected by the vulgar. Then the well-to-do have no need of useful friends, but do need agreeable ones. Some associates they must have, and these must be such as they find to their taste. For, although they may put up with what is disagreeable for a time, they cannot any more than other people stand it for ever – even the absolute good would be too much for us at last, if it got to be a bore. So the rich look out for friends who shall be agreeable. Of course they should require them to be good as well – good in themselves and good for them – since in that case their friendship will be everything a true friendship ought to be. But princes and potentates, it would seem, prefer to have their friends specialized for different services; some are useful to them, others agreeable, hardly any are both. For what these great personages seek are not pleasant companions who are also good, nor profitable friends to serve some high purpose, but witty talkers when they want amusement and, when they want value for the connexion, practical men of business – characters rarely combined in one man. We have said that the good man is also both useful and agreeable, but he does not become the *friend* of a superior in rank who is not his superior in goodness as well. If it happen otherwise, the inferior in rank is not in a position to make up for the difference by giving more than he gets. But how many important people possess this moral superiority?

We have been speaking of friendships formed on a basis of equality.

To resume. The friendships of which I have been speaking are founded on equality. Each party wishes for, and receives from the other identical benefits, or else they exchange equivalent amounts of different things – so much pleasure for so much profit.*

* It has already been remarked that these friendships are comparatively unreal and impermanent. They are both like and unlike the same

But we may have friendships between unequals.

CHAPTER SEVEN

BUT there is a different kind of friendship, and in this the parties are unequal. Examples are the friendship between father and son or, generally, between an older and a younger person, the friendship between husband and wife, and that between every ruler and those who accept his rule. But there are variations between these friendships themselves. That between parents and children is not the same as that between rulers and ruled; nay, the friendship of father for son is not the same as that of son for father, nor that of husband for wife the same as that of wife for husband. For each of these has a distinct excellence and function, and has different reasons for feeling affection, with the result that their loves and likings reveal some differences. Well, then, in friendship of this kind the parties do not, and ought not to expect to, receive identical benefits each from the other. In a parent-children friendship the children perform the duties which they owe to those who gave them life, and the parents do *their* duty towards their offspring. When this happens the friendship between them will be lasting and good. But in all those friendships where the parties are not upon the same footing it is necessary as well that the feeling between them should be equalized according to a ratio or proportion. That is to say, the more virtuous friend should receive more affection than he bestows, and so should the more useful, and in every case whichever has the superiority. It is when the superiority is balanced by an equivalent amount of affection

thing, so that from one point of view they are friendships but from another they are not friendships at all. Because of their resemblance to the friendship that is based on goodness they do appear to be friendships, for pleasure is an element in the one, utility in the other, and these are attributes of friendship too. But that is proof against calumny and has permanence, whereas the others never stay long the same, besides exhibiting other differences. Consequently, owing to this dissimilarity between them and it, they seem not to be real friendships.

that we get in a manner that equality which, we agree, is of the essence of friendship.

We must, however, distinguish between equality in friendship and equality in justice.

We may observe, however, a difference between equality in friendship and equality in justice. In the sphere of the just the 'equal' or, as we say in that context, the 'fair' means primarily what meets the case, and what may be quantitatively equal is a minor consideration. But where friendship is concerned it is the other way about. This comes out very clearly when friends drift far apart in respect of virtue or vice or wealth or anything else. They cease to be friends, and this appears to them to be a natural development. The clearest case is that of the gods, for they are utterly superior in everything worth loving. But we see it also in the case of royalty, for those in less exalted station do not expect to be friends of the king, nor does a common chap aspire to the friendship of saints and sages. We cannot of course in such cases fix the exact point up to which and no farther men can go on being friends; for friendship may keep crumbling away, and survive for all that. But when a great gulf is fixed, as between God and man, there can be no friendship. This has given rise to the question whether it is not a mistake to say that friends wish the *greatest* of goods for each other – that they should be gods, for example. If they do cherish such wishes for them, they will no longer have them for friends, and so shall not have certain goods, for friends are goods. They will thus be defeating the very object of their wishes. If then we were right in saying that a friend, truly so-called, wishes his friend well for that friend's sake, we are bound to conclude that the latter must continue to be exactly the sort of person that he is. Therefore he will content himself with wishing for his friend the greatest goods available to a human being. And perhaps not all of these. For everybody who forms a wish thinks first of himself.

An inequality between friends may be reduced to equality by a deeper affection from the inferior to the superior.

CHAPTER EIGHT

IT is plain that most people would rather get than give affection, the reason being that they like the feeling of being honoured. That accounts for their fondness for flattery, since a flatterer is a friend who is, or professes to be, of an inferior status, and so pretends to make up for this by loving the friend more than the friend loves him. Now to be loved is felt to be next thing to being honoured, and to be honoured is the ambition of most men. Yet they do not seem to prize this for its own sake but for some accidental concomitant. While the majority of men like to have notice taken of them by important personages, this is because of the expectations that are aroused. They fancy that, if they want something, they will get it from the great man; so they are charmed by his condescension as an indication of favours to come. But those who desire to be honoured by the good and the wise are really seeking to be confirmed in the favourable opinion they have of themselves. Thus their pleasure comes from their confidence in the judgement of those who tell them they are fine fellows. It is different with affection, which men like to receive on its own account. From this we may conclude that to be loved is better than to be honoured, and that friendship is to be desired in and for itself.

Now friendship surely consists in giving rather than accepting affection. Think, for example, of the joy that mothers have in loving their children. Sometimes they give them out to nurse, still knowing and loving them, but not asking to be loved in return if they cannot have that too. They are content if they see their babies getting along nicely, loving them even if they cannot do their duty by *her*, because they do not know her. Friendship then showing itself more truly in giving than in receiving affection, and love for his friends being considered a laudable trait in a man, it would seem to follow that the special excellence of friends consists in their bestowing this affection. So the kind of friends who stay friends, and whose friendship is lasting, are those who give each other that amount of affection which is proportionate to their deserts. By doing this even friends who are not equal may come closest to being friends in the full sense, for it would put them on an equality – *caritas est paritas*. But charity is not only parity, it is also similarity, in particular the similarity of those who are alike in goodness. For, having an internal principle which keeps them steadfast, they are constant in friendship to one another, neither asking nor rendering ignoble services, you might even say making them impossible, since a man shows his goodness not only in doing no wrong himself, but in not allowing his friend to do it. On the other hand the vicious are inconstant friends, for they have no consistency in their own characters. They are friends only for the brief period in which they find pleasure in each other's degradation. More lasting are the friendships of those who are found useful or agreeable to their friends, but they last only so long as they provide each other with useful or agreeable attentions. Generally speaking, the utilitarian partnership has the appearance of a friendship between opposites, as when a rich man makes friends with a poor man, or an ignoramus with a savant, each being prepared to give a *quid pro quo* for something he does not have himself but would like to have. It would be possible to put under this heading of 'the attraction of opposites' the relation between lovers or a friendship between a handsome and an ugly person. This is the reason why lovers sometimes seem to us absurd when they expect to get as much love as they give. If we suppose the lover and his beloved to be equally lovable, the expectation is reasonable enough. But the thing becomes ludicrous if this condition is not satisfied. The probability is, however, that the attraction of absolute opposites is accidental, not essential. What they really desire is the mean * between them. The dry, for instance, is not seeking to become its opposite, the wet, but to reach an inter-

* We know that this is the good.

mediate position. We may say the same of the hot and all the other things which have opposites. However, this is somewhat beside the point and we need not pursue the matter here.

Friendship is a social phenomenon.

CHAPTER NINE

IT has already been observed in connexion with friendship and justice that they deal with things and persons in the same way. In every association there is some rule of justice governing the relations between the partners, and some friendly feeling is also presupposed. At any rate people on the same ship or in the same battalion address each other in friendly terms, and so do the partners in any common enterprise. But such friendship goes only as far as the need they have to work together, for that is the extent of their mutual obligations. And, as the proverb truly says, 'friends have all things in common,' for friendship is an expression of community. Brothers and comrades go shares in everything, other friends share this or that part of their possessions and to a greater or less extent according to the warmth of their friendship. Thus what is right in one kind of friendship is not right in another. There is a different set of rights and obligations between parents and children than there is between brothers or comrades or fellow-citizens, and so throughout the other forms that friendship may take. There are therefore also different ways in which those who make such friendships may violate their obligations to one another, and the wrong thus done is aggravated in proportion to the closeness of the tie uniting them. Thus it is worse to swindle a comrade than a fellow-citizen, to refuse to go to the aid of a brother than to the aid of a stranger, to assault your father than someone else. And with an intensification of friendship there naturally goes an increase in the sense of obligation between the friends, because the same persons are involved and their obligations of friendship are co-extensive with their obligations in justice.

But all associations may be regarded as parts of the association we call the state. Thus when people associate in their travels it is to secure some advantage – they are providing themselves with some of their means of subsistence. Well, political societies too are believed to have been originally formed, and to continue in being, for the advantage of the citizens. It is this advantage which lawgivers have in mind when they frame a constitution, and the current definition of justice is 'the common interest'. The other associations, however, aim at certain specific advantages. Sailors combine for the purpose of making money from the profits of a voyage, soldiers join forces in order to exploit the profits of war, whether they are hoping for loot or conquest or the capture of a city. In the same way the members of an electoral division or parish have a common purpose when they offer sacrifices and unite in the celebrations connected with them.* It appears then that all these associations are parts of the grand association which is the body politic, and there will be a correspondence between the secondary friendships I spoke of and these partial or limited associations.

This provides us with a basis or analogy on which we can make a classification of political constitutions.

CHAPTER TEN

THERE are three forms of political constitution together with an equal number of perversions or corruptions of these. The three constitutions are: kingship, aristocracy, timocracy. The last is the form of constitution that is based on a

---

* In this way they duly honour the gods and at the same time provide themselves with delightful periods of relaxation. It is significant that the traditional sacrifices and festivals are held *after* the gathering in of the harvest – they are all of the harvest-home type. The explanation is that the end of harvest was the season of year when the celebrants had least to do.

property qualification or *timema*, which makes it natural to describe it as a 'timocratic' constitution, although most people are in the habit of calling it just a 'polity', by which they mean a 'constitutional form of government.' Of these three constitutions the best is kingship, the worst timocracy. The perversion of kingship is tyranny. Both are monarchies, but they are poles asunder. The tyrant thinks of nothing but his own advantage, the king studies the good of his subjects. He can hardly be called a king unless he has enough of his own and is better off in every way than his subjects; but if he enjoys these advantages there is nothing else he needs and he will be in a position to consult the interests of his subjects without bothering about his own.* Tyranny is the exact opposite of such a rule in this respect, that the tyrant pursues his private interests. I may add that tyranny is more certainly the worst of the perverted, than timocracy of the true, constitutions. For the worst is that which is the opposite of the best.

When kingship undergoes a change it is in the direction of tyranny, for it must, be a change for the worse, and tyranny is the degenerate form of monarchy. So a bad king becomes a tyrant. Aristocracy changes into oligarchy, the result of deterioration in the character of the rulers, who do not take merit into account in their handling of the public resources but reserve for themselves all or most of the good things going and keep re-electing the same ministers, because their grand object is to make money. Power remains in the hands of a few, but these are men of bad character instead of the best members of the community, as in an aristocracy. Timocracy passes into democracy – indeed they are next-door neighbours. For timocracy, too, regards itself as government in the interests of the people, all citizens who can satisfy the property qualification being supposed to have the same political status. Of these three perversions the least bad is democracy, for the deviation it makes from timocracy (or a 'polity') is slight. Such are the ways in which the several constitutions generally change, for it is in these ways that a

* A king who cannot supply his own wants will be king only in name.

change is most easily effected and is least revolutionary in character.

Aristotle now develops the analogy with the family.

Now something like these various forms of government can be traced in family life, on which they seem to be modelled. The relation of a father to his sons resembles kingship, since a father has the interests of his children at heart. That is why Homer calls Zeus 'Father Zeus', for paternal government is the ideal of kingship. But in Persia paternal government resembles tyranny, for Persian fathers treat their sons as slaves. Again, the relation of master to slaves is a kind of tyranny, for it is the master's interest that is the object of its activities. Here, however, an autocratic system is clearly normal and right. When it is exercised by a father over his children, as in Persia, it is wrong, because forms of government should vary with the type of persons governed. Husband and wife live together in a sort of aristocracy. That is to say, the man is master, as is right and proper, and manages everything that it falls to him to do as head of the house. But whatever can be suitably performed by the wife he hands over to her. But when he manages everything without exception, he is turning his government into an oligarchy; for he is going beyond his just claims and what is due to him as the natural superior. But sometimes it is the wife who takes charge, as may happen when she is an heiress. In that event authority does not go by merit but by money and influence, as in oligarchies. Brothers form a sort of timocracy; they are equals, except in so far as they may differ in point of age. The difference is important because, if it is really considerable, the friendship between them ceases to have a brotherly character. Democracy is most completely expressed in households where there is no master, for all the members are then on an equality. It is also in force in households where the master is weak, and it is Liberty Hall.

The quality of the affection in these relations varies with their nature.

CHAPTER ELEVEN

EACH of these forms of government exhibits a form of friendship co-extensive with what is just under that government. The friendship of a king for his subjects expresses itself in benevolence, in which he excels them, for doing good is his business. As a good man he provides for the well-being of his flock, as Homer understood when he called Agamemnon the 'shepherd of the people.' The love of a father for his children is also of this nature.* The rule of a father over his children, or of a family progenitor over his descendants, is as much a natural thing as the rule of a king over his subjects. So when you have these friendships you have a surplus of benevolence on one side; and this is why parents receive honour as well as attentions, so as to restore the balance. In these, then, what is just from one side is not equivalent to what is just from the other, but is proportioned to the merit of the parties; and this, as we saw, is true of friendship as well.

The affection between husband and wife is the same as that which exists between the government and the governed in an aristocracy. For the degree of it is measured by the relative merits of husband and wife, the husband, who is superior in merit, receiving the larger share of affection, and either party receiving what is appropriate to it. And the claims of justice in this relationship are satisfied in the same way. As for the friendliness between brothers, it is like what we get between the members of some club or association. You have equality of rank and age, and where you have that you have as a rule a similarity of sentiments and habits.

* There is a difference, however, in the magnitude of the benefits. For a child owes to its father what is regarded as the greatest blessing that can befall it – its existence, to which we must add its nurture and education; in fact we consider ourselves under these obligations even to our forbears.

This is the kind of sympathy one finds between the citizens of a timocracy. For the timocratic ideal is that all shall be equal as well as good. Hence political power is shared among the citizens equally and in turn, and the result is that the friendship between them is friendship upon terms of equality.

But in the perverted constitutions friendship, like justice, goes but a little way, and least in the worst; for under a tyranny there can be little or no kindness between ruler and ruled. They have nothing in common, so there can be no friendliness between them, just as there can be no justice. The relations between them are those of the skilled work-man to his tool or of the soul to the body. No doubt the in-strument is in every case all the better for the manipulation it receives from the user, but there can be no friendship or justice in our dealings with inanimate things. We cannot even have it towards a horse or a cow, nay, towards a slave in his character of slave. For the slave has nothing in com-mon with his master; he is a living tool, just as a tool is an inanimate slave. There can therefore be no friendship of a master for a slave as such, though there may be for him as a man. For clearly there must be some form of justice involved in the relations between one man and another who is cap-able of acting legally or being a party to a contract. Simi-larly, friendship is possible with any man so far as he is a human being. We cannot then maintain that there is much room for friendship and justice between rulers and ruled under a tyranny. They are most adequately realized in democracies, the citizens of a democracy being equal and having many things in common.

Aristotle takes a brief survey of the family pieties.

CHAPTER TWELVE

COMMUNITY or association is, as I said before, essential to any friendship. But we may have to make a special class for the friendship between kinsmen and that between the members of a social fraternity. For the character of an association is less marked in them than in friendships between fellow-citizens or fellow-tribesmen or fellow-voyagers, etc., which seem to be built upon some compact or mutual understanding. And with these may be classed the exchange of hospitality with foreigners. But friendship between kinsmen is itself divisible into more than one variety, although all seem to be developments of the love of parent for child. Parents love their children as parts of themselves, while children love their parents as the authors of their being. Again, parents have better grounds for recognizing their children than the children for knowing their parents. He who gives life feels a more intimate connexion with him to whom he gives it than conversely, because that which owes its origin to a thing belongs to that thing,* whereas the originator does not belong to the originated at all, or at any rate not so much. Then the love of parents extends over a longer period, for it begins as soon as the children are born, whereas it is only after the lapse of some time, when they have acquired the capacity for reflection or at least for taking notice, that children begin to love their parents. If we take all this into consideration, we shall see why it is that of the two parents it is the mother that is the most devoted to the children. Yet however that may be, it is certain that parents love their children as themselves in the sense that one's offspring is a kind of second self. Children for their part love their parents as their begetters.

Brothers love one another on the ground of having the same parents, the identity of their relation to the parent stock identifying them with one another. Hence we speak of people as being 'of the same blood' or as having 'the same roots', with other expressions of that sort. With brothers then it is, so to speak, a case of identity in separation. At the same time brotherly affection is greatly encouraged by their having the same upbringing and pretty much the same age. We have proverbs like *Men of a year like to draw near* and *Familiarity breeds friendship*. No wonder then that fraternal

* e.g. a tooth or a hair or anything of the kind belongs to the owner of the tooth, hair, etc.

affection is like comradeship. The attachment of cousins and other relatives is an extension of the affection between brothers going back to their common ancestry, and their mutual sympathy is greater or less according as they are more nearly or more distantly connected with the common ancestor.

The affection of children for their parents (like man's love of God) is the sort of feeling one has for what is good and superior. For their parents have bestowed on them the greatest of blessings – they have given them life and nursed them and provided for their education when they reached school age. Besides this, family affection has more pleasure and profit in it than has any friendship between unrelated persons in proportion as family life provides a better chance of going shares in everything.

Friendship between brothers has the same characteristics as friendship between comrades, and has them more markedly if the brothers are good men or resemble one another in some other way. For (a) brothers are attached to each other by a specially close bond, and are born and bred in the love of each other. (b) Having a common parentage, and having been brought up together and received the same education, they come to resemble one another in character. (c) The test of time has been applied to them longest and given the most trustworthy results. (Friendly feelings among more distant relations vary in intensity as the closeness of the relationship.)

The love between husband and wife is evidently a natural feeling, for Nature has made man even more of a pairing than a political animal in so far as the family is an older and more fundamental thing than the state, and the instinct to form communities is less widespread among animals than the habit of procreation. Among the generality of animals male and female come together for this sole purpose. But human beings cohabit not only to get children but to provide whatever is necessary to a fully lived life. From the outset the partners perform distinct duties, the man having one set, the woman another. So by pooling their individual contributions they help each other out. Accordingly there is general agreement that conjugal affection combines the useful with the pleasant. But it may also embody a moral ideal, when husband and wife are virtuous persons. For man and woman have each their own special excellence, and this may be a source of pleasure to both. Children too, it is agreed, are a bond between the parents – which explains why childless unions are more likely to be dissolved. The children do not belong to one parent more than the other, and it is the joint ownership of something valuable that keeps people from separating. If we ask how a husband should conduct his life in his behaviour towards his wife, or generally how a friend should conduct himself towards his friend, we must apparently say that it comes to the same thing as asking how they are to behave justly towards one another. And this behaviour will obviously be different between friends and strangers, between comrades and between fellow-students.

The last two chapters of Book Eight are devoted to a consideration of the claims which friendship imposes on (a) equals and (b) unequals.

CHAPTER THIRTEEN

So, as I said at the beginning of this lecture, there are three forms of friendship and, with each of these forms, two kinds of friends – those who are equal and those who are unequal.* Those who are equal must make this equality appear in their friendship by contributing an equal amount of affection together with the other requisites of their friendship. Those who are unequal must do this by making a return in affection for the superiority of their friends in that in which these friends are superior.

* Two equally good men may be friends, or one of the friends may be a better man than the other. There is the same possibility in the case of those who make friends for the sake of the pleasure or the utility of the friendship; they may be equal or they may be unequal in the amount of pleasure or utility they confer.

Complaints and recriminations are heard most often, if not exclusively, in the kind of friendship which has a utilitarian object. This is natural, for in friendship which has no other motive than goodness the friends are only anxious to benefit one another, this being a distinguishing mark of goodness and friendliness. Since each strives to outdo the other in kindnesses, there is no room for complaints or quarrels. Nobody can be angry with one who is fond of him and seeks to treat him well. On the contrary every decent person so treated is anxious to repay the benefits. And the author of most of these is getting back what he desires from his friend, and so will not grumble at him. Nor are complaints likely to be made among friends who associate for the pleasure they communicate to each other. For in the enjoyment they find in the company of one another they are at the same time getting what they desire to have. It would be patently absurd to complain that one did not find one's companion amusing, when one can leave his company the moment one likes. It is in the utilitarian brand of friendship that we hear complaints. For there the motive is profit, with the result that the friends are always pressing for more and more of that, each thinking that he is not getting his fair share. He grumbles that he does not receive what a man of his merit should have. Besides, the friend who confers the benefit is never able to make it all that the recipient would like.

In the same way as justice is divided into written and unwritten, so utilitarian friendship seems to carry with it a *moral* or a *legal* obligation. The consequence is that, if complaints arise, it is mainly at a time when the relative position of the friends is not the same at the end of their association as it was when the association was formed. If it was formed on certain fixed or stated terms, it has a legal character, whether it is a business transaction involving the immediate exchange of a commodity or a more liberal arrangement extending the period of repayment, though with a clause specifying the terms of the repayment. In such an arrangement the obligation should be clearly stated and unambiguous, though there is an element of goodwill in postponing the date of repayment. This will explain why in some communities you cannot bring an action at law in such cases, the assumption being that, when people enter into an arrangement in which the good faith of the parties is involved, they must not complain if it is broken. As for the moral type of utilitarian friendship, it is not expressed in set terms. The gift, or whatever it is that passes between the friends, is given as to a friend. Still the giver expects to get back the equivalent or better, since it is implied that what he has given is not a free gift but a loan; and, if he finds himself in a different position at the end of their friendly relations than at the beginning, he will cherish a grievance. This sort of thing happens because most men if not all, though they would like to do the fine thing, actually choose what serves their interests. Now it is a fine thing to confer a benefit without looking for a *quid pro quo*, but the profitable thing is to be the beneficiary. So, if it is within one's power, one ought in repaying a kindness to give as good as one got, and to do so unasked. For the man who has to be pressed to return a kindness is not the man to make a friend of. If one has made such a friend, one should recognize that it was a mistake to begin with and that one has accepted favours where one ought not, namely, from a man who was not a friend and was not acting simply as such. One ought in such a case to treat the service done as a business transaction, and so bring the connexion to an end. One might also, if pressed on the subject, enter into an agreement to repay what one had received if and when one was in a position to do so. (If one were not, the presumption is that the giver could not on his side have expected repayment.) If possible, then, the service should be paid for. But one should be very careful at the outset as to who it is by whom the service is conferred and what are the terms of it, in order that one may either accept it on these terms or refuse to accept it at all.

But disputes may arise when an attempt is made to put a value on the services rendered. Is the standard to be the advantage accruing to the recipient or the sacrifice made by the benefactor? And in the former case is the repayment of the service to be made in accordance with this standard? The recipient seeks to depreciate the value of the service rendered, arguing that it cost the man who gave it nothing worth mentioning and could have been had from somebody else. The giver insists that on the contrary it strained his resources, that no one else could have given it, that it was given at a time of danger or on some such pressing occasion. Perhaps the best solution is to say that, where the friendship has been formed for its utility, the service should be measured by its value to the beneficiary. For the appeal for aid comes from him, and when the other supplies it, it is with the expectation of getting something of equal value in return. It is then the value of the service to the beneficiary that is the true measure of the assistance given; and the proper course for him is to give full value for the relief experienced, or even more, for that will be the finer gesture.

In true friendship between good men we do not hear complaints. In it the benefit is considered to be measured by the intention expressed in the deliberate action of the benefactor. For intention is the mainspring of character and moral excellence.

CHAPTER FOURTEEN

QUARRELS also spring up in friendships where there is inequality between the friends. Each regards himself as entitled to more than he has, and when you get a state of affairs like that, a rupture is inevitable. When one of the friends has a better moral character than the other he thinks that more is due to him on the principle that goodness should always have the preference. But then the more useful friend puts in a similar claim, arguing that one who has no useful contribution to make to the partnership is not entitled to an equal share in the profits; it is expecting a man to be a philanthropist, not a friend, if he is not to draw from the friendship any advantage at all proportionate to the efforts he has made to make it a success. Such a man takes the view that a friendship ought to be like a partnership in business, where the partner who contributes the largest amount of capital pockets the lion's share of the profits. On the other hand the man who is short of capital, and the less virtuous of the friends, argue in just the opposite sense. 'What is the good,' they say, 'of being friends with the virtuous and the influential, if there is to be nothing in it for us?'

Well, it would appear that there is something in the claims of both one side and the other, and each should receive a larger share from the friendship. But not a larger share of the same thing. The morally superior friend should get the larger share of honour, and the hard-up friend the larger share of the cash. For honour is the meed of goodness and beneficence, while penury can only be relieved by making some money. A good illustration of this may be taken from public life. The citizen who contributes nothing of value to the community finds no honour in it. It is the man who benefits the community who receives what it has to give, namely, honour. You cannot make money out of the public and be honoured at the same time. And that the public benefactor should be honoured is only fair; for nobody will stand being fobbed off with the smaller share in everything. Accordingly when a man suffers in pocket as a result of holding some public office he is repaid in honour; it is the corrupt official who gets paid in cash. This then is the method which should be put into operation in a friendship between unequal parties. The party who gets financial or moral aid should give in return what he can, and that is honour. For friendship asks for no more than the possible; it does not insist on full value. That is not always possible. For instance, we cannot sufficiently honour the gods or our parents. No one could ever pay them the honour they deserve, but a man earns a good report if he serves them to the best of his ability. From this we may infer that it cannot be right for a son to disown his father, though a father may disown his son. For a debtor ought to pay his debts, and nothing that a son may do can pay for the blessings he has received, so that he is permanently in his father's debt. On the other hand a father may dissolve the legal connexion with his son for the same reason as leads a creditor to discharge his debtor. Yet the probability is remote that a father would break off all relations with a son who was not vicious in the extreme. For, setting aside natural affection, a father would not be human who spurned the assistance of his own son. But a bad son will look on the duty of supporting his parent as something to be evaded or at best grudgingly undertaken. For the world prefers receiving benefits to bestowing them. That, it avoids as a thing unprofitable. . . .

BOOK NINE

Aristotle proceeds to discuss friendship between people whose qualifications for it, and consequently whose contributions to it, are different. He begins by considering certain initial problems, of which the first is this. When a service done by one of the friends has to be repaid by the other, how is the amount of the repayment to be assessed? And he answers that the criterion should be the value of the service in the estimate of the recipient.

CHAPTER ONE

In all dissimilar friendships (i.e. where the parties have different qualities) it is, as has been said, a ratio or proportion that restores equality and preserves the friendship. We find an illustration of this in the relations between citizen and citizen. The shoemaker in return for his shoes gets their value in another medium. So does the weaver and so do other craftsmen. In the exchanges, however, men have invented a common measure in the shape of money, to which everything is referred and which serves as a measure of their mutual services. But a common measure is not everywhere applicable; it cannot for instance be applied to the relations between lovers. There it sometimes happens that the lover complains that his devotion is unrequited. (It might be, of course, that there is nothing about him to attract love.) On the other hand the object of love frequently complains that he who promised everything now fulfils none of these promises. Such recriminations occur when the lover looks for pleasure and the beloved for gain, and neither now has the quality which is sought. When such motives inspire the friendship, it is sure to be broken up when the objects for which it was formed no longer exist. For neither loved the other for what he was in himself, but for something he happened to have. Since *this* was not permanent, the friendship was not permanent, and that will be found true of all friendships of that nature. But the friendship which is based upon goodness of character is permanent, because each friend is loved for himself. (See above.)

Quarrels break out when the friendships turn out differently from what the parties desire. Not to get what you have set your heart on is almost as bad as getting nothing at all. One is reminded of the story about the harper and his patron. The patron promised that the better the harper performed, the more he would pay him. Next morning, when the musician asked him to make good his promise, the patron replied that he had already paid for the pleasure he got by the pleasure of anticipation he had created in the breast of the harper. Now, if pleasure was what both desired, this might have proved not unsatisfactory. But if one of the two is out for pleasure and the other for gain, and the one has his wish and the other not, the partnership will not work out fairly. For it is what a man needs that he is interested in getting, and it is only to get that, that he is prepared to give what he has to give.

When terms have not been agreed on beforehand, which of the parties is the proper one to assess the amount to be repaid – the man who proposed or the man who accepted the service? Evidently the latter; for one would say that the person who proffers a service puts it in the power of the other to accept it or not. Protagoras, we are told, acted on this principle. When he lectured on a subject he used to ask the pupil to put his own value on what he had learned and accepted that as his fee. But in this matter some teachers prefer to be guided by Hesiod's rule:

> Even with a friend let his reward be fixed
> Beforehand, and thereafter paid in full.

But such as take their fees in advance, and then carry out none of their extravagant promises, naturally find themselves the target of complaints as not having done what they undertook to do. However, I suppose the Sophists are driven to adopt this course because nobody would give them money for their knowledge after finding out what it amounted to. Anyhow, these persons, taking their fee and then doing nothing to earn it, inevitably meet with complaints.

When an agreed price for the service to be rendered has not been fixed in advance, the party who proposes to render it may be moved solely by regard for the friend to whom he makes the proposal. In that event, as I have said, no complaints will arise, for the friendship of the good for the good does not admit of these. The return made should be in proportion to the intention of the benefactor, for we judge a friend and even goodness itself by the intention in each case. This consideration no doubt should guide the conduct of those who are to pay a teacher who has imparted his knowledge of philosophy. His services cannot be measured in money, and honours here would not meet the case. But presumably it would be considered enough if he, like the gods and like parents, got such return as the indebted party has it in his power to make. On the other hand the motive of the giver may not have this disinterested character. In that event no doubt the best course is to make a return representing the value of the service as agreed on by both parties. Failing such an agreement, it will appear both necessary and just that the assessment of value should be made by the party who had the benefit of the original offer. For when the man who made the offer has received in return the value of the service done him he will have recovered from the beneficiary what is truly owing him for service done. The practice of fixing the price at what the purchaser is willing to pay is that which is followed in the open market. In some communities there exists no legal procedure under which an action for breach of a voluntary covenant can be brought, the law taking the view that when you have trusted a man you must carry the transaction through on that basis. For it is thought fairer that the man who was trusted should fix the value of the commodity rather than the man who gave the credit. For in general the owner of a commodity puts a higher price on it than the man who wants it, since everybody sets a high value on his own property and his own gifts.* But of course the recipient ought to value what he has received not at the price which seems fair to him *after* he has received it, but at what he thought it worth before he got it.

Next comes the problem of assessing the claims of different friends. In the case of relations none has an absolute claim to preference. Each claim has its place in the scale of values.

CHAPTER TWO

THE matter we are discussing involves a number of questions such as these. (*a*) Is there any limit to the respect and obedience due from a son to his father? (*b*) When one is ill, ought one to put oneself entirely in the hands of a doctor? (*c*) In electing a general at Athens ought one to vote for a candidate who is more of a soldier than a politician? (*d*) In doing a service ought one to render it to a friend rather than a man of high character? (*e*) Ought one to repay a benefactor for his kindness rather than launch out on a present for a comrade – supposing, that is to say, that one is not in a position to do both?

Naturally it is not easy to lay down exact rules in all these contingencies. For the contingencies themselves vary indefinitely in importance, ethical quality and urgency. It is clear, however, that no one is entitled, he only, to unlimited deference. And as a general rule one ought to pay for benefits received rather than make free gifts to comrades, just as one ought to repay a loan rather than present the money to a friend. Yet of course we must allow for exceptions. Suppose I am kidnapped and subsequently ransomed; next suppose my ransomer is kidnapped. Am I to ransom him in turn, whoever he may be, from the brigands, or my own kidnapped father? Why, even if my ransomer has not been captured but is merely asking back the money he paid for my ransom, am I to pay *him* instead? It might be thought a

* The payment, however, is made to the amount fixed by the recipient.

man's duty to ransom his father rather than himself. Well, as I said, the general rule must be – repay the debt. But if there is a special degree of honour or urgency in making a gift of the money, then let the balance turn in favour of the gift. For now and again justice is actually not served by returning the original obligation, as for instance when A has done B a service knowing him to be a good man, and then B is faced with the demand to repay the service to A, who, he is convinced, is a bad character. Even if it is a loan that is in question, there may be circumstances in which it would be wrong for the borrower to make a loan in turn to the lender. When A lent the money to B it was to an honest man from whom he felt sure that he would recover it. But B has no assurance that *he* will get his money back from A, who is a rogue. Now if this is the truth about A, it is not playing the game for him to ask B to lend him money in turn. Even if it is not the truth, but people believe it, they would not think it strange on B's part to refuse the request.

As I have so often insisted, discussions of feelings and actions admit of no more definiteness than belongs to the matter under discussion.

It seems pretty clear then that everybody has not the same claim upon us and that there is some limit to what even a father may expect from his son.* Therefore since parents, brothers, comrades, benefactors all have different claims upon us, we must render to each his special and appropriate service. And this in fact is what people do. If it is a marriage they have on hand, they invite their relations, for family affairs interest them as members of the family, while there is felt to be a particularly strong reason for relations to turn up at funerals. Public opinion would no doubt favour the view that parents have the first claim on their children for maintenance as something due to them; it may even be regarded as a finer thing for a man to support the parent-stock of his being than to supply his own vital needs. As we honour the gods, so ought we also to honour our parents. Yet not in every way. Even a father should not be honoured in the

* So Zeus, the father of the gods, does not receive *all* the sacrifices.

same way as a mother, nor as a philosopher is honoured or a military chief, but in the way proper to a father; and similarly a mother should be honoured in the way that is proper in a mother's case. Younger men should pay their elders the honour to which their age entitles them by rising at their approach and giving up their seats to them, and similar courtesies. On the other hand, in our dealings with brothers and intimate friends what is needed is the readiness to say whatever we think and share whatever we have. As for kinsmen, fellow 'tribesmen', fellow citizens and the like, our constant endeavour should be to give them all their due. This means comparing the fair claims of each group on the basis of their degree in kinship and their virtue or usefulness. Now it is comparatively easy to make out the necessary distinctions when we are dealing with people of the same description. But when they are not of the same kind it is a more troublesome business. For all that we must not shirk it but must discriminate between their claims as well as we can.

The kind of friendship that may be justifiably broken off.

CHAPTER THREE

ANOTHER problem for the casuist is whether or not a friendship should be broken off when the friends are no longer what they originally were to one another. If the friendship was formed for the sake of the usefulness or pleasure it promised, it seems arguable that there is nothing to excite surprise in breaking off the connexion when these inducements no longer exist. For it was these that formed the attraction and, when they have been exhausted, one must expect the friendship to die. Yet a man would have some ground for complaint if his friend had been pretending to love him for his character when all the time he was loving him only for the profit or pleasure he got out of him. For, as I said in my introductory remarks on the subject, when friends quarrel it is generally when the character of their friendship is not what they assume it to be. Therefore when a man has fallen into the mistake of thinking that his friend loves him for his character when he does nothing of the sort, he has only himself to blame. On the other hand, if he has been deceived by the false pretences of the other, he is justified in blaming his deceiver, who is actually worse than a coiner in proportion as what he falsifies is intrinsically more precious than coins.

Suppose another case. I have made a friend of a man in the belief that he is a person of good character, and he turns out – or one gets that impression – to be a scoundrel. Am I to go on treating him as a friend? Surely that is out of the question, if it be true that we cannot love everything but only what is good. Is it not even wrong? For surely we must not be lovers of what is evil, or let ourselves become like that, but remember what was said before, that like makes friends with like. Should we then, in such a case as I have imagined, break off the friendship on the spot? Not, I suggest, invariably but only when the friend is incurably bad. So long as he is capable of redemption our duty is to give him our support. That duty is all the more imperative because the support is moral and not financial, character being more precious than money and closer to friendship. Not that it would be thought strange if one broke off such a connexion, for the man I made my friend was not like that. It is he who has changed and, if I cannot save him, what can I do except let him go?

But now suppose one of two friends has become neither better nor worse, but the other has advanced far beyond him in virtue. Should the more virtuous friend continue to cultivate the other? It may turn out to be impossible. This appears most clearly when the difference in merit has become pronounced, as may happen to boyhood friends. If one of them stays a boy in intelligence while the other becomes a man of eminent ability, how can they go on being friends with their now divergent tastes and different likes and dislikes? Spiritually and intellectually they will have nothing in common, and in these circumstances friendship, as we saw, becomes impossible; for friendship involves being together, and that is now impracticable. Is one then to behave towards an old friend exactly as if he had never been a friend at all? Surely one ought to remember the former intimacy and, just as we feel bound to show more favour to friends than to strangers, so we should for old acquaintance' sake keep in touch with former friends, provided that the reason for our severing relations was not an exceptional degree of wickedness on their part.

Aristotle takes up again the question of how friendship is to be distinguished from other, kindred feelings. It would seem that the distinguishing marks of friendship are best explained if we consider a friend as an alter ego.

CHAPTER FOUR

THE characteristic element in our friendship for our neighbours, and the points which distinguish and delimit the various forms of friendship, seem to have their origin in the sympathetic feelings with which we regard ourselves. The definition of a friend is (*a*) one who desires and performs the good, or what appears to him to be the good, of another for the sake of that other. Or we may define a friend as (*b*) one who desires the existence and preservation of his friend for the friend's sake.* Others describe a friend as (*c*) one who is inseparable from another or (*d*) has the same ideals; or (*e*) as one who shares the joys and sorrows of his friend.† Friendship (as well as a friend) is definable by one of these five marks. But each of them appears also in the feelings which a good man entertains towards himself.‡ For (*d*) there is no

* We have a parallel to this in the feeling of mothers towards their children, and of old friends who have fallen out but retain a kindness for one another.

† This trait is also specially characteristic of mothers.

‡ One might say, in the feelings of other men too, in so far as they suppose themselves to be virtuous. But, as I have said, we certainly must take true virtue and the truly good men as our standard in every case.

conflict between the mind of a good man and the rest of his nature, and he desires the same things with every part of it. Also (*a*) he wishes whatever things are good for him – both what are really and what are apparently good – and seeks to realize them in his actions, the good man showing his character in this, that he labours to establish the good. And this he does for his own sake, that is, for the intellectual part of his being, which *is*, we believe, the essential man. Again (*b*) he desires his own life and safety, more especially that of the rational part of his soul. For existence is good in the eyes of the good man, and everyone desires his own good. No man would deliberately choose to have all the blessings in the world for his own at the price of becoming somebody else. (In fact, as things are, the good belongs to God alone.) It is always his wish to be the man he is, whatever he may be. And we must believe that the thinking part of a man is the man himself almost or altogether. Again, (*c*) the good man is glad to hold converse with himself, for he has pleasant memories of the past and fair hopes for the future, on which he can dwell with satisfaction; nor has he any lack of topics upon which to exercise the speculative powers of his mind. Lastly, (*e*) he has a complete and undivided consciousness of his joys and sorrows. For it is always the same things that please or vex him, and not one thing at one time and another at another – hardly ever does he change his mind. It is then because the good man has these distinguishable feelings towards himself, and because he feels towards his friend as he feels towards himself – for a friend is a second self – that friendship also can be regarded as an expression of one of these feelings, and friends as those who experience them.

The question may be raised whether it is possible for a man to feel friendship for himself; but it is best to dismiss it for the present. All that need be said here is that it is a possible view to hold that such a friendship may exist, if we think of a man as a dual or composite being. To which we may add that devoted attachment to someone else comes to resemble love for oneself.

We have been describing the feelings of the *good* man towards himself. But most people, though falling below his moral standard, appear to have them too. The probability is that men have their share of them just so far as they have the approval of themselves and take themselves to be virtuous. For completely debased and criminal types never have them or even the pretence of them. It is hardly too much to say that no worthless person has them. For people of that kind are divided against themselves; their desires do not coincide with their wishes. In this they resemble the incontinent, who choose harmful pleasures instead of what they themselves recognize as good. There are some again whose cowardice and laziness prevent them from doing what they believe is in their own best interests. Of these there is a third class – habitual and dangerous criminals, hated for their depravity, who actually seek to escape from life by committing suicide. Again, the bad crave for company and avoid their own society, because when they are by themselves they have many disagreeable recollections and expect to have more, whereas being with others gives them a chance to forget. Possessing no lovable quality, they have no love for themselves. Consequently such men have no sympathetic consciousness of their own joys and sorrows. For the soul of them is divided against itself. One part of it, being depraved, feels pain in denying itself certain things, while another part has a sense of gratification – one part pulling this way and the other that – and they are like to be torn in pieces. If it is impossible to feel pain and pleasure at the same time, at any rate a feeling of pleasure is followed after a little by a sense of remorse in a man of this type, who can only wish that he had never indulged in such gratifications. For a bad man is always full of regrets. From this we may see that a bad man is never on good terms with himself, because he is devoid of any lovable quality. If then a state of mind like this is wretched to a degree, one ought to strain every nerve to avoid wickedness and attain to virtue. Only then will one be at peace with oneself and become dear to another.

Next comes an account of Eunoia, *'well-wishing' or 'goodwill'.*

CHAPTER FIVE

EUNOIA or goodwill bears some resemblance to friendship, but is not in fact friendship, for we may feel goodwill towards strangers and persons who are not aware of our feeling – a thing impossible between friends. We remarked that at an early stage of this discussion.

Nor is goodwill the same as love or liking. For it is without intensity and excludes desire, and you never have love without these. Besides, some intimacy is necessary for affection, whereas goodwill may be the birth of a moment. At any athletic contest, for instance, the spectators feel well disposed and sympathetic towards the competitors. This sympathy, however, is not translated into action. The goodwill is, as we said, the birth of a moment, the kindly feeling superficial. Goodwill then is not friendship. But it is the beginning of friendship, as the pleasure one derives from looking at a person is the beginning of a lover's passion. Nobody falls in love who has not been first delighted by the sight of beauty, although it does not follow that a man who is delighted by the beauty of a person is in love. It is love when one longs for the absent dear one and desires his presence. Similarly men cannot be friends unless they have come to cherish a kindness for one another, although they may have that feeling without becoming friends. All they wish is the good of those for whom they have a kindness; they would not actively help them to attain it, nor would they put themselves about for their sake. We might then by a new application of the word 'friendship' define goodwill as inactive or potential friendship, which, when the lapse of time has ripened it into intimacy, becomes actual friendship. It is to be distinguished from the friendship based on utility or pleasure, which can never produce goodwill. True, goodwill towards his benefactor is felt by anyone who has received a benefit; and this is only proper. But if a man's motive for doing somebody else a service is merely the hope that he will make a good thing out of it, one can hardly say that he has a kindness for the man he is serving so much as a kindness for himself. I might as well say that a man is my friend whose attentions have an interested motive. It is a fair generalization that goodwill is created by some fine quality in the person towards whom it is felt. It stirs in a man when some other person seems to him beautiful or brave or the like, as may happen – to use my former illustration – when we watch the competitors in some manly contest.

We have next to consider Homonoia, *'unanimity' or 'concord'.*

CHAPTER SIX

EVIDENTLY akin to friendship is another feeling – unanimity or concord. This makes it something more than agreement in opinion, for that might be found in people who do not know one another. Neither do we call it concord when people agree in theory about a speculative matter, such as the constitution and behaviour of the heavenly bodies; you may agree with a man in his astronomy without feeling that you would like to be a friend of his. But we say there is concord in a state when the citizens agree about their interests, adopt a policy unanimously and proceed to carry it out. This implies that we have concord only where a practical end is in view – an important end capable of attainment by the interested parties, whether these be the entire population or only two persons. For example, there is concord in a state when the citizens pass a decree that all the public posts shall be elective, or that an alliance be formed with the Spartans, or that Pittacus shall be sole head of the government.* But when there are two candidates for power, like Eteocles and Polynices in the *Phoenician Women* of Euripides, then there is discord or civil strife. For it is not concord when

* This would have to be at a time when Pittacus himself was willing to accept such a position.

two people have the same idea, no matter what. They must have it in connexion with the same person, as when 'the lower orders' and their 'betters' share the idea that government should be in the hands of 'the best'. Then all concerned get what they want. From this it appears that concord is, what it is generally said to be, friendship between the citizens of a state, its province being the interests and concerns of life.

Now this conception of concord is realized among good men, for such are in harmony both with themselves and with one another, having pretty much the same ground to stand upon. For the wishes of good men have a permanent character, and do not ebb and flow like the tides; moreover, they are directed to what is both just and expedient, and it is ends of that nature which they are at one in seeking. But bad men are incapable of achieving more than a trifling degree of concord as of friendship, since they invariably want more than their share in such advantages as may be going, while at the same time they shirk as much as they can of the trouble and expense of public service. And, while each hopes to secure these advantages for himself, he keeps a critical eye on his neighbour to prevent *him* from gaining them. And in fact, unless they do watch one another, the public interest is sacrificed. The result is discord, everybody trying to make everybody else do his duty, but not doing it himself.

Why is it that the recipient of a benefit is not so fond of his benefactor as the benefactor is of him?

CHAPTER SEVEN

I t is commonly believed that a benefactor has friendlier feelings towards the recipient of his kindness than the recipient has for his benefactor, and the apparent paradox invites discussion. It is generally thought that the explanation is to be sought in the fact that the parties are related to one another as creditor to debtor. When a man has borrowed money he would be glad to see the last of the man from whom he borrowed it, whereas the lender is genuinely anxious that nothing should happen to the borrower. In the same way a benefactor wants the man he has obliged to go on living, so that he may get something from him in return as a proof of his gratitude. Paying back, however, is what the beneficiary hates to think about. Epicharmus would probably say that those who maintain this opinion 'take a poor view' of human nature. But I am afraid human nature does incline that way – most of us have short memories and are more anxious to get than to give a benefit. Yet it is arguable that the true reason has a deeper cause, and that the relation of borrower and lender is not a fair parallel. It is not real affection that the creditor feels; he wants his debtor to go on living merely because he wants his money back. The benefactor on the other hand has a sincere kindness and affection for the man he has assisted, even if he gets no immediate, nor any probable future, good out of him. This is equally true of the artist or craftsman. Every artist loves his work better that he would be loved by it, were it to be endowed with life. I think we may say this is particularly true of poets, who dote on their own verses with a mother's love. It is much the same with the benefactor. The object of his benevolence has come to be its object as a result of his own efforts; and so he loves him more than that which is made can love its maker. The reason is that everything desires and loves just *to be*. Now we realize our being in action (for we exist by living and acting), and the man who has made something may be said to exist in a manner through his activity. So he loves his handiwork because he loves existence. It is part of the nature of things. What is potential becomes actual in the work which gives it expression.

But another factor comes in. The man who has helped another may be considered to have done a fine thing. The consciousness that this is so has the effect of making him pleased with the person he has helped, but the latter cannot feel that there is anything noble in *his* relation to his benefactor. At most it is profitable, and what is profitable is contemplated with less pleasure and affection than what is noble. So for the doer of the good deed the deed abides – for what is noble does not pass away quickly – but the usefulness for the beneficiary is transient. Now there are three things that give pleasure: the activity which achieves fulfilment in the present, the hope that looks to the future, the memory that looks back to the past; and of these the sweetest and most dearly loved is the realized moment. As for memory, if it be of beautiful and noble things it is indeed sweet; but if it be of things useful it is less sweet or hardly sweet at all. On the other hand it seems to be just the opposite with anticipation.

Again, loving may be viewed as an active, being loved as a passive, experience. It is therefore natural that affectionate and kindly feelings should exist in the more active of the two persons, that is, in the benefactor.

Then, again, all men have a special feeling for what they have won with toil and trouble. So those who have made money love it more than those who have inherited it. Now it will be agreed that there is no trouble involved in receiving some good thing, but bestowing it costs something of an effort.* It would seem then that this special feeling is another characteristic of benefactors.

How far, and with what justification, may a man love himself?

CHAPTER EIGHT

ANOTHER problem is whether one ought to love oneself or another most. The world blames those whose first thoughts are always for themselves and stigmatizes them as self-centred. It is also generally believed that a bad man does everything from a selfish motive, and does this the more, the worse he is.† On the other hand the good man is supposed

* That is why mothers are fonder than fathers of their children; it cost the mother more pains to bring them into the world.

† A bad man is often accused of 'doing nothing until he has to.'

never to act except on some lofty principle – the loftier the principle, the better the man – and to neglect his own interest in order to promote that of his friend. It is a view which is not borne out by the facts. Nor need this surprise us. It is common ground that a man should love his best friend most. But my best friend is the man who in wishing me well wishes it for my sake, whether this shall come to be known or not. Well, there is no one who fulfils this condition so well as I do in my behaviour towards myself; indeed it may be said of every quality which enters into the definition of a friend – I have it in a higher degree than any of my friends. For, as I have already observed, all the affectionate feelings of a man for others are an extension of his feelings for himself. You will find, too, that all the popular bywords agree on this point. ('Two bodies and one soul,' 'Amity is parity,' 'The knee is nearer than the shin.') All the proverbs show how close are the ties of friendship, and they all apply best to oneself. For a man is his own best friend. From this it follows that he ought to love himself best. – Which then of these two opinions ought we to accept in practice? It is a reasonable question, since there is a degree of plausibility in both.

No doubt the proper method of dealing with divergent opinions of this sort is to distinguish between them, and so reach a definite conclusion on the point of how far and in what way each of them is true. So the present difficulty may be cleared up if we can discover what meaning each side attaches to the word 'self-love'. Those who make it a term of reproach give the epithet of 'self-loving' to those who assign to themselves more than they are entitled to in money, public distinctions and bodily pleasures, these being what most men crave for and earnestly pursue as the greatest blessings, so that they contend fiercely for the possession of them. Well, the man who grasps at more than his fair share of these things is given to the gratification of his desires and his passions generally and the irrational part of his soul. Now most men are like that, and we see from this that the censorious use of the epithet 'self-loving' results from the fact that the self-love of most men is a bad thing. Applied to them, the censorious epithet is therefore justified. And unquestionably it is people who arrogate too much of such things to themselves who are called 'self-loving' by the ordinary man. For if anybody were to make it his constant business to take the lead himself over everyone else in the performance of just or temperate or any other kind whatever of virtuous actions, generally claiming the honourable role for himself, nobody would stigmatize *him* as 'a self-lover'. Yet the view might be taken that such a man was exceptionally self-loving. At any rate he arrogates to himself the things of greatest moral beauty and excellence, and what he gratifies and obeys throughout is the magistral part of himself, his higher intelligence. Now just as in a state or any other composite body it is the magistral or dominant part of it that is considered more particularly to *be* the state or body, so with a man; his intelligence, the governing part of him, *is* the man. Therefore he who loves and indulges this part is to the fullest extent a lover of himself. Further, we may note that the terms 'continent' and 'incontinent' imply that the intellect is or is not in control, which involves the assumption that the intellect is the man. Again, it is our reasoned acts that are held to be more especially those which we have performed ourselves and by our own volition. All which goes to show that a man is, or is chiefly, the ruling part of himself, and that a good man loves it beyond any other part of his nature. It follows that such a man will be self-loving in a different sense from that attached to the word when it is used as a term of reproach. From the vulgar self-lover he differs as far as the life of reason from the life of passion, and as far as a noble purpose differs from mere grasping at whatever presents itself as an expedient. Hence those who are exceptionally devoted to the performance of fine and noble actions receive the approval and commendation of all. And if everyone sought to outdo his neighbour in elevation of character, and laboured strenuously to perform the noblest actions, the common weal would find its complete actualization and the private citizen would realize for himself the greatest of goods, which is virtue.

Therefore it is right for the *good* man to be self-loving, because he will thereby himself be benefited by performing fine actions; and by the same process he will be helpful to others. The bad man on the other hand should not be a self-lover, because he will only be injuring himself and his neighbours by his subservience to base passions. As a result of this subservience what he does is in conflict with what he ought to do, whereas the good man does what he ought to do. For intelligence never fails to choose the course that is best for itself, and the good man obeys his intelligence.

But there is something else which we can truly say about the good man. Many of his actions are performed to serve his friends or his country, even if this should involve dying for them. For he is ready to sacrifice wealth, honours, all the prizes of life in his eagerness to play a noble part. He would prefer one crowded hour of glorious life to a protracted period of quiet existence and mild enjoyment spent as an ordinary man would spend it – one great and dazzling achievement to many small successes. And surely this may be said of those who lay down their lives for others; they choose for themselves a crown of glory. It is also a characteristic trait of the good man that he is prepared to lose money on condition that his friends get more. The friend gets the cash, and he gets the credit, so that he is assigning the greater good to himself. His conduct is not different when it comes to public honours and offices. All these he will freely give up to his friend, because that is the fine and praiseworthy thing for him to do. It is natural then that people should think him virtuous, when he prefers honour to everything else. He may even create opportunities for his friend to do a fine action which he might have done himself, and this may be the nobler course for him to take. Thus in the whole field of admirable conduct we see the good man taking the larger share of moral dignity. In this sense then it is, as I said before, right that he should be self-loving. But in the vulgar sense no one should be so.

It has been questioned whether the possession of friends is necessary to happiness. Aristotle has no doubt that it is so, and gives his reasons.

CHAPTER NINE

ANOTHER debatable point concerning the happy man is this. Will friends be necessary to his happiness or not? It is commonly said that the happy, being sufficient to themselves, have no need of friends. All the blessings of life are theirs already; so, having all resources within themselves, they are not in need of anything else, whereas a friend, being an *alter ego*, is only there to supply what one cannot supply for oneself. Hence that line in the *Orestes* of Euripides:

When Fortune smiles on us, what need of friends?

Yet it seems a strange thing that in the process of attributing every blessing to the happy man we should not assign him friends, who are thought to be the greatest of all external advantages. Besides, if it is more like a friend to confer than to receive benefits, and doing good to others is an activity which especially belongs to virtue and the virtuous man, and if it is better to do a kindness to a friend than to a stranger, the good man will have need of friends as objects of his active benevolence. Hence a second question. Does one need friends more in prosperity than in adversity? There is a case for either of these alternatives. The unfortunate need people who will be kind to them; the prosperous need people to be kind to.

Surely also there is something strange in representing the man of perfect blessedness as a solitary or a recluse. Nobody would deliberately choose to have all the good things in the world, if there was a condition that he was to have them all by himself. Man is a social animal, and the need for company is in his blood. Therefore the happy man must have company, for he has everything that is naturally good, and it will not be denied that it is better to associate with friends than with strangers, with men of virtue than with the ordinary run of persons. We conclude then that the happy man needs friends. What then is the meaning of those who uphold the other view? What truth is there in their arguments? The answer may be this. Most people look upon their friends as assets. Well, the ideally happy man will not lack friends of that sort, for he possesses every advantage already. Neither will he feel the need of friends chosen for their agreeable qualities, or, if he does, it will only be for a short time now and again, for the life of the happy man is pleasant in itself and has no need of an imported pleasure. So, as he does not feel the need of useful or pleasant friends, he is supposed not to need any at all. This inference can hardly be sound. As I said at the outset, happiness is an *activity*. Now an activity is demonstrably something that is in course of doing, not something that has already come into existence as a material object. Suppose then that the following statements are true, as they evidently are. (*a*) Happiness consists in living and acting. (*b*) The activity of a good man * is good and, being good, intrinsically pleasant. (*c*) The consciousness that a thing is one's own is pleasant. (*d*) We are better able to study our neighbours than ourselves, and their actions than our own. (*e*) Good men derive pleasure from the actions of other good men their friends, inasmuch as such actions possess the quality of being good and the quality of being their own or as good as their own, both naturally pleasant qualities. If these five propositions are true, it follows that the perfectly happy man will have need of virtuous friends. For he elects to give his mind to the contemplation of actions that are good and his own, and the actions of a good man who is his friend may be so described. Besides, we all assume that the happy man ought to enjoy life. Now the solitary man has a hard time of it. It is not easy to keep up a continuous activity by oneself; in the company of others and in relation to others it is not so difficult. Consequently the activity of the good man, which is pleasurable in itself, will be less discontinuous if he has friends about him. And this will help him to enjoy without intermission that

* See above.

pleasurable feeling which should be part of the happy man's existence.* There is this too, that association with virtuous persons may form in a way a training in virtue. What does Theognis say?

> From good men goodness may be learned.

As we probe more deeply into the question we are led to think that a virtuous friend is in the nature of things desirable for a virtuous man. For that which is of its own nature good – I have remarked this before – is in itself good and pleasing to the good man. The life of the lower animals is defined as the capacity for sensation, of man as the capacity for sensation *plus* thought. But 'capacity' or 'potentiality' is a relative term, and a capacity finds its realization in an activity. It would seem then that to live in the proper sense of the word is to feel sensations or to think thoughts. Now life is good and pleasant in itself, for it is not a mere welter of sensations but a definite thing, and definiteness enters into the very nature of goodness. Now what is naturally good is good for the good man, and it is this that has made it pleasant in the eyes of all. We must not build our argument upon a vicious and debased life, or a life passed in pain, for such an existence is indefinite or chaotic, like the vice and pain that belong to it.† But now consider the following propositions. (*a*) Life as such is good and pleasant.‡ (*b*) A man who sees is aware that he is seeing, a man who hears that he is hearing, a man who walks that he is walking. So too in our other activities there is something in us that is conscious of them, so that if we perceive a thing we are conscious that we are perceiving it, and if we think we are aware that we are thinking. (*c*) To be conscious that we are per-

* Note that a good man, just because he is good, takes pleasure in virtuous actions and is disgusted with those which spring from wickedness in much the same way as a musician likes good music and is irritated by bad.

† The point about pain will be clarified in the sequel.

‡ This seems to be proved by the fact that all men desire it, and most of all the virtuous and perfectly happy. For their way of life is in the highest degree desirable and their existence the fullest felicity.

ceiving or thinking is to be conscious of our existence.* To be conscious that one is alive is pleasant in itself, life being of its very nature a good thing, and the consciousness of possessing a good thing being pleasant. (*e*) Life is desirable, especially for the good, because for them existence is good and therefore pleasant.† (*f*) The good man feels towards his friend as he feels towards himself, since his friend is a second self to him. – If we accept these propositions as true, our conclusion must be that, just as a man's own existence is desirable for that man, so to the same or nearly the same extent is the existence of his friend also desirable for him. But what makes existence desirable is the consciousness of goodness, and such a consciousness is pleasant in itself. So a man ought to have a sympathetic consciousness of his friend's existence, which may be attained by associating with him and conversing and exchanging ideas with him. For that is what is meant when human beings speak of 'living together' – it does not mean grazing together like a herd of cattle.

If then the entirely happy man finds existence desirable in itself as something essentially good and pleasant, and if the existence of his friend is only less desirable for him than his own, then a friend must be considered something to be desired by the happy man. But what is desirable for him he must have, if he is not to suffer some diminution of happiness in that particular. Therefore the man who is to be happy will have need of virtuous friends.

Should there be a limit to the number of one's friends? Aristotle thinks that some limitation is always necessary.

CHAPTER TEN

SHOULD we then make all the friends we can? Or, as Hesiod has put it – aptly most people think – when he is on

---

* We have already observed that existence is sense-perception or thought.

† Pleasant, because they take pleasure in the perception of what is essentially good.

the subject of hospitality:

> Neither keep board for many nor for none,

will it be perhaps the best policy in friendship also to avoid being friendless on the one hand and having a superfluity of friends on the other? It would undoubtedly be a suitable policy to follow in dealing with friends made on the score of their usefulness to us, for repaying the services of a large number of people is a whole-time job, for which life is too short. So more friends than we need to give our own lives sufficient scope are superfluous and a hindrance to living well. Nor do we need more than a handful of friends of the amusing sort; we don't want too much honey in our food. But there is a secondary question. Ought we to have all the *good* friends we can? Or is there a limit to the number of friends, as there is to the population of a city? Ten people would not make a city and a hundred thousand would exceed its natural proportions. Probably the ideal number cannot be precisely fixed but is anything between certain limits. So also the number of one's friends should be limited – I suggest the largest number with whom one can be intimate, since, as we saw, intimacy is the surest guarantee of friendship. But it is obvious that one cannot associate closely with a large body of people, dividing oneself among them. It is also requisite that one's friends be friendly with one another, if they are all to form as it were a happy family. But when the numbers are large such a result is not easily achieved. It is difficult also to sympathize sincerely with the joys and sorrows of more than a few, for it may easily happen that one is moved to rejoice with one and grieve with another simultaneously. It may be suggested then that it is as well not to aim at forming as wide a circle of friends as possible but to restrict oneself to a number sufficient for a group of people living on terms of intimacy with one another. It would seem in fact impossible to be the devoted friend of many for the same reason as makes it impossible to be in love with several persons. What we mean by love is affection for a friend carried beyond a certain point; and an emotion of that intensity is naturally concentrated on a single object. Even warm friendship can be felt only for a few. The truth of this seems to be proved by the experience of actual life. The number of those whose affection for each other amounts to comradeship is not large; the famous friendships of this kind are between one man and another – Pylades and Orestes, Achilles and Patroclus, and some others. The man with a host of friends who slaps on the back everybody he meets is regarded as the friend of nobody.* He is the ingratiating or obsequious type. Now it is possible to be friendly with many as one citizen with another without being obsequious. It is possible even for a man of the highest character to have many such friends. What is not possible is to have many friends whom we love for their own sake and for their goodness. Enough, if we have even a few of that quality.

To the question whether friends are more needed in prosperity or adversity Aristotle replies that they are needed in both.

CHAPTER ELEVEN

Do we need friends more in prosperity than in adversity? The question is pertinent, because we seek them in both. The unlucky are in need of help, the fortunate of companions and – since they wish to be bountiful – objects of their bounty. We may say then that friendship is more necessary in adversity – so it is useful friends who are needed in that condition – but it is more honourable in prosperity. So the prosperous seek not merely friends but virtuous friends, since one would prefer such to be kind to and associate with.

I should have said that the mere presence of friends is welcome in prosperity and adversity alike. Grief is lightened by the sympathy of friends, so that one may raise the question

---

* Unless we count his relations to his fellow citizens as a kind of *political* friendship.

whether they actually share the burden of grief or if it is just the solace of their company and the thought that they are sympathetic that mitigates the pain. Whether in fact it is that or something else that makes the sufferer feel better need not be discussed here. In any case the feeling I have mentioned appears to be a fact of experience. Yet the pleasure of having our friends come to see us is evidently not always unmixed. Just to set eyes on them is delightful, especially if one is suffering from some reverse of fortune, and it does to a certain extent help us to get over our sorrow. For a friend – a tactful friend – is a comfort both to see and to hear, knowing as he does one's character and one's likes and dislikes. On the other hand it is painful to observe the pain felt by one's friend at one's misfortunes, for everybody tries to avoid being the cause of pain to his friends. For this reason men of a masculine temper make a point of not involving their friends in their private troubles, and, unless he is quite case-hardened, a man hates the idea of giving them pain; and generally he will not let them lament with him, because he himself is not given to lamentation. But the weaker sex and womanish men are greatly pleased by those who mourn and sigh with them, and love them as true friends and sympathizers. However, it is our plain duty in all things to model our conduct on that of the nobler nature.

In prosperity on the other hand the society of friends makes our leisure moments pass delightfully, while we have the gratifying consciousness of their pleasure in whatever good befalls us. This might lead to the reflection that we ought to press our friends to share our good fortune – for beneficence is a fine impulse – but that we should be slow to ask them to share our misfortunes on the principle that we should keep to ourselves the largest portion of what might do them hurt.* If we are to call our friends to our aid, it should be above all when they will be of great service to us without much trouble to themselves. Conversely, it is surely fitting that we should visit a friend in misfortune readily and

* Hence the saying, 'Enough, if *I* suffer.'

without waiting to be invited.* But the case is altered when we visit those in prosperous circumstances. We should go readily when it is a matter of assisting them in some of their affairs. (Even they need friends for that.) But we should be chary of going if it is to give ourselves a good time, for there is something ignoble in an eagerness to profit by somebody's munificence. At the same time we should no doubt be on our guard against presenting the appearance of churlishness by saying no to every offer of help. It is a situation that does occasionally arise.

Our conclusion then is that the company of friends is desirable in all circumstances.

A little chapter on the value and influence of friendship.

CHAPTER TWELVE

WELL, then, are we to say that, just as lovers find their chief delight in gazing upon the beloved and prefer sight to all the other senses – for this is the seat and source of love – so friends find the society of one another that which they prefer to all things else? For in the first place friendship is a communion or partnership. Secondly, a man stands in the same relation to his friend as to himself. Now the consciousness which he has of his own existence is something that would be chosen as a good. So the consciousness of his friend's existence must be a good. This consciousness becomes active in the intercourse of the friends, which accordingly they instinctively desire. Thirdly, every man wishes to share with his friends that occupation, whatever it may be, which forms for him the essence and aim of his existence. So we find friends who drink together, and others who dice together, while yet others go in together for physical training, hunting or philosophy. Each set spend their time in one another's

---

* It is the part of a friend to do a service, particularly to those in need of it, even if they do not call on us to do it; service of that kind is more creditable to both parties and gives both of them more pleasure.

company following the pursuit which makes the great pleasure of their lives. As their wish is to be always with their friends, they do what these do and take part with them in these pursuits to the best of their ability. But this means that the friendship of the unworthy is evil, for they associate in unworthy pursuits; and so becoming more and more like each other they turn out badly. But the friendship of the good is good and increases in goodness in consequence of their association. They seem to become positively better men by putting their friendship into operation and correcting each other's faults. For each seeks to transfer to himself the traits he admires in the other. Hence the famous saying:

From noble men you may learn noble deeds ...

BOOK TEN

This book consists of two roughly equal parts, the first resuming the discussion of pleasure, the other summarizing Aristotle's teaching on the subject of Happiness. The first chapter considers the importance of the position which pleasure must hold in any theory of ethics.

CHAPTER ONE

OUR next task, I take it, is to discuss the nature of pleasure. There is general agreement that the love of pleasure is one of the great elementary instincts of human nature, so that pleasure and pain are the instruments used in the education of the young to keep them on a straight course. Also to like and dislike the right things seems to be of primary importance in the task of forming a virtuous character. For pleasure and pain continue to affect us through life and they exercise a decisive influence on our progress towards goodness and happiness for the simple reason that we choose what is pleasant and shun what causes us pain. So we can hardly omit all discussion of a subject so momentous, especially as there is nothing like unanimity on the questions involved.

One school maintains that pleasure is the supreme good, another on the contrary that it is wholly bad, some of its members very likely from a conviction that it is so, others believing that it is in the interests of morality to represent pleasure as a bad thing, even if it is nothing of the sort. They argue that most people have a leaning that way or even are enslaved to their pleasures, so that they have to be driven in the opposite direction, since only so will they reach the mean. But we may doubt if this is sound reasoning. When the question is one of the emotions and their translation into action, words are less convincing than deeds. So whenever our explanations are contradicted by the palpable facts they are laughed out of court, and the truth suffers in consequence. If a man who passes a general censure on pleasure is observed on occasion to desire it himself, this inconsistency is thought to betray a conviction of his that *all* pleasure is desirable, for the ordinary man is incapable of drawing distinctions. We see then that true theories are invaluable for the conduct of our lives as well as for the acquisition of knowledge. They accord with the facts and therefore carry conviction. So they encourage those who understand them to live in harmony with them.

So much by way of preface. Let us now pass in review the theories that have been propounded on the subject of pleasure.

The doctrine of Eudoxus that pleasure is the good. His arguments and their refutation.

CHAPTER TWO

I T was Eudoxus who held that pleasure is the supreme good. His reasons may be briefly stated. 'All creatures, endowed with reason or not, manifestly seek it. What is desirable is always good, and what is most desirable is best. Hence the fact that all creatures are attracted to the same point shows that the centre of attraction is the supreme good for all, since a particular thing finds its particular good in the same way as it finds the food particularly suited to it. Now that which is good for all and which all seek to have is the supreme good.' So far, however, as this line of reasoning had cogency it was less on its merits than from the high character of its author, who had the reputation of being a man exceptionally free from the vice of self-indulgence. So, since no one believed that he was pleading the cause of pleasure, it was widely accepted that what he had said must really be true.

Eudoxus was further of opinion that the goodness of pleasure was no less clearly demonstrated by consideration of its opposite. Pain is something which by its very nature disposes men to shun it. By parity of reasoning its opposite, pleasure, must be an essentially desirable thing. He held, too, that the most desirable thing is that which we choose for its own sake and not as a means to something else. Now pleasure is by common consent a thing of that sort; we never ask a man why he seeks pleasure, because we assume it to be desirable in itself. Another of his arguments went like this. The addition of pleasure to any good thing whatsoever has the effect of making that thing – justice, for example, or temperance in our conduct – more desirable; but only the good can make what is good more good. – Yet all this argument seems to prove is that pleasure is *a* good, not that it is better than something else. Of course every good thing is more desirable when another good is added to it than it is by itself. It is pretty much the argument which Plato uses to *refute* the view that pleasure is the supreme good. The life of pleasure, he argues, is more desirable with intelligence than without it. Now if pleasure *plus* something else is better than pleasure by itself, pleasure cannot be the supreme good. For the supreme good does not become more desirable by the addition to it of something else. It is evident also that nothing can, any more than pleasure, be the supreme good, if it is rendered more desirable by the addition of something intrinsically good. ...

On the other hand, the view now current in the Academy, that pleasure is not a good at all, is equally open to objection.

Those, however, who oppose Eudoxus by asserting the contrary proposition, that what all creatures desire to have is not good, are surely talking nonsense. What all men believe to be so, I say is so; the man who destroys this foundation for our belief is not very likely to say anything more convincing. If indeed it were only the irrational creatures that are eager for pleasure, there might be something in the paradox. But, seeing that intelligent beings behave in the same way, what meaning can we attach to it? It may be indeed that even the meaner animals have an instinct, overriding the faculties with which nature has endowed them, which seeks the good that is fittest for them. – Nor does the argument from the converse appear to be any sounder. Those who state it say, 'If pain is bad, it need not follow that pleasure is good. There can also be an opposition between two evils, or between an evil and something that is neither good nor evil.' That is true enough, but it has no bearing on the points we have stated. If both pleasure and pain are evils, both ought to be avoided. If they are neither the one nor the other, neither ought to be avoided or both should be avoided alike. As a matter of fact what we see is people avoiding pain as evil and choosing pleasure as good. Therefore it *is* as good and evil that they are opposed.

CHAPTER THREE

AGAIN, the fact that pleasure is not a quality does not prove that it is not a good. Virtuous activities and happiness are eminently good things; yet neither are qualities.

Another argument appears in Academic discourses to the effect that pleasure cannot be good because it admits of more and less – in other words is indefinite, while the good is definite. Now if they come to this conclusion as the result of observing that people who feel pleasure feel it in greater or less degree, the same argument will apply to justice and the other virtues. For those who pursue these virtues are distinctly spoken of as more or less virtuous.* But if they go by the pleasures themselves, it is to be feared that the ground for their argument is incorrectly stated. For if we accept their view that there are two kinds of pleasure, the pure and the mixed, it is only the mixed that they can regard as indefinite.

Then why should not pleasure be like health, which is a definite thing, yet for all that admits of degrees? The elements are not combined in the same proportion in everybody to produce health; they are not even always combined in the same proportion in the same person; and when it is

* A man may be more just or act more justly than another, or be more brave, or behave more soberly than another.

in process of being destroyed the proportion is still maintained for a time, involving a variation in degree. Why then should it not be the same with pleasure?

Another argument used in the Academy runs as follows. Postulating that the supreme good is perfect, and that a motion or a process whereby something comes into being is imperfect, they attempt to show that pleasure is a motion or process of this nature. It does not seem to be a good argument. Pleasure can hardly be a motion, for it is a recognized property of any motion to be quicker or slower, if not absolutely,* then relatively. But pleasure has no velocity whether absolute or relative. You can *become* pleased quickly, as you can fly into a passion quickly, but you cannot *be* pleased quickly, or quickly as compared with someone else, in the way you can walk or grow or do something like that faster than some other person. It is possible to pass into a pleasurable state of feeling quickly or slowly, but to exercise the pleasurable activity, in other words to be pleased, is a thing that cannot be experienced quickly. And – we may go on to ask – in what sense can pleasure be a process of becoming? Nobody supposes that any thing comes out of *anything*. What people do believe is that, when a thing is destroyed, it goes back into that which brought it into being. And – I am still quoting the Academy – when pleasure is the genesis of something, the destruction of that something is pain. They add that pain is a deficiency of our natural condition and pleasure its 'replenishing'. But it may be objected that these happen to our *bodies*. If pleasure is a replenishing of the natural state, it will be the thing that is replenished that will feel the pleasure. Therefore it is the body that feels pleasure. But that is not the general opinion. – Pleasure then is not a process of replenishment, though the man in whom the process is going on may feel pleasure, as he would feel pain when having a surgical operation performed upon him. It is not the *operation* that feels the pain. – This notion that pleasure is a natural replenishing was probably suggested by

* The motion of the universe, for instance, is absolute, for it cannot be compared with any other motion than its own.

the pains and pleasures connected with eating; when we have felt the distress occasioned by the sensation of emptiness, it does give us pleasure when this sensation is followed by replenishment. But not all the pleasures are like that. The pleasures of knowledge, for instance, have no preliminary pains; neither have some pleasures derived from the senses, such as those of smell, and many sounds and sights; to which we may add memories and hopes. If these are processes by which something is produced, what is it that is produced? No deficiency of anything has arisen to be replenished.

When people cite instances of scandalous pleasures to show that all pleasures are not good they may be answered in more ways than one. First, we may simply deny that these pleasures are pleasant. They may be pleasant to ill-conditioned persons, but that does not compel us to believe that they are pleasant in themselves or to anybody except these persons. We might as well believe that what is healthy or sweet or bitter to a sick man is really so, or that what looks white to a man who has something the matter with his eyes is really white. Then one might argue as follows. While the actual pleasures are desirable, their sources may render them undesirable. For instance, wealth is desirable, but not as the price of selling one's country. Health is desirable, but not if it involves indiscriminate eating. Thirdly, we may argue that the pleasures differ in kind. Those which come of some fine experience or exalted sentiment are different from those of a baser origin; it is impossible to taste the pleasures of a just man unless you are just, or the pleasures of a musician unless you are musical, and so in other cases that one might quote. Again, the possibility of distinguishing between a flatterer and a friend seems evidence that pleasure is not a good or else that pleasures differ in kind. For the object of a friend in his association with another is believed to be to do his companion good, the object of the flatterer to give him pleasure. The flatterer meets with reproach, but a friend is praised because as a companion he aims at other things than giving pleasure. Again, nobody would choose to pass through life with the mental outlook of a child, even if he continued to take unlimited pleasure in the things that children like. Nor would any one deliberately seek enjoyment in doing something very disgraceful, even if the consequences were never likely to be painful. Not to mention that there are many things which we should earnestly desire to have, even if they brought no pleasure in their train – things like sight, memory, knowledge, moral and intellectual excellence. Pleasure may be the inevitable concomitant of these things; but if so, it makes no difference. We should choose to have them even if no pleasure were got out of them.

It seems then to be proved that pleasure is not the supreme good, and that not every pleasure is to be desired; also that there do exist certain pleasures which are in themselves desirable, these being distinguishable from the baser pleasures by their specific qualities and the nature of their sources. ...

Aristotle passes to his own view of the nature of pleasure, and he begins by saying that it is neither a process nor the end of a process.

CHAPTER FOUR

PLEASURE, its nature and quality, may be set in a clearer light if we resume our discussion of it from the beginning.

Let us start with a parallel. Sight – the act of seeing – may be regarded as perfect at any moment of its duration; it does not need the addition of something which shall come into existence at a subsequent moment and bring its specific quality to its perfected state. Now pleasure also seems to have this character. For it is indivisible, and there is never a moment at which you can catch it and say, 'The specific quality of this pleasure will not be perfectly fulfilled unless it is prolonged for a certain time.' Consequently pleasure cannot be a form of motion or progression. For every motion or change takes time, and is a means to some end. Take the building of a house. It is perfect when it has completed what it set out to do. Thus a motion is regarded as perfect from two points of view, either (*a*) as lasting through the whole period of its duration, or (*b*) at the moment of reaching its end. The particular motions distributed over the time which it takes to complete the whole process are imperfect and are different in kind both from the whole and from one another. One may illustrate this from the building of a temple. The fitting together of the stones is a distinct process from the fluting of columns, and both are different from the construction of the temple as a whole. The last is a perfected process, nothing further being needed to produce the end proposed – the completed temple. But things like laying the foundations and framing the triglyphs are imperfect processes because they are restricted to a part of the whole. This means that they differ in kind from the process of constructing the whole temple; nor is it possible to surprise a specifically perfect motion at any *moment* within the whole process; one finds it only throughout the process. It is the same with walking and all the other modes of locomotion. We may assume that locomotion is a movement from one point to another, and it may take various forms – flying, walking, jumping, etc.* Thus the starting point and the goal of a racecourse are not the same as the terminal points of a section of the course, nor those of one section the same as those of another. If I draw a line to represent the racecourse and divide it into two sections, the passage of the racer along one section is not the same as his passage along the other. For he does not merely traverse a certain line but one that is in a certain place, and the line to which I point is in a different place from this other line to which I am *now* pointing. But a detailed treatment of motion will be found in my treatise on Physics. We may say, however, that motion is not perfect at any particular moment. The movements, the sum of which makes up the whole, are imperfect. They also differ in kind, because the starting-point and the end of a motion form a species of the genus formed by the movements. In contrast with this the specific quality of a pleasure is perfect at any

* Of course there may also be differences in walking itself.

moment. It is clear then that pleasure is not a motion; on the contrary it is something whole and perfect.

We may be led to the same conclusion if we consider that every motion takes time. This is a limitation which does not apply to pleasure; for a pleasant sensation is indivisible and can be felt only at the moment.

From these considerations another point emerges. It is incorrect to speak of pleasure as resulting from a motion or from a process giving rise to it. Such a description is not universally apt; it applies only to things which have parts and are divisible. A glance, a geometrical point, an arithmetical unit – such things are not brought into existence as the result of a process. Neither then is pleasure, for pleasure is an indivisible whole.

Pleasure accompanies and perfects the healthy exercise of our activities directed to good ends.

CHAPTER FIVE

EACH of the senses when it is functioning has an object, and it functions perfectly when it is in good condition and is directed to the finest thing which it is capable of perceiving.* It follows that the active exercise of a sense is at its best when the organ of that sense is (*a*) in the best possible condition, (*b*) directed to the best possible object perceptible by it. This activity will also be the most perfect and the most pleasurable. For there is a pleasure peculiar to each of the senses as there is to reflection and philosophic or scientific speculation. And the activity of the sense is most pleasurable when it is most perfect, and most perfect when the organ is in a sound condition and applied to the best of its objects; and the pleasure perfects the activity. It does not, however, perfect it in the same ways as the thing perceived and the perceiving faculty, when these are good, perfect it. Thus in

* That is about as good an account as we can get of the perfect functioning or activity of a sense, assuming that it makes no difference whether it is the sense itself or the organ of the sense that acts.

another sphere health and the doctor are both causes of our being healthy; but not in the same way.* The pleasure also perfects the activity, not as the disposition which issues in that activity perfects it by merely being present in the agent, but as a culminating perfection like the bloom which comes to those who are in the flower of youth. So long then as that which thinks and that which is thought, that which perceives and that which is perceived, are as they should be, there will be pleasure in the use of our minds and our senses. For here we have a subject and an object, the former acting on the latter, and so long as these continue in the same relation to themselves and to one another, the same result will naturally follow.

Pleasure wanes and waxes with the activity concerned.

How is it then that no one can feel pleasure continuously, so that the relation does not remain unchanged? The cause is probably fatigue. We cannot exercise our powers without some remission. It follows that pleasure also must have its breaks, since it is attendant upon the exercise of our faculties. For the same reason some things please us while they are novelties, but give us much less pleasure at a later stage. That is because at first the mind is stimulated and grapples energetically with the object presented to it, as happens in the case of sight when we fix our eyes on something. Afterwards the activity is less intense and slackens, and as a result the pleasure also grows faint.

* That each of the senses has its own pleasure is clear from the circumstance that we speak of sights and sounds as pleasant as well as things more obviously such. It is also clear that we feel the pleasure most keenly when the organ of the sense employed is both in the best condition and operating on the best object; and when both the object and the organ are good there will always be pleasure, when there is something to cause it and someone to feel it.

The desire for pleasure is vital.

The view may be held that all men seek pleasure because all desire life. Life is a form of activity, and when a man engages in an activity it is always in connexion with those objects and by means of those faculties which he likes best. Thus the musician exercises his sense of hearing on musical sounds, the student uses his brains upon the problems of science, and so on. The pleasure which supervenes upon these activities perfects them and so perfects life, which all men desire to have. It is understandable then that we seek pleasure, for it perfects life for each of us, and life is a desirable thing. But the question whether we desire life for the sake of pleasure or pleasure for the sake of life is one which must be dismissed for the moment. At least we may say that they appear to be bound together too intimately to admit of separation. There is no pleasure without some activity, and every activity is crowned with pleasure.

There follows an analysis of pleasure into its kinds, differences between which are caused by differences in the activities which give rise to the varieties of pleasure.

This leads to the opinion that pleasures differ specifically from one another. Things different in kind must, we surmise, end in different sorts of perfection. That they do end differently may be seen in the case of natural organisms, like animals or trees, and artistic creations, like a picture, a statue, a house, an article of furniture. In the same way we surmise that what perfects one kind of activity must differ in kind from what perfects another. Well, the intellect functions in a different way from the senses, and it follows from this that the pleasures which perfect the activities of intellect and sense are also different in kind.

But an even better illustration of this truth may be seen in the fact that activities are hindered by the pleasures derived from other activities. Thus amateurs of the flute are incapable of attending to a reasoned argument when they hear somebody playing the flute, because good flute-playing gives them more pleasure than the activity which is engaging their attention at the moment. The result is that the pleasure of the music paralyses their power of following the argument. The same thing happens when a man tries to do two things at once. The more agreeable activity jostles the other out of the way (all the more effectually if it is particularly agreeable), ending in the complete abeyance of the other. So if it gives us very great pleasure to be doing a particular thing, we are not much good for anything else. And when we find one occupation only faintly amusing, we start upon another. For instance, the people who munch *dragées* in the theatre munch hardest when the acting is poor.

Well, since our activities are accentuated and prolonged and improved by their own pleasures, and impaired by the pleasures of other activities, it is clear that pleasures differ widely among themselves. Indeed, alien pleasures produce pretty much the same effect on our activities as do the pains peculiar to these activities when these are bad. The pain resulting from an activity makes that activity impossible. Suppose you find writing or ciphering a great bore; you stop writing or doing sums because it is an activity which you find unpleasant. Activities, then, are affected in one way by their pleasures and in exactly the opposite way by their pains, where by 'their' pleasures and 'their' pains are meant those which attend the activities themselves and not their consequences. Alien pleasures, as I remarked, have much the same effect as pains; if they do not, like pain, destroy an activity, they come very near it.

Activities differ in their ethical quality and may be divided into those which are worth our pursuing, those which are to be avoided, and those which are neutral. The same division therefore is applicable to the pleasures, each activity having a pleasure of its own. Thus the pleasure peculiar to a virtuous activity is morally good, that peculiar to a vicious activity morally bad. Even desires for good things are praised, desires for base things censured, on moral grounds. But the pleasures felt in the exercise of our activities have a closer affinity with the activities than the desires which stimulate them to function. For the desire is both distinguishable in its nature from the activity and precedes it in time, whereas the pleasure is so closely attendant upon the activity, or rather so much a part of it, that it becomes a question whether they are not the same. Not that we can really suppose that pleasure, which is felt, is feeling or thinking – that would be absurd – but because they are inseparable they appear to some to be identical.

Activities being thus diverse, the pleasures attending them are also diverse. Sight is superior to touch, hearing and smell to taste, in purity. In this way then the pleasures may be distinguished. The pleasures of the intellect surpass in purity the pleasures of sense, while both sorts differ among themselves in this respect.

It is thought that every animal has a pleasure, as it has a function, of its own. It is the pleasure of exercising that function. The belief may be verified by observation of particular animals. Take a horse, a dog, a man – each has a pleasure peculiar to himself. Heraclitus says a donkey would rather have the sweepings of a granary than gold. He is right; a donkey prefers something to eat. Different species of animals have different species of pleasures. But do animals of the same species have different kinds of pleasure? One might expect the answer to be no. But in man at least there is no small variation in this respect. One man's meat is another man's poison. What is painful and shocking to some gives pleasure to, and arouses sympathy in, others. Even if we confine ourselves to sweet things, we encounter the same phenomenon. What tastes sweet to a fever patient tastes differently to a man in sound health. An invalid and a robust man never agree as to when it is warm. Examples might be multiplied.

It is only the good man's pleasures that are real and truly human.

But in all such cases we are guided by the belief that the truth is that which seems to the good man to be true. If this be a sound principle, as it surely is, and if goodness – that is, the good man in respect of his goodness – is the standard by which we measure the true value of everything, it follows that the true pleasures are what seem to him to be pleasures, and the really pleasant things those which he finds pleasant. And if some things displease him which produce an agreeable impression on others, there is nothing to surprise us in that. Humanity is subject to corruption and abnormality in many forms, and what seems pleasant to persons in such a condition is not really pleasant at all. Clearly then we are bound to affirm that the admittedly disgraceful pleasures are pleasures only to the depraved. But with regard to the reputable pleasures, what or what sort of pleasure should we affirm to be distinctively human? I suggest that the answer may be found after a review of the human activities. For these are attended by their own pleasures. That being so, we must affirm that it is that or those pleasure or pleasures which perfect the activity or activities of the perfect and perfectly happy man when they are human in the full meaning of the word. The others, like the activities which they crown, will be pleasures only in a secondary or greatly reduced way.

A recapitulation of what has been said of Happiness.

CHAPTER SIX

HAVING finished our discussion of the different forms of goodness, friendship and pleasure, it remains for us to produce a sketch of happiness; for happiness we regard as the end to be sought in human life. We may, however, shorten the discussion by recapitulating what was said before. We stated then that happiness is not a condition – not a state of mind or disposition of character. If it were, it might belong to a man whose whole existence was passed in sleep, while he lived the life of a vegetable, or to the victim of some appalling misfortune. So if we cannot accept this but feel that we must rather insist that happiness is some form of activity; * if, moreover, activities may be classified into those which are necessary to some end desirable for the sake of something beyond themselves, and those that are desirable in and for themselves, clearly happiness must be classed among activities desirable in themselves, and not among those desirable as a means to something else. For happiness is not in need of anything – it is self-sufficient. As for activities, they are desirable in themselves when all that is asked of them is their own exercise. Actions which are in conformity with goodness evidently have this character, for the performance of morally good and beautiful actions is desirable on its own account.

Reasons why we must not identify Happiness with Amusement or what we call 'enjoying ourselves'.

But amusements also are desirable on their own account. We do not go in for them for the sake of something else – in fact they tend to do us more harm than good by leading us to neglect our health and our finances. Yet such pleasures are the great resource of those whom the public regards as happy, and it explains why those who have a ready talent for these pastimes are popular in the most exalted circles. They make themselves agreeable by providing the sort of amusement that their patrons like, and so they are always in request. Hence these amusements are thought to be necessary to happiness, because the occupants of thrones devote their leisure to them. But what persons of that kind do proves little or nothing. Good morals and sound sense are not inevitable concomitants of power, and it is good morals and sound sense that prompt our best activities. If these per-

* See above.

sons, who have never tasted pure and liberal pleasure, have recourse to carnal delights, that is no reason why we should think them the most desirable. Children are sure that the things they prize most highly are the best, and so it is natural that, as children and adults have different notions of what is valuable, so should good men and bad. To repeat what I have said more than once, it is the things that are valuable and pleasant in the eyes of the good man that are really such. Everyone considers the activity most natural to his own disposition to be the most desirable. So the good man considers activity in the way of goodness to be most desirable. It is not in amusements that happiness is to be found. Certainly it would be strange if the end of life were amusement, and we are to labour and endure hardness all our days merely for the fun of it. Almost every objective we choose is chosen for an ulterior purpose. But not happiness; happiness is an end in itself. To make a serious business of amusement and spend laborious days upon it is the height of folly and childishness. The maxim of Anacharsis, *Play so that you may be serious*, may be taken as pointing in the right direction. For amusement is a form of rest or relaxation, and rest we need because we cannot always be working. Rest then is not an end but a means to future activity. Also we believe that it is the life lived in accordance with goodness that is the happy life; and such cannot be divorced from seriousness or spent in amusing oneself. We maintain, too, that serious things are intrinsically better than funny or amusing things, and that the activity of a man, or of some organ or faculty of his, is more serious in proportion as it possesses a higher excellence. Such an activity then is itself superior and therefore more conducive to happiness. We may add another argument. Anybody can enjoy fleshly pleasures – a slave no less than a Socrates. But nobody is prepared to give a slave a life of his own; that is, nobody is prepared to give him a measure of happiness. So – once more – happiness does not consist in pastimes and amusements but in virtuous activities.

In the two following chapters Aristotle gives reasons for thinking that Happiness in its highest and best manifestation is found in cultivating the 'contemplative' life.

CHAPTER SEVEN

BUT if happiness is an activity in accordance with virtue, it is reasonable to assume that it will be in accordance with the highest virtue; and this can only be the virtue of the best part of us. Whether this be the intellect or something else – whatever it is that is held to have a natural right to govern and guide us, and to have an insight into what is noble and divine, either as being itself also divine or more divine than any other part of us – it is the activity of this part in accordance with the virtue proper to it that will be perfect happiness. Now we have seen already that this activity has a speculative or contemplative character. This is a conclusion which may be accepted as in harmony with our earlier arguments and with the truth. For 'contemplation' is the highest form of activity, since the intellect is the highest thing in us and the objects which come within its range are the highest that can be known. But it is also the most continuous activity, for we can think about intellectual problems more continuously than we can keep up any sort of physical action. Again, we feel sure that a modicum of pleasure must be one of the ingredients of happiness. Now it is admitted that activity along the lines of 'wisdom' is the pleasantest of all the good activities. At all events it is thought that philosophy ('the pursuit of wisdom') has pleasures marvellous in purity and duration, and it stands to reason that those who have knowledge pass their time more pleasantly than those who are engaged in its pursuit. Again, self-sufficiency will be found to belong in an exceptional degree to the exercise of the speculative intellect. The wise man, as much as the just man and everyone else, must have the necessaries of life. But, given an adequate supply of these, the just man also needs people with and towards whom he can put his justice into operation; and we can use similar language about the temperate man, the brave man, and so on. But the wise man can do more. He can speculate all by himself, and the wiser he is the better he can do it. Doubtless it helps to have fellow-workers, but for all that he is the most self-sufficing of men. Finally it may well be thought that the activity of contemplation is the only one that is praised on its own account, because nothing comes of it beyond the act of contemplation, whereas from practical activities we count on gaining something more or less over and above the mere action. Again, it is commonly believed that, to have happiness, one must have leisure; we occupy ourselves in order that we may have leisure, just as we make war for the sake of peace. Now the practical virtues find opportunity for their exercise in politics and in war, but these are occupations which are supposed to leave no room for leisure. Certainly it is true of the trade of war, for no one deliberately chooses to make war for the sake of making it or tries to bring about a war. A man would be regarded as a bloodthirsty monster if he were to make war on a friendly state just to produce battles and slaughter. The business of the politician also makes leisure impossible. Besides the activity itself, politics aims at securing positions of power and honour or the happiness of the politician himself or his fellow-citizens – a happiness obviously distinct from that which we are seeking.

We are now in a position to suggest the truth of the following statements. (a) Political and military activities, while pre-eminent among good activities in beauty and grandeur, are incompatible with leisure, and are not chosen for their own sake but with a view to some remoter end, whereas the activity of the intellect is felt to excel in the serious use of leisure, taking as it does the form of contemplation, and not to aim at any end beyond itself, and to own a pleasure peculiar to itself, thereby enhancing its activity. (b) In this activity we easily recognize self-sufficiency, the possibility of leisure and such freedom from fatigue as is humanly possible, together with all the other blessings of pure happiness. Now if these statements are received as true, it will follow that it is this intellectual activity which forms perfect happiness for a man – provided of course that it ensures a complete span of life, for nothing incomplete can be an element in happiness.

Yes, but such a life will be too high for *human* attainment. It will not be lived by us in our merely human capacity but in virtue of something divine within us, and so far as this divine particle is superior to man's composite nature, to that extent will its activity be superior to that of the other forms of excellence. If the intellect is divine compared with man, the life of the intellect must be divine compared with the life of a human creature. And we ought not to listen to those who counsel us *O man, think as man should* and *O mortal, remember your mortality*. Rather ought we, so far as in us lies, to put on immortality and to leave nothing unattempted in the effort to live in conformity with the highest thing within us. Small in bulk it may be, yet in power and preciousness it transcends all the rest. We may in fact believe that this is the true self of the individual, being the sovran and better part of him. It would be strange, then, if a man should choose to live not his own life but another's. Moreover, the rule, as I stated it a little before, will apply here – the rule that what is best and pleasantest for each creature is that which intimately belongs to it. Applying it, we shall conclude that the life of the intellect is the best and pleasantest for man, because the intellect more than anything else *is* the man. Thus it will be the happiest life as well.

CHAPTER EIGHT

THE moral as distinct from the intellectual life will, though only in a secondary degree, be happy too. For the moral activities are human *par excellence*. When we display courage or justice or any other virtue it is in our dealings with our fellow men, when we are careful to observe what is due to each in all contracts and exchange of services, indeed in our actions and feelings of every kind, all of which are manifestly human experiences. Some of these, we think, are actually the products of our bodily constitution – goodness of character is felt to have in many ways an intimate connexion with the passions. Prudence, too, is bound up with moral goodness, and goodness with prudence, because the first principles from which prudence starts are given by the moral virtues, for which the right standard is set by prudence. But these virtues, thus closely linked with the passions, go to form the composite being called man. Now the virtues of our composite nature are essentially human. Therefore the life that is lived in the performance of these virtues, and the happiness that ensues from such a life, must also be purely human. But the happiness of the intellectual life is something quite distinct from this. We must leave it at that, for a detailed discussion would go beyond the scope of the question before us. It would further appear that such happiness stands in need of external accessories to but a small extent or less than the happiness founded on moral goodness. The necessaries of life are required by both, and in equal measure.* Granted; in this respect the difference between them may be small. But there will be a vast difference in what they require for the exercise of their powers. Thus the liberal man will need money to practise his liberality, as will indeed the just man to meet his obligations.† The brave man will need strength if he is to do something brave, and the temperate man the opportunity of being intemperate. (Otherwise how can he, or the possessor of any other virtue, prove that he possesses the virtue?) Another question is whether it is the purpose of an action or the action itself that is the most decisive factor in producing moral goodness on the assumption generally made that goodness depends on both. Well, the perfect character will obviously need both for its formation. But many extraneous things are needed for the performance of virtuous actions, and the greater and finer the actions, the more numerous will be these accessories. On the other hand

---

* It does, however, look as if the politician took more trouble about ministering to bodily needs and the like than the philosopher.

† Mere wishes or intentions remain in the vague, and even the unjust *pretend* that they wish to act justly.

the student of intellectual problems has no need of all these paraphernalia; perhaps they are rather a hindrance to his thinking. Yet after all he is a man and a member of society and, in so far as he is that, he will choose to act on moral grounds. And this means that he will have need of external goods to permit him to live on the human level.

That perfect happiness is a speculative activity will further appear from the following considerations. The gods in our conception of them enjoy the most complete blessedness and felicity. But what kind of actions can we rightly attribute to them? If we say 'just actions,' how absurd it will be to picture them as making contracts and restoring deposits and all that sort of thing! Shall we say 'brave actions. then? Can you imagine the gods seeking glory by facing dangers and alarms? And what of liberal actions? Whom are they to be liberal to? What an odd idea that the gods actually possess coined money or something like it! Then there are temperate actions. But what could temperate actions mean in their case? What a piece of vulgarity to commend the gods for not having flagitious desires! And if we go through the whole list we shall find that all forms of virtuous activity must be paltry for the gods and unworthy of them. Nevertheless men have always thought of them as at least living beings and, if living, then doing something, for we cannot suppose that they are always asleep, like Endymion. But if from a living being there is taken away action, not to mention creation or production, what is left him but contemplation? We must conclude then that the activity of God, which is blessed above all others, must take the form of contemplation. And from this it follows that among human activities that which is most akin to God's will bring us the greatest happiness. What also goes to show the truth of this is the fact that the lower animals cannot partake of happiness, for they are utterly incapable of contemplation. The life of the gods is altogether happy, that of man is happy so far as it includes something that resembles the divine activity; but none of the other animals can be properly described as happy, because they are in no way capable of speculation or contemplation. Happiness then covers the same ground as contemplation and those who have the greatest power of contemplation are the happiest, not accidentally but as an essential element of their contemplation. For contemplation is itself beyond price. – We conclude that happiness is a form of contemplation.

But after all the philosopher is human, and so will need the added help of external goods. For human nature is not equal to such intense intellectual effort, if it must rely entirely on its own resources. The thinker must have a sufficiency of health and food and whatever else is necessary to keep him going. Yet, though it may be true that a man cannot be completely happy without external goods, it must not be thought that a man who is to be happy will find it necessary to have them in lavish measure. Self-sufficiency does not depend upon a superabundance of means, nor does conduct, and a man may perform noble actions without being master of land and sea. A competence is enough to enable a man to behave in a virtuous manner.* A competence then is all that we require, for a man will have a happy life if he acts as a good man acts. One may add the testimony of Solon and Anaxagoras. Solon – rightly of course – described the happy as men, moderately supplied with this world's goods, who had performed noble actions and lived a sober life. For there is nothing to prevent a man of moderate estate from doing what is right. Anaxagoras evidently did not think of the happy man as rich or powerful when he said that it would not surprise him if the many looked upon such a man as an oddity. For the many go by externals and have eyes for nothing else. – It thus appears that our view is in harmony with the opinions of the wise.

The opinions and arguments of such men do, of course, go far to convince us. But, when we are treating of conduct, it is experience of the facts of life that is the test of truth, for here it is experience that has the last word. We are bound

* We have concrete evidence of this in the fact that private citizens are to all appearance not less given to good actions than princes – are rather more so in fact.

then in our ethical studies to bring our preliminary statement of the case to the test of the facts of life. If this is in harmony with the facts, we can accept it; if it is not, we must look upon it as just a theory.

And may we not say that the man whose activity is of the intellect and who cultivates that and keeps it in the best condition is also the man whom the gods love above all others? For if, as most of us believe, the gods concern themselves with human affairs, it is only reasonable to believe that they delight in that part of us which is best and most akin to themselves – I mean the intellect – and that they reward with their blessing those who value and honour it most highly. For the gods care for what is dear to them, and what they do is right and good. Now we cannot doubt that it is the wise man who possesses these qualities to the fullest extent, and so he will be dearest of all men to the gods. And, if he be so, we cannot but suppose that he will also be of all men the happiest. So here we have another reason for believing that the wise man is the happiest man.

Such then is our theory of ethics. But theory is not practice and has no effect on the practice of the average man.

CHAPTER NINE

Assuming then that we have adequately discussed, at least in outline, the subjects of happiness and the different forms of goodness together with friendship and pleasure, may we consider the task we set before us as now complete? Or would it not be better to say that in the science of conduct the end, as we have so often had occasion to say, is not to obtain a theoretical acquaintance with the different points at issue, but rather to put our theories into practice? If that be true, it is not enough to *know* about goodness; we must endeavour to possess and use it, and in some way to see to it that we become good. Now if discourses on the theory of ethics were enough in themselves to make men good,

Many and great the rewards they would win,

as Theognis has it. And they would deserve them, and all we should have to do would be to provide ourselves with such discourses. But the plain truth is that, while theories may very powerfully stimulate and encourage generous youth, and may inspire a character naturally noble and sincerely loving the beauty of goodness with a passion for virtue, they are unable to push the many in the direction of lofty principles. For it is the nature of the many to yield to the suggestions of fear rather than honour, and to abstain from evil not because of the disgrace but the penalties entailed by not abstaining. Living under the dictates of passion, they chase the pleasures fit for such natures and the means of gratifying them, and they shun the pains which are the opposite of these pleasures. But the honourable and the truly delightful – of that they have no conception, having never tasted genuine pleasure. What theory, what homily can ever reform people like that? To uproot by argument habits long embedded in the character is a difficult, perhaps an impossible, task. We may, I take it, regard ourselves as fortunate if we can get some portion of goodness by acquiring for ourselves all the recognized means of becoming good.

To become good we must have a suitable nature rightly directed by habit and education.

Now some thinkers hold that goodness comes by nature, others that we acquire it by habit, others that we are made good by teaching. The bounty of nature is clearly beyond our control; it is bestowed by some divine dispensation on those who are in the true sense of the word 'fortunate'. As for arguments and teaching, it is to be feared they are not efficacious in all instances. Like a piece of land, which has to be prepared for the seed that is to grow there, the mind of the pupil has to be prepared for the inculcation of good habits, if it is to like and dislike the things it ought. The man who is passion's slave will not listen to or understand the logic of anyone who tries to dissuade him from going on as he is doing. When a man is in that state, what chance have you of changing his mind by argumentation? In fact one may venture on the broad statement that passion is not amenable to reason but only to force. We must then have a character to work upon which has a natural bias towards virtue, loving the noble and hating the base.

Education in goodness is best undertaken by the state.

Yet it is far from easy to obtain a right training in goodness from youth upwards, unless one has been brought up under right laws. To live a hard and sober life is not an attractive prospect for most, especially when they are young. For this reason the nurture and the pursuits of young persons should be regulated by law, for hard conditions and sober living will cease to be painful when they have become habitual. Of course, it is not enough to receive the right nurture and supervision in youth. We must also practise what we have learnt and make a habit of it when we are grown up. So we shall need laws for the regulation of adult behaviour as well, for the whole indeed of our lives, for people are by and large readier to submit to punishment and compulsion than moved by arguments and ideals. Hence some believe that, while lawgivers are under an obligation to encourage and inspire the citizens in the pursuit of virtue for its beauty, not doubting that those who have been well brought up will respond, they are also bound to inflict chastisement and penalties on the disobedient and ill-conditioned, and to deport the hopeless cases altogether. They take the line that, while the good man no doubt, living as he does with some kind of moral standard, will listen to reason, the degraded, who are all for pleasure, must be chastised by pain like beasts of burden. This is also the reason they give for maintaining that the punishment for transgressors should take the form of those pains which come nearest to being the opposite of their darling pleasures.

Be that as it may, I repeat that, if a man is to turn out well, he must have been properly educated and trained, and must thereafter persevere in good habits of life and do no wrong either with or against his will. This result can be produced only by submitting one's life to the guidance of intelligence in some form and a right system with truth in it. Now a father has not got the power to enforce obedience to his authority, nor indeed, broadly speaking, has any individual, unless he happens to be a king or something equivalent. But law, emanating as a rule from a certain wisdom and intelligence, does have the power of compulsion. We dislike people who thwart our inclinations, even if they are entirely justified in doing so, but we do not grumble at the law when it orders what is right. Yet Sparta, with perhaps one or two other places, is the only state in which the lawgiver seems to have been at pains to regulate the nurture and day-to-day life of the community. In the majority of states the problem has not been faced, and every man does as he likes with his life in the manner of the Cyclops in Homer, 'laying down the law for children and wife.'

Private instruction, however, may fairly take the place of public education, if the parent qualifies himself to perform the task of the legislator.

The best that could happen would be the institution of a sound system of public supervision of these matters. But, if they are entirely neglected by the state, it is the plain duty of the private citizen, to help his own children and friends to become good men or, if that is beyond him, at least to make it his ambition. But what has been said suggests that his success in this will be greater, if he acquires the art of legislation. So much is clear – if you are to have state supervision, it must be exercised through the laws and, if it is to be good, the laws must be good. But whether they are written or unwritten, whether they are to direct the education of one person or more, would seem to be questions of no greater importance than they are for music or physical training or any other form of education. Paternal advice and domestic habits have their influence in the family, just as law and custom command obedience in the state. And they have it in even greater measure because of the blood-relationship and the benefits flowing from that which unites the father and the family, whose natural affection and obedience are original assets in his favour. One may go even farther. Private education, like individual treatment in medicine, is superior to public. It is a general rule in medicine that rest and fasting are beneficial in fever cases. But it may be the wrong treatment in a particular case. We may take it, too, that a professor of boxing does not make all his pupils adopt the same style. It would appear then that individual attention permits of greater accuracy in dealing with particular cases, for then the individual has a better chance of getting the treatment that suits him. For all that, the best treatment of a particular case will be given by the doctor (or trainer or whoever the instructor may be) who has a general knowledge of what is good for all, or for all of a particular class. For, as their names imply, the sciences are sciences of the universal. This is not to deny that in a special case it is perfectly possible that treatment may be successfully applied by someone who has not had a professional training but has an empirical knowledge derived from detailed observation of the results of particular treatments. Thus some people appear to be their own best physicians, although they would be quite incapable of doing anyone else good. Still there can surely be no question that anybody who wants to be fully qualified in the art and science of a subject like education must proceed to the study of general or universal principles and familiarize himself with these in the only way possible. For science, as I said, deals with the universal. This surely permits us to assume that anyone who aspires to make people (few or many; it makes no difference) better by supervision must do his best to acquire the art of legislation, if he accepts, as no doubt he will, the principle that we can be made good by laws. We need such a legislator, because predisposing to virtue the first man that comes along is not a task for everybody. It can only be done by one (supposing him available) who has the scientific knowledge to do it. That is just as true of legislation as it is of medicine and the other professions which call for a technique and practical good sense.

Reasons for believing that it is useless to study political science under its professed teachers, the Sophists.

The next question we have to ask ourselves is this. From whom and by what method can we acquire the art of legislation? In the other arts and sciences one learns from the expert. The experts in this field are the politicians; for legislation, as we saw, is a branch of political science. Is the future legislator, then, to learn his business from the politicians? But the cases are perhaps not the same – political science is perhaps unlike other arts and sciences. In these the men who carry on and impart their skill to others are the same as those who practise it; witness doctors and painters. But in political science the Sophists, who profess to teach the subject, are never practising politicians. The practising politicians for their part seem to rely more on a natural gift strengthened by experience than upon a habit of thinking about principles. At least we never find them writing or speaking about the principles of political science, though to do this would surely be more to their credit than composing speeches for the law courts or public meetings. Nor do we find them making politicians of their sons or their friends. Yet surely that was the logical thing for them to do, if they were really capable of it. For they could not have left a finer legacy to their country, nor is there anything they would rather have for themselves, and therefore for their nearest and dearest, than statesmanlike qualities. Not but what experience does seem to contribute a good deal to success in politics. If it were not so, familiarity at first-hand with political problems would never have turned anybody into a

statesman. We may conclude that aspirants to a knowledge of political theory must have practical experience as
well.

On the other hand, those Sophists who profess to teach
politics are on the face of it very far from making a success
of their profession. The fact is that they do not know in the
least what political science is or what it is about. If they did,
they would not identify it with rhetoric or give it an even
inferior status. Neither would they imagine that it is a
simple matter to make a constitution by the method they
suggest, which is this. You collect all existing laws that have
won general approval and then select the best – a process
which your collection has made possible. As if that very selection did not call for brains, and as if a correct judgement
were not the great difficulty here no less than in music! It is
only the experts in an art who can form a correct judgement
about its products and understand by what means and by
what method these can be perfectly produced and what elements can be combined harmoniously. The amateur may
congratulate himself if he is clever enough to see whether the
result is on the whole good or bad. (You may observe this
in the criticism of painting.) Laws may fairly be described
as products of the art of politics. How then can a collection
of laws enable a man to become a master of legislation or to
pick out the best of them? You do not see men becoming
qualified in medicine by reading handbooks on the subject,
and that although the authors attempt not only to describe
how to treat cases on general lines but go into details on
methods of curing and treatment for special classes of patients, classifying them according to their physical condition
and habits. Such instructions are allowed to be useful for the
practitioner, but the layman can make no use of them at all.
It is not unlikely then that collections of laws and constitutions will be serviceable enough to those who are capable of
examining them critically and of judging what is a wise enactment and what is not, and what is the proper spirit that
should animate legislation for communities of different
types. But merely to go through a collection of such prece-

dents without the right habit of mind will not enable us to form a correct judgement of them unless by a kind of instinct, though the process may not improbably do something to improve our political intelligence. . . .

And with that Aristotle passes to the subject of politics.

318